Consciously Live What You Feel

Life's Little Secrets Book Series
Book One

Consciously Live What You Feel

Spiritual Transformative Education

TERRANCE G. SWEJKOSKI

Conscious Clarity Center, Inc.

Traverse City, Michigan

Published and distributed in the United States by: Conscious Clarity Center, Inc.: https//consciousclaritycenter.org

Editor: Karen Petersen, Traverse City, Michigan

Cover Design: Ann Powell, Sarasota, Florida

The author of this book does not dispense medical advice or prescribe the use of any technique as a form of treatment for physical, emotional, or medical problems without the advice of a physician, either directly or indirectly. The intent of the author is only to offer information of a general nature to help you in your quest for Spiritual well-being. In the event you use any of the information in this book for yourself, the author and the publisher assume no responsibility for your actions.

The events related to the author's experiences, including conversations that occurred, have been re-created to the best recollection of the author. Some situations have been modified, compressed or expanded; and names and identifying details of certain individuals have been changed for confidentiality purposes.

FIRST EDITION
First Printing, 2017

ISBN-13: 978-0-9994399-0-6

Printed in the United States of America

Dedicated to everyone that has ever said, "There must be something greater to this life than what is seen on the surface."

"Meditation is not some "thing" you do; it is the experience of Being that which you are." – Terrance G. Swejkoski

Table of Contents

Introduction

Higher Self controls everything you do when you are not clouded by the smokescreen of fuel that is burning at a very low-energy level. During these moments of feeling inspired to do something is when you are actually in touch with your purpose for being here. It's when thoughts are limited and Spirit angels are allowed to shine through the dogma of the daily life situations that you are the most connected with Highest Self. At these moments, which are the spaces between the thoughts, is when you are connecting with the Universe in ONENESS.

You are a Spiritual Being having a human experience on Earth. However, you have been training since the birth of the body that you are a physical body only and once the body dies, you will as well.

The purpose of this book is to awaken the Higher Self within you through the process of Spiritual Transformative Education and to bring your true purpose into the conscious awareness of True Self.

This book, "Consciously Live What You Feel", is Book One in the *Life's Little Secrets Book Series*. Let me explain the process of how the writing took place so that you better understand the significance of the words and how the series came to manifestation of itself.

During a period of deep refection in the silence of meditation, I was being guided for several months to bring conscious clarity to many questions I had related to the statement, "There must be something greater to this life than what is seen on the surface." It was during one of these periods of deep silence that the blueprint for this book series was brought to light.

The still, silent voice within communicated through a higher power than I had ever experienced before and the words flowed to the paper as if written by someone else while I merely transcribed what was being said. All the questions were transcribed in one sitting and the energy of the experience opened up my mind to the unlimited possibilities that had been hidden from me before that evening.

Once the blueprint questions were reviewed and categorized, over a period in excess of ten years of meditative silence sessions, the answers began manifesting through the stillness of non-thought. Each question was asked and answers appeared very much the same way that the blueprint had become reality. If an answer did not appear within a meditative session, no words were transcribed during that period. I was patient and simply waited for the higher power within to guide my hand as I surrendered to what I now know as Source Energy guidance.

The "Consciously Live What You Feel" book is focused on the Soul Merge level of the *Conscious Clarity Energy Process™* which assists you in understanding the purpose of ego and eventually brings Spiritual Body awareness to the forefront of your life during the Soul Merge process. It is at this point you will make a choice to stay a prisoner of ego and live a life controlled by other egos focused on fear and scarcity or you will make the shift to Spiritual Body awareness through Soul Merge and change your life from an ego-based mediocre existence to a love-based miraculous life of peace and abundance.

I know it's hard to believe from the ego's point of view that all is well, no matter what the life situation. When we are going through a time of pain, may it be physical or emotional; it's difficult for the mind to accept that this is the way it was planned out. This is why it's important to embrace the knowledge laying dormant in your Highest Self on a daily basis to understand this acceptance and surrendering process. Through the power of meditative silence you will become in touch with all the solutions to all your questions.

When you are feeling emotions that don't feel good, it's a clue that you are off track. When you are feeling emotions that are good, it's a clue you are on track and living your life from a state of inspiration or in alignment with higher Source Energy.

It is my wish that you become inspired to follow the realignment process of your Four-Body system outlined in detail in this book. Dig deeply into your emotions and forever live a life based upon the Love, Peace and Light within you which is found in understanding the true definition of Oneness!

Namaste – Terrance G. Swejkoski
Traverse City, Michigan

Part One

Understanding Ego

Chapter 1

Know Who You Really Are

How Did You Forget Who You Really Are

You are not a human being; you are a Spiritual Being having a human experience. Let that sink in for a few minutes before continuing. Don't think about it, just sit with it. My goal is to assist you in remembering who you really are and to realign you with your true Higher Self!

Beginning the moment you were conceived, the essence of which you really are began to be clouded by the good intentions of your parents, teachers and society as a whole. This is no one's fault; it is simply a statement of fact.

The personality/ego is part of the whole separation process that comes from being born into human form at a very low vibration. You are placed on Earth at a vibration level in line with the collective consciousness of the planet at the time of your human form's birth. If you attempted to enter the body at your Highest Self vibration, the body would immediately disintegrate. Therefore, it was necessary to lower your initial energy vibration level to align with your birth environment.

Not all people experience the same type of birth process. It depends mostly on the parents you choose before coming here and the life-form situation those parents have decided to live in. For now, it's important for you to at least consider the idea that you wrote out your entire Life Plan, from the day of your birth to the day of your death, prior to arriving here on Earth.

As you begin the journey into the *Conscious Clarity Energy Process™,* if you are to even consider getting back in touch with your true Higher Self, you must be prepared to step into areas of realization that will be very uncomfortable for the personality/ego (hereafter simply known as ego) to grasp. This is the challenging part for most people; this whole experience, including taking this study course, is a process that you agreed to long before you made the decision to come into form on this planet. I will provide the details of why you are here later in later chapters. If you allow some open-mindedness while we start out, I promise I will explain exactly why you should at least consider what I'm saying and trust it has the potential of being absolute truth.

It will require a considerable amount of time for you to adjust to this concept before your ego will adapt sufficiently to be comfortable with this new awareness. All the information and proof you need to begin to accept this truth will grow as you continue to read on.

24

There has been a fog or smokescreen placed in front of you such that you have fallen into the typical life-form "what's in it for me" trap, which clouds the true essence of your greatness. The ego does not want you to become consciously clear - it wants control. It wants to pilot *The Train of Life™* in its own unhealthy manner.

There is no longer a planet of beings that experience reality in three dimensions; it moved into the higher awareness of a fourth dimension reality many years ago, likely without you even knowing it.

Ponder that for now ...

How Do I Get In Touch With My True Higher Self

Ego (in its current state) will do whatever it can to block you from understanding your true Higher Self, your pre-determined wisdom and natural right to greatness. The mind fabricates a series of road blocks which hide the truth from you. Your life is a process and, as with any process, it takes a series of small steps to move forward. To simplify this, I use the analogy of *The Train of Life™* to explain the many challenges and uncertainties of the form-based life process. (See Illustration B, *The Train of Life™*)

Upon arrival in the mother's host body, you are totally devoid of all unnecessary thought patterns. You are clear and your focus is on the Original Source Agreement or Life Plan intended for you. However, beginning at the instant of conception, the mind clutter starts to form from the input of

25

well-meaning people, which has an effect on the ego of the new human body during its development. This constant clutter builds as you continue to spend sensory time on Earth. It has been determined in various scientific studies that by the time the body reaches adulthood the mind has approximately 60,000 thoughts every day. The unfortunate part of this whole scenario is that most of those thoughts are the same thoughts you had the day before.

The good news is that there is a place you can go to purge many of those unnecessary thoughts and, thereby, eliminate mind clutter. Through meditation, prayer and silence, elimination of cluttered thoughts will bring you back into direct contact with your true Higher Self. It's the only place you can go to temporarily escape from the constant clutter of thought, which, of course, the ego uses to stop you from achieving your Life Plan greatness.

Just for a moment think of what would be different in your life today if you limited those 60,000 random thoughts to just a few. If you can discover how to reduce unnecessary thoughts, then you can learn to replace them with the ultimate creation model, which is the true intention for your life.

In Illustration A, *Original Source Agreement*, I demonstrate the connection between Source Energy, Higher Self and ego. Study this for awhile and see if you resonate with one aspect of this Life Plan strategy more than the others. Or are you in harmony with all three?

If you are not in harmony, it's because the ego/Engineer conducting your life path has placed a fog or smokescreen on

The Train of Life™. In reality, what this has done is lower your energy vibration level and separate you from the Conductor/Higher Self. My goal is to help you to reconnect with the true essence of who you are. When you discover how to merge the ego and Soul together, then, and only then, will you see a miraculous change in the way your life moves forward. Through raising your energy vibration in small segments every day, you will again move in alignment with your true purpose for being here.

What Is the Body

The body is a nothing more than a form-based vessel which houses your true Higher Self. Always remember you are a Spiritual Being having a human experience. For too long, you have lost touch with this truth and now is the time to get back on track with the true intention for your purpose on this Earth.

The Body is actually comprised of four levels of Self. For now, simply review the following levels which are aligned in the proper sequence below:

1. Spiritual Body
2. Mental Body
3. Emotional Body
4. Physical Body

The form/body, which is comprised of the last three levels of Self, is a limited, sensory, form-based vessel which is only here to be of service to you. Your current reality may be only based upon things that you identify with which are produced to survive, rather than thrive in this limited sequential time-based world. What proof of this can be found in our world? All form-based things are only here for a short period of time. When you begin to realize there is a greater power within that is actually conducting this wonderful symphony called life, you will then see the challenges of the experience or process you are now living with greater clarity.

You are meant to be happy by living in this life situation in a state of pure bliss. However, the daily things that come your way have clouded the Conscious Clarity of your true purpose. The intention for your Life Plan is to always have the Engineer of *The Train of Life*™ directly connected to the Conductor. As with any train, it's actually the Conductor that determines the path the train takes. However, when the Engineer steps in and changes the course, based upon free will and without the guidance of the Conductor, all Hell breaks loose!

The human body is comprised of an amazing physical form, based completely upon the by-products of the sequential birth/death process. And, because it is form-based, it is limited as to what it can do without the guidance of the Higher Self. That is why it is important (mandatory) for you to get back in touch with the Higher Self, because it is formless and limitless which means it can guide you in alignment with your True Life Purpose.

The human body was chosen to house you because of its unique abilities to co-exist with other form-based life forms on Earth. The intention for this wonderful process of life was to always be happy while helping to raise the collective consciousness of the planet. This is where the mind comes into play. And yes, that is meant literally; you are experiencing a wonderful play or movie of which the body is the lead character. Your body was given a mind so that you could make decisions based upon free will. Therefore, the type of life you live is a direct result of those decisions that only your physical mind perceives as reality.

Please keep in mind that your Higher Self made the Original Source Agreement (See Illustration A) with Source Energy prior to the birth of the body. This agreement has every possible scenario of your path already planned out for you. It's your free will that allows you to make a choice at every junction in life as to which segment or direction you take and, in truth, there are no victims. At some level of the creation process (during the development of the Source Agreement), you signed up for everything past, present and future. It's really as simple as choosing to move forward in light by only doing good things which increases energy vibration, or doing things that dim the light which in turn decreases energy vibration.

However, no matter which path the ego chooses for the body, there is always a way to tell whether or not you are in harmony with Higher Self. This is based upon the wonderful creation of the Emotional Body. The emotions you feel can be either positive or negative and will give the body clues or alerts as to how you are doing. The challenge is whether you move forward and thrive or choose to remain stagnant and only survive. Your emotional body will never let you down; it always provides clear signals. The problem is the mind. It will place a smokescreen upon what is truly meant for you if you allow it to do so. Yes, the mind makes the choices, but those choices are typically cluttered with past stories that manipulate you into false beliefs. Once you learn how to purge those limiting beliefs from the mind, then life energy vibration increases exponentially.

The good news is the first part of your Total Self, the Spiritual Body or inner Spiritual Self (Conductor), will always provide pure guidance. Once you discover how to tap into this communication source, your perceived reality will change, allowing you to thrive during the life process rather than simply to survive.

What Is the Soul

The Soul is the formless entity or Higher Self (True Self), which is the true essence of who you are. The Soul is the eternal Being that is housed within the current form based physical body. Review Illustration A to clearly visualize how the Higher Self relates to the other aspects of the Four Body System. The Soul is the Conductor of *The Train of Life*™, and therefore, is responsible for keeping the ego in alignment with the Original Source Agreement's true intention.

Once you realize that the purpose of Life is to understand who you are and what part you play in this ever-changing, multidimensional process, you will clearly see the intention of the Soul Merge process. The evolution of the planet will make sense to you and you will feel privileged to be a part of this wonderful process to increase the mass consciousness of the world.

The Soul, which I refer to as the Conductor, is truly the part of you that is least understood by the ego. This is because most of people currently only understand third dimensional life and have little knowledge that the fourth dimension of life even exists. Therefore, you may feel as though this is beyond your comprehension at this moment in sequential time. Simply be patient; everything will become clearer as you progress through the *Conscious Clarity Energy Process*™.

There will be many enlightening moments during this process when you begin to see how you have been blinded by the well-meaning intentions of other people in your life. However, in the words of the Christ energy, "Forgive them, for they know not what they do." You must remember, everyone is doing their best at any given moment based upon what they have learned from other people in their own life. Once the mass consciousness rises above the third dimensional reality into the fourth dimensional reality, a new baseline will be established. This will be the greatest moment in the evolution of the planet and will prepare us for quantum leaps in understanding how the Universe works in harmony as One.

We are now seeing more people on the planet opening their hearts to a level of higher energy vibration in which they now see clearly what was clouded by a fog or smokescreen previously. As this awareness grows based upon the Conductor of life consistently providing guidance through your emotions and intuition, you will naturally fall into a new life pattern. This will take time, so be patient and gentle with yourself and allow this awareness to build naturally as you progress. Remember, this is a process, one that has been planned out long before you were born into the body. At this point, all that is necessary is that you learn to accept the different parts of the Four Body System and understand that the Conductor is in charge, not the ego.

The reality is that the younger you are, the easier it will be for you to accept the intention of the *Conscious Clarity Energy Process™*. This is mainly due to the simple fact that you have not been as blinded by others' egoistic intentions for you. You will be more open to listening and learning than those with deeply embedded belief systems, which stem mostly from lower energy vibration input. However, no matter what age we may be, deep inside we all know the truth and it will be laid out for us in great detail as we progress based upon listening to our Higher Self connection.

The planned intention for the Conductor is to always be directly connected to the ego and to consistently keep the ego on the path of the Original Source Agreement. Once you truly accept that you were responsible for the details of this agreement, you will never again feel as if you are a victim of the circumstances surrounding your own personal Train of Life™. How this all relates to your progression will be explained in the next chapter.

How Did I Get Here

Prior to birth conception, you participated in a Life Plan meeting with Source Energy (God). During this meeting an Original Source Agreement was made, which was based upon the input from all the cast members you personally selected to be part of your Train of Life™ process.

Note: It is extremely important that you anchor this statement into your consciousness now. If you are having difficulty believing this right now (due ego's manipulation), then simply don't believe it. However, I ask that you keep your mind open to the possibility that it is true. (As you progress with the *Conscious Clarity Energy Process*™, you will remember this Life Plan meeting.)

Your true purpose for deciding to become a form-based human is to assist the Universe with increasing Planet Earth's energy vibration or mass consciousness. To assist you in doing so, you were given a set of unique talents to bring to the Earth which are in harmony with the "Source Energy Master Plan". I understand that you may be skeptical; however, as I stated before, you will remember this Life Plan meeting later on. There is a specific reason you do not remember it right now. So for now, please, again, proceed based upon the premise that this is all true.

The intent of the Original Source Agreement, as shown in Illustration A, is to provide a comprehensive plan for a happy, harmonious Train of Life™ experience. The agreement was made between Source Energy (also known as God, Higher Power, Life Force, Mother Nature, etc.), your Higher Self and all the lifetime participants in your Life Plan. If you think about your Life Plan in the form of a movie, you are the lead star, the co-author, the director, the choreographer and the casting director. Source Energy is the producer or Highest Self and has veto power over any aspect of the plan by connecting with your Higher Self or Conductor. Therefore, if you are not in alignment with the script which you personally wrote, Source Energy will step in and provide you a gentle nudge to assist you in moving in the right direction.

All of the possible scenarios, including all the variables based upon your ego's free will choices, are part of your Original Source Agreement. This means every possible script change, inconsistency, diversion or challenge has been taken into account, knowing that ego has a choice to pilot *The Train of Life™* either from lower self inputs or the Higher Self guidance of the Conductor. As difficult as it may be to believe right now, there are absolutely zero scenarios that were overlooked while formulating your personal Life Plan. Remember, you chose all the cast members and they all agreed to be part of your Life Plan without exception.

It is your responsibility to move *The Train of Life™* forward on a straight or linear, progressive path that consistently gains momentum in raising energy vibration or to

34

deviate from the Life Plan and drive *The Train of Life™* around a predetermined series of life challenges. All the final choices are yours and yours alone. You create your own reality based upon the free will enabled choices that you make in each moment.

When you finally accept that you are the One totally responsible for your own Original Source Agreement, you will no longer consider your lower self a victim of circumstance. You will accept that you are the one accountable for your choices and learn to listen to the Higher Self guidance preprogrammed into your Four Body System. You will no longer blame any other entity for how your life is progressing or regressing, because you will be living from a higher state of awareness. This state of awareness knows when mistakes are made and will bring you back to true reality when needed, provided the ego listens!

Going back to *The Train of Life™* analogy, you can clearly see that the ego (Engineer) and Higher Self (Conductor) are always meant to be connected. Since the time of ego's first breath, the Higher Self has been there as the observer empowering you with unconditional Love to always be your Higher Self and do what is best for the betterment of humankind. It is up to you to get back in touch with who you really are by listening to the guidance from within the cosmic energy system. This can be very difficult at times, especially during times of ordeal because of the constant bombardment of cluttered thoughts which cause you to forget who you really are.

Please understand that just because you may be off-track for a period of time, it does not mean you have to continue on the same diverted life course. The past never equals the future and the future is always based upon your choices in the current moment. Therefore, let your current moments be based upon keeping your mind present and in touch with the Conductor of life.

Now, let's start to understand why it's so difficult to remember the Original Source Agreement meeting as it was intentionally planned out before birth.

Why Don't I Remember Everything

During a storm, clouds and fog make it impossible to see clearly what's directly in front of you. The mind is no different. If your mind is filled with a series of unnecessary, cluttered thoughts, it's impossible to see the Original Source Agreement with clarity. Yes, you will feel subtle changes of energy in alignment with the agreement; these are sometimes referred to as déjà vu experiences by the mind. However, the majority of the time you will be lost in mind-cluttered thoughts. The best way to get clear is to purge the mind of those unnecessary thoughts.

Earlier you learned the mind has some 60,000 thoughts every day and that most of those thoughts are the same thoughts you had yesterday. You will discover how to purge those unnecessary thoughts later in the *Conscious Clarity*

Energy Process™, but for now, let's concentrate on determining where they came from in the first place.

To better examine the process that caused the mind clutter, I created Illustration B, *The Train of Life*™. This illustration summarizes the various "burdens of influence" from well-meaning individuals. I will summarize this shortly, but first let's recap what you have learned so far.

The human body is comprised of a four body energy system which powers *The Train of Life*™. The last three parts, mind, emotion and physical being are all part of the ego. The ego is the Engineer piloting *The Train of Life*™ forward on the intended linear life path. The first part of the four body energy system is the Spiritual Body or Soul, which is the Conductor or Higher Self. The Conductor is responsible for observing the Engineer and directing *The Train of Life*™ down the tracks based upon the Original Source Agreement or life path. The Conductor is in direct contact with Source Energy: the Highest Self.

The following summarizes the various components of *The Train of Life*™ analogy. I will present a detailed discussion of each component as we progress. For now, my intent is for you to focus your attention on the foundation or underlying principles of the *Conscious Clarity Energy Process*™.

<u>*The Train of Life*™ Summary (See Illustration B)</u>
<u>Engine/Engineer (Personality/Ego) / Lower Self</u>:

The primary Engine or driving force of *The Train of Life™* is the ego, which is designated as the Engineer. The Engineer dynamics are based upon the last three parts of the Four Body System. The intention of the Engine is to move forward with the Original Source Agreement based upon free will or choices made during the life process, but only at the current energy vibration or state of consciousness.

During the life process, commencing upon conception, there are influences directed at the Engineer from well-meaning people. These people are represented as the Baggage Cars located between the Engineer and Conductor. These include all the influences or dramas brought with you collectively during the life situation and are then visualized by you as a direct aspect of your perceived reality. The Baggage Cars start to manifest from infancy to adolescence and finally into adulthood. As your life progresses, you have a choice to keep adding more and more burden of influence from the Baggage Cars and to use this information for personal guidance or you can listen to Inner Guidance from the Conductor/Higher Self. Unfortunately, most people continue to live from a three-dimensional perspective; therefore, Baggage Car influences pilot their life.

Inner Guidance/Conductor/Higher Self:

The observer and Spiritual level of Inner Guidance is the Conductor or Higher Self. The Conductor is in direct contact with Source Energy (God) and constantly relays subtle messages to the ego from the inner consciousness level. The Conductor's energy vibration is in harmony with the true purpose for being on Earth and is responsible for overseeing every aspect of ego's form-based life situation. The Conductor has the power to maintain direct connection with the Engineer and will pass along messages from Source Energy when necessary. These messages come in many different forms and sometimes are in response to ego's choices.

The Conductor is always actually in charge of moving forward with the Original Source Agreement. However, usually the communication connection between the Conductor and Engine is clouded or fogged over by the Engine's smokescreen, which is produced by the influences of the people in the Baggage Cars. The good news is that the Conductor is always consciously clear of the intended path of *The Train of Life™*. When the Engine is producing a smokescreen, the Conductor can see right through it. However, if the smokescreen is too heavy, the Engineer cannot hear the messages clearly that are emanating from the Conductor. This causes a very low-energy vibration in the last three quadrants of the Four Body System.

Baggage Car Influence/Life Situation Drama:

The Baggage Cars consist of all the well-meaning people that you have decided to bring along with you on your life path. These cars house both positive influences and negative influences. It is always the Engineer's choice to either let them continue along with you or to uncouple or detach them from your Train of Life at any time. The Conductor is always there to give guidance, but the Engineer makes the choice as to who stays and who is released.

The level of influence from these people will be determined by the energy vibration they impart based upon their own level of consciousness. The energy you absorb from these well-meaning people will determine the direction the Engine ultimately takes on the predetermined life path. Also, the energy level of these people will produce the fuel for your train. Therefore, the higher the energy source or fuel used, the clearer your Train of Life™ path will be.

The density of the fuel determines your ability to remember the Original Source Agreement and the Conscious Clarity of the smokescreen produced. Typically, the first Baggage Cars are lighter in energy but progressively become darker as more burden of influence is added to *The Train of Life™* over time.

In the next chapter, I will begin to explain Energy Transformation and how it affects your daily life situations. For now, spend some additional time reviewing *The Train of Life™* illustration and how the Baggage Cars may be influencing your life.

What Is the Energy Within Me

All energy has an assigned vibration or frequency to it. All things (anything that is form-based) vibrate at a lower frequency than formless energy does. The difference between form and formless is based upon the Lower Self and the Higher Self, respectively. Therefore, all things, including thought, are based upon ego or that of the illusion called the life situation.

Right now our discussion will be based upon the formless energy that is within us. This is also known as the Spirit/Soul or Higher Self Energy. This energy is the controlling factor behind all that is seen in the life situation. This energy is always stepped up to the level of conscious contact with Source Energy, which is the highest energy and can be accessed easily during meditation. Source Energy is beyond typical human comprehension. However, our Higher Self can easily connect with Source Energy on a daily basis if we choose to do so. This connection is made in the space between the thoughts, better known as stillness or silence. Once you discover how to become still by quieting the mind, direct connection is established and you will have daily contact (also known as channeling). During this contact, you are capable of seeing all the solutions to all life situation challenges. You will also start to remember your Original Source Agreement and see how your gifts or talents are directly linked to the process of increasing the collective consciousness of the world.

The energy within you is the Spiritual Body guiding everything you do at the levels beyond the mind. Most people do not know how to connect with this life-giving Source, in fact, most are not aware it even exists. Once the ego's smokescreen is cleared (as previously mentioned), you will be in a totally different frame of mind, will accept the inner guidance as truth and will clearly connect with Source Energy. For now, be patient and gentle with your Lower Self, because it will take time to fully comprehend what is being presented to you. For most of you, because you have been manipulated for so long by the outside egoistic influences, it will take a substantial effort on your part to reconnect at the level of Source Energy understanding. This is totally normal under the circumstances of the current mass consciousness level. However, once you break through the smokescreen and gain momentum, connection with Source Energy will be automatic no matter what the outside circumstances are in your daily life situation. Then, you will begin to live a life of acceptance rather than one of immediate reaction to outside circumstances.

Please take the time to thoroughly review Illustration C which details the Energy Transformation process. In the illustration, you will clearly see how your Higher Self energy has been stepped down such that it was in alignment with the consciousness of the parents you chose prior to your Earth birth. Without this stepped down process, the physical body would have immediately disintegrated when you entered the form-based vessel. Furthermore, it was important for the energy to be grounded to the Earth prior to increasing it slowly in the form-based body. You will discover later how to increase this energy vibration to realign in total harmony with Higher Self. Once you discover how to do this, you will no longer live your daily life situation from the ego's perspective. Everything changes quickly once the Soul is merged within the Chakra Energy System of the body.

The process to increase the energy vibrations to a level of greater understanding is necessary for you to comprehend the later sessions in the *Conscious Clarity Energy Process™* and to begin to understand the Soul Merge process.

In the Original Source Agreement, you formulated a series of Life Plan Categories which allows you to slowly increase your energy vibration. These categories include Spiritual Life, Emotional Well Being, Physical Health, Family Relationships, Career, Financial Freedom, Soul Merge and Happiness. Two of these, Spiritual Life and Soul Merge, are core categories with an immediate higher-energy vibration to provide the other categories a boost whenever needed.

These life situation categories have a series of triggers associated with them called emotions or feelings. The purpose of these triggers is to assist you with awareness pertaining to whether or not you are in alignment with your Original Source Agreement.

How Do I Explain My Feelings

Pre-programmed reminders have been taken out of context for far too long. Typically, most people take feelings or emotions at face value; they only see the surface result. They use them as a reason to justify actions that the mind (ego) has concocted after making a judgment or making up a story on what the feeling means and only from a physical viewpoint. I'm not saying that all actions of the mind based upon emotion are misdirected; I'm simply saying the actual intent for using one's emotions as a balancing tool has been adversely manipulated by the ego. The result is that the true spiritual guidance system is being placed in the ego's smokescreen more than you may realize.

To maintain simplicity for now, I will focus on the two key primary root emotions: first, there is Love and second there is fear. You will soon discover how all other emotions are derived from these two root emotions.

LOVE

The Original Source Agreement is based upon pure Love with no exceptions. Highest Energy Source does not understand any other emotion. The Original Source Agreement was always meant to have you do "only good things" based purely on Love. When action is based upon Love, only good comes from it. Feel that for a few moments. Just sit still and contemplate what your life would be like if everything you did was from a feeling of Love, knowing that everything in life would move forward based upon only good things happening to those around you. Now, take it a step further and imagine that everyone on the planet did the same. Do you have a problem with that? Do you believe that is simply unrealistic or a fantasy? Now, ask yourself why you believe what you believe.

Here's the truth: if you answered anything other than "it's totally realistic for everyone to live from a base of Love", your ego has stepped in based upon fear. You may not see it on the surface, but the truth is if you are feeling only Love and transmitting that feeling to the mind, it should stay intact. The only thing that can change that feeling is thought. A mind based on anything other than Love is producing "fear-based manipulations" in an attempt to control your Lower Self. This vulnerability is based upon Lower Self thoughts of limitation and a deeply rooted false belief that you are in some way not worthy of Love.

FEAR

The concept of fear is completely an ego (mind) creation meant to do only one thing: to keep you under the ego's manipulative control drama. Fear is the cancer of the world which will continue to spread unless we all do our small part in creating a life based upon the Original Source Agreement intention. Just do good things. It's really that simple!

The typical reaction to "just do good things" is "how can I do only good things when there is so much unrest in this world?" That is the exact point being made here; the ego wants turmoil and fear. It's the fear that gives ego its power over you. Once you discover how to eliminate fear, ego will get back on track and listen to the Higher Self guidance. The best way to do this is to live your life in a constant state of awareness and acceptance. It doesn't matter what other people are doing or what they are saying. It's not your responsibility to even care what others are doing and saying. If you simply accept what is happening in this process of life, you will do yourself a world of good. Yes, there are many things that are difficult to accept, especially if they seem to go against the intended concept of Love. However, if you make a personal commitment to only do good things, no matter what those around you are doing, don't you think that higher energy vibration will eventually overpower that which is lower energy? Of course it will. Just try it. Begin by only doing good things for a few minutes. Then expand that out into hours, then days. See what happens.

Fear is an overrated, limiting emotion only used as an attempt to control you. You are truly much greater than that!

The simple truth is that you have two choices: either live from a state of Loving awareness or live from a state of fear and desperation. Remember, only Love has the power to overcome all things the mind manipulates into a negative emotion and all negative emotion produces more fearful thought patterns. Only you can decide which direction to take and the direction one chooses is based upon free will and you make those choices every moment of your life!

Who Decides What Comes Next

In the last section, you discovered there are two root choices in the life process: to live through Love or to live through fear. It's really that simple. The only thing (again, "thing" means form, of the ego) that complicates this simple choice is the mind through all its stories and limiting false beliefs. Remember, all the choices and possible scenarios to everything that has occurred or will occur in your lifetime was been written by you in the Original Source Agreement prior to your conception. Only you are responsible for the choices you personally make in life. All that others can do is influence you and, when it comes down to it, you make the final choice based upon your own beliefs.

Therefore, "who decides what comes next?" is answered with a simple "you do", period. End of story. No further explanation required. You make the choices. Who you are today is based upon the sum total of all the choices you have made up until this very moment in time. There are no victims in life. There are only different perceived realities which are always based upon your free will choices.

Most people have a hard time believing that their perceived reality is based only upon their own choices. The truth of the matter is that it's okay; it's not your fault that you have that limited perspective. You have been fed so much misinformation by the egos of well-meaning family members, friends, teachers and acquaintances for so long that you simply forgot who you really are. You are living life in the smokescreen of all this misguided influence and have lost Conscious Clarity of your True Self. You are the co-creator of the total Master Plan of the Universe. What you "decided" to write in your Original Source Agreement is all part of this ever-changing life process. Your Spiritual Higher Self knows this without question and it is your responsibility to remind your ego of this true reality.

Your life process will build in momentum only when you finally accept the fact that you can change each scene, each co-star, each outcome and the final ending of your Life Plan process at any time. You have the power to move your life situation in whatever direction you would like to see it progress. Yes, this may require some actual dedicated work on your behalf. Your thoughts equal your perceived reality. Only you can make the choices necessary to move forward with the intended life of happiness you so rightly deserve and already planned for yourself.

Your life can be happy every day. The way to manifest that into reality is by taking small steps at a time. If your life is not what you expected it to be at this point, all you need do is look at the choices you made. Once you see the choices clearly, ask yourself how your life would be different if you made different choices. Don't beat yourself up about it, be gentle, simple look at your life today and be honest with yourself. Once you see the picture in your mind's eye of how your life would be different had you made different choices, simply make a commitment to make better choices from this moment forward. That improved picture you are seeing is the actually reality you had planned out; however, somewhere along the path you took a detour!

The past cannot be changed and the truth of the matter is that every experience has brought you where you are today. Your past taught you many valuable lessons which you would not have learned if you had not experienced what you did. That is the key: "you have gone through it" and you need not stay in any place other than the current moment. We have all been taught to dwell on the past. Many believe that the past will repeat itself. I am here to tell you that that is simply a lot of bull. The past only repeats itself if the same manifested realities are brought into play based upon making the same choices/mistakes.

The truth is that the past never equals the future. The future is always based upon the choices made in the current moment and only the current moment really matters. Stop listening to what the know-it-alls are telling you. Get out of the smokescreen and get yourself back in charge of the life process you originally planned out for yourself.

Ask yourself which emotions have been piloting your Train of Life™. Then eliminate those self-defeating emotions from your consciousness. Make an effort to purge all negative emotion one small step at a time. Once you decide to have a life filled with peace, joy and harmony, your happiness will evolve to a level you never dreamed possible in your current state of mind. When you live in awareness, it's easy to feel these false beliefs creeping into your life and you will learn to quickly dismiss them before they clutter your mind or create unnecessary drama.

Manifested reality always feels better when you are feeling the essence of which you really are; the peaceful, loving, compassionate Spiritual Being which can be brought to the forefront of your life at anytime through living in a meditative state of mind and silence.

Why Is Everything So Different When I Am Peaceful

Whenever you are consciously in touch with the Higher Self, meaning you are in a state of Conscious Clarity, you will feel blissful. This state of deep Knowing and understanding is only achieved when you stop identifying with the labels placed upon you by outside influences which only confuse and distort truth.

The Higher Self is a ray of light vibrating at a much higher frequency that the Lower Self. By allowing life situations to fall away, you will feel the essence of which you are clearly and without judgments of any kind! While living in this higher state of awareness, the ego will be put aside and the Conductor of *The Train of Life*™ will be in the foreground. When the Conductor is vibrating at this higher frequency, the mind is at ease and not following the clutter of outside influence.

When the Spiritual Body is focused and powerful, the sequential time illusion will not matter. At moments of Higher Self total connection with mind, minutes will feel like seconds, hours like minutes and days like hours. You will feel a sense of calm, deep inner peace and the connection with Source Energy will be at its highest level. It is at these times answers to all your questions will bubble up from inside as if by magic. It is at these times that you will see your Original Source Agreement as if it is being presented to you as a manuscript. You will sense the connection with other higher-energy beings and will clearly understand what the next step is on your life path.

When vibrating at this higher energy level, it will be possible for you to have clear conversations with other higher-energy beings that are typically not resonating within your normal range of limited sensory perception. However, as you continue to increase your energy vibration, you will gradually hold onto the higher-energy fields for longer periods. And, once the Soul Merge transformation is completed, you will naturally maintain higher energy frequencies. Once the merge occurs, you will experience a feeling of lightness of which you have never felt before in your ego-conditioned body. There will be no going back from that moment on. Your energy vibration will have increased its amplitude to a point of no return and everything in the external world of form will look different to you.

This is something that is difficult to explain in words as it is only experienced in the deeper realms of Knowing and feeling at the higher-energy vibration levels.

Once you transition into this higher energy field, the form-based things in your life will not have the same impact on your realigned life. This level of awareness will allow you to see through false, limiting beliefs and a new way of living will result. The Spiritual Body moving into the forefront of your daily life will be noticed by many. However, they will not have the words to explain what they are experiencing in your presence. To them, it will seem as if you have had some type of experience in your life that has all of a sudden made you happy. You will be asked questions about what's different; some people will be happy for you while others will become jealous or try to bring you back down to their level of vibration. This will be an exciting time for you as it will be a time that you experience a surge of followers or many people will simply fall away. Simply allow the changes to occur as they may as you move forward in Spiritual Evolution.

Each time your energy vibration is anchored in at a higher level by a major uplifting choice in your consciousness you will experience a shedding of these lower energies. This is completely normal. People will either join you or be left behind.

To provide an example of this, I'd like to share a short story with you:

Until I was in mid-life, I was a heavy drinker. I would have at least one drink every day as soon as I arrived home from work. I used to call it my happy pop, though I didn't realize just how unhappy I was in my life situation. Of course, the reason I was so unhappy was due to allowing my ego to control me.

The sad part is that I wasn't really aware of being unhappy. I just had the belief that after a perceived hectic day of work, it was normal to have something to drink to calm the nerves and relax. Here's the problem with that: the alcohol wasn't actually calming me; alcohol was literally placing me in a state of lower energy vibration, well below my current life situation resonant frequency. Therefore, I felt better, because I was no longer aware of the life situation that was causing my unhappiness. The really sad part was that all the people I chose to hang around with at the time were all doing the exact same thing. We would "party" every weekend to the point of no return.

Then one day I had a wake-up call: a life situation presented itself where I made a conscious choice to stop drinking. When that choice was made, my friendships changed along with that choice. No one could believe I was no longer choosing to take part in the drinking part of the parties. Oh, I was still around, but the outcome was much different. I found that I became a better listener and that people would either open up to me more about their life situations or the exact opposite would happen: they would not talk to me at all. What a wake-up call that was and a necessary one, too.

That was a very interesting time in my life; it was a time of anchoring into a new higher energy, one that stepped up my energy vibration to the point that I was determined to find out exactly why I did the things I did. It was a time of deep Soul-searching and realigning with the true Higher Self. It all started because I had felt a few moments of inner peace and I knew from that moment of discovery that I never wanted to be unable to find that feeling again.

How Can I Be Peaceful All the Time

Once you discover that being peaceful is your normal state of being in harmony with your Original Source Agreement, you will begin to clearly see flashbacks from when you created your Life Plan. The more you sit in silent awareness the more you will experience increases in energy vibration of the body and memories will bubble up with Conscious Clarity.

Increasing energy vibration can be accomplished in many different ways:

A few of the natural ways to remain peaceful are through the practice of being meditative, prayer, listening to chants, feeling the power of inspirational high-energy music or observing nature in its natural silent beauty. These are the times when you will actually feel God communicating with you directly. It may appear only in a brief moment, but rest assured, when that moment comes, you will know it. When you are in direct conscious contact with the Source Energy, all words are channeled through you in a miraculous non-sensory silence, the language of inner peace. How you achieve that level of communication is determined by you and you alone. There are many paths, but only you know which path resonates for you.

One of the proven ways to begin reconnecting with Source Energy is to take yourself on a journey back in time to when you were a child.

"As you travel back in sequential time, you will remember more moments of inner peace."

Simply begin drifting backward; reflect on when the mind clutter was at a lower point of influence. Take yourself back a few years at a time. Simply erase the drama of each year by only focusing on all the good times and leave the rest behind. Good memories will take you back to an ever-growing recollection of pleasant moments. Even if a great deal of pain was experienced as a child, the good memories will overpower the ones that were unpleasant if you consciously focus your attention on the intention of only the peaceful times. As you travel back in sequential time, you will remember more moments of inner peace. By the time you reach infancy, you will actually open up to a level of awareness that you never dreamed possible.

Personally, I *now* clearly remember sitting in a meditative state of being as a young child of approximately three or four years old. Of course, at the time I had no idea that meditation was what I was experiencing. I placed no label on it; it was just natural for me. I knew I was having a direct conversation with God, the Highest Source of all formless energy. And today, as I become more and more peaceful, those memories continue to increase in clarity each day.

As a child, I had a special place selected, a place to escape from the sensory perceptions of the low-energy life that surrounded me during most of my childhood. As the years went on, my Conscious Clarity was increasingly clouded by the fog of low-energy life situations. However, my special meditation place always stayed intact. It was and still is within reach whenever I feel the need to check out of life situation drama and return to the true reality of inner peace. (Review Illustration B, *The Train of Life™* and Illustration E, *Life Energy Fuel Source*; they provide an excellent visual picture of the different energy levels and the resultant factors of each.)

Every night, I visit the deepest realms of the Universe and am consciously clear of it prior to falling into a deep sleep (awareness). For a long time, I thought everyone experienced this same silent peaceful awareness. I knew as a child that this was the place to go to cleanse the mind from life situations that troubled my peaceful Self. I knew somewhere deep inside I was more than I was lead to believe by the people surrounding me. However, as most people do, I allowed my outer ego to be manipulated into becoming overpowered by the daily low energy of my living environment. Having grown up in the heart of Detroit, Michigan on the East Side, I was taught quickly to either be tough or die. That was the false reality of the outer experience I was presented with each day. However, deep inside I was always in contact with my Higher Self. I had a deep inner knowledge that my life situation could be and would be better at some point and I would somehow rise above the limiting current physical aspects of my life situation.

Knowing what I do today, *The Train of Life*™ has become a straightforward path focused on moving ahead through quantum leaps of faith powered by the wisdom of the experiences that have molded my Being. I now clearly understand the essence of which I am and have committed the rest of this human experience to leading others back to the peace and tranquility of Higher Self energy.

I now know that it's always a choice to live in a state of inner peace and harmony, no matter what outside influences, driven by egos, do to hamper that natural state of Being.

What Do Most People Think They Are

The vast majority of humankind believes they are the body which is controlled by the mind and interface with other forms on a limited level. They believe they were born and they will eventually die. They totally identify with their roles in their limited areas of involvement with the rest of humanity. They believe their existence is totally based upon what they can see from a five-sensory perspective and nothing outside of their perception is real. This is the typical third-dimension type of individual, living life day in and day out in survival mode based upon cause and effect. The truth is it is totally natural to have this limited perspective based upon the current collective consciousness of the world.

The reason for this belief is simply because it is exactly what they have been taught by well-meaning individuals since their time of conception. The same beliefs have been passed down since the beginning of humankind. Therefore, if they can identify with it, in form, through one of the five senses, it must be reality and all there is. All of these traits are form-based, having nothing to do with the essence of which you really are.

If you believe you are only what you can perceive through the five senses, you are living a life based upon limitation, birth & death, good & evil, dark & light, victim & controller and mind & material possessions. You believe you are father, mother, son, daughter, priest, rabbi, boss, worker, president, laborer or any of the other thousands of labels the mind (ego) has placed upon your worth as it is perceived by the judgment of other humans or self-judgment.

The main problem with believing that you are only a form-based individual looking out for only your needs and the needs of your immediate family, employer, ministry or any other form-based labeled entities is that once you lose one of those roles part of you perceivably dies. If you are totally identified with only form, once the form is gone, what remains? In the mind's eye, you are in some way less than you were before. If you identify with the body and mind only, you place limitations on every *thing* in life as you perceive it. You will stay trapped in the body and never allow the Spiritual essence which you truly are, to shine forth and guide your life situation.

<u>Examples:</u>

If you are a person that believes the way you look really matters, when the body naturally begins aging, you will feel as though you are less. If you had a perfectly toned physical body with tight skin, low fat content and a pleasing appearance (all based upon judgment/visual perspective), once the body begins to atrophy, how will you perceive yourself? Or worse, how will others perceive you? How much would you be willing to spend on cosmetic surgery in an attempt to regain your youth? Does it really matter?

If you are the president of a large corporation in charge of thousands of people with high influence in all parts of society and world affairs, how do perceive yourself? Do you think you are greater than anyone else? Do you place yourself on a pedestal of power? Do you think you know more than anyone else? Are you living a life of material abundance? Are you truly happy and fulfilled with life? Now, take it all away, you no longer have the title president, your money is gone, all your material items are gone. How do you perceive yourself now? Are you less in your mind's eye? What about the people around you, how do they perceive you now? Does it really matter?

If you are a wife and mother raising a beautiful family how do you perceive yourself? Do you see yourself as a teacher that allows a child to think for themselves and grow through their own choices? Or, are you a mother that believes, without you, your children cannot make it in this world? If you perceive yourself as only the leader of the household, including raising the children, taking care of your husband's needs and managing the daily ins and outs of the household, how will you perceive yourself when the daily role of mother is gone and the children are grown and gone on their own? How will you be perceived if all your household roles are gone? Will you continue to try to control your children or will you allow them to live their own lives on their terms? What happens if your husband decides to leave and you no longer hold the title of wife? How will you be perceived by others with the label divorcee? Will you be less in your mind's eye? How will you cope with these form-based matters? Does it really matter?

The simple truth is that when you only identify yourself as being that which is perceived in form (including mind), you can never be more than form. As far as the mind or ego is concerned, you will always have someone else judging who you are based upon a label, or worse, based upon the labels you place on yourself. You will always live life based upon limiting belief patterns which have been deeply anchored to a false perception of which you are not.

If you are now living this way, it is by choice. And, if it is a choice, you can choose to make a different choice. Life is really not complicated; it is the form-based stories that are complicated. It is the lower self and low-energy vibration of form-based thinking that is complicated. This is also known as wrong-mindedness thinking.

You can step out of the typical third dimension patterns of form-based, control dramas at any time you choose to. There are no justifiable reasons to stay stuck in an identity based life; there are only excuses for not moving forward.

Why Do I Feel Alienated

Making the decision to no longer live based upon only a form-based perception of life came to me as an "aha" moment many years ago in Vietnam while serving as a United States Marine. It was during a near-death experience when all the lights came on and a reconnection was made with the Highest Source. At that time, I had another glimpse of the true essence which I am. At that exact moment, it became crystal clear. The only downside is that I allowed my ego to regain control of my mind, which took me on a journey of low vibration, ego and society-based adventures, all of which were perceived as happiness on the surface. However, the truth is that although I had a perception of happiness, my ego placed a smokescreen around me that clouded my Higher Self guidance system.

There were many signs which alerted me to what was really happening, however, I allowed my manipulative ego to dismiss them. I can remember to this day, there were times that I asked myself, "Why do I feel alienated?" There were times that my Higher Self would clearly show me the true path that was meant for me and this was really weird for me at the time. It was a time before anyone was openly discussing fourth dimension Self and the connection we have with Source Energy. I was torn between my perceived realities of happiness and my true inner Self guidance. I had no one to talk to about this revelation; my ego did a great job of keeping the true intentions of my Original Source Agreement hidden in a vast cloud of fog. Throughout those challenging times, I was constantly given hints that there was a better way. My ego chose not to listen and I continued to live a life of conflict within myself in a tug-of-war between ego and Spirit, never really knowing for certain what to believe.

Therefore, I know from firsthand experience how some of you are feeling about making this shift from ego and form-based life to one of inspiration and dedication to Love, compassion, true happiness and inner joy. The one promise I can honestly make with an open heart is that once you finally make the decision to live from your Higher Self, you will be happy beyond your ego's perceived definition. Because Joy will emulate from within you!

When you discover how to be truly happy, all the daily drama around you means nothing. This includes all the material possessions which you may now find as a necessity for your happiness. Once you make the transition to living life from the inside out, as opposed to the outside in, the material stuff will be nice to use, however, you will quickly discover it is not yours to keep. All the material stuff is temporary; only you are eternal, only you (the Spiritual Self) are part of the whole package. You are part of the totality of Oneness that allows all things to manifest into form. You are the formless, the all powerful true essence of the Highest Source. You are only here for one purpose: to share with everyone and the Universe with the intention of raising the mass consciousness of the world as you now know it.

Never doubt your ability to do great things in this lifetime. You are truly a power for good, the good of all humanity, and it is your responsibility to start living your life based upon the Original Source Agreement created in unison with Source Energy. With an open mind you will be able to quickly make the modifications necessary to place yourself back on track through balancing all the categories of your life situation for the benefit of all. Yes, you will be the minority, but the rewards are well worth it.

Therefore, if you feel alienated at times, it's because most people have not reached a level of higher spiritual awareness (energy vibration) to resonate with your current life experience and changes.

Is It Possible To Always Stay Balanced

Once you are following the balanced path of your Original Source Agreement, you will feel it. There will be a deeply inspired inner Knowing that you are moving in the right direction. Your life will begin to create momentum and you will feel the natural progression of being on your own Train of Life™ as opposed to following others. You will feel the spiritual power of Higher Self shift into control of everything you do. It's a feeling of pure bliss that can only be experienced as it exists beyond the mind's comprehension. To attempt to put words to it only serves the ego's need to manipulate, to gain control of that which it cannot have from a form-based perspective.

To experience this type of harmony consistently, it is necessary to live a balanced life in which your Train of Life™ gains momentum and the Conductor guides you in your originally intended direction. Review Illustration D now as it details the eight specific categories to focus on.

The following summary of each category will assist you with understanding the basic foundation behind each area. By using *The Train of Life™* analogy, it will be easy to plant a deeply rooted knowledge base into the reasons you do what you do. Then you will begin to understand how you can change what you do such that it aligns with your Original Source Agreement.

It's time for you to ride your own train; get off the tracks of other peoples' agendas and move forward on the planned mission for your life. The journey is never-ending, but the scenery along the way can now change miraculously.

Categories of Life Balance – A Process of Harmony

The list of categories is in random order, but needs to be balanced to achieve a truly fulfilled life. I recommend reviewing each and assigning a perception number from 1 – 10 for each category, where 10 = complete fulfillment and 1 = needs major attention.

The idea is to give yourself some type of measuring tool, such that you can monitor your progress as you move forward. You could just as easily use percentages, where 100% = complete fulfillment and 10% and below needs major attention. Use whatever rating system works best for you. This is not meant to be a judgment, it is simply meant to be a measuring tool for the mind to understand how you are feeling.

Each Life Plan category represents one of the eight wheels on each personality train car, including the passenger cars; see Illustration D, *Life Plan Balance*. The hub, Highest Self in the center, represents your connection with Highest Source Energy where you can always go for guidance (an increase of energy) if you feel you are out of balance and need a surge of higher energy to boost your power.

The key is to balance the eight categories equally such that *The Train of Life™* is rolling smoothly, grounded on the path of your Original Source Agreement. Therefore, if you are out of balance in one category, then the rest will feel the burden and T*he Train of Life™* will feel sluggish. One point I'd like to make perfectly clear: even if your energy vibration is low, you can still move forward easily if there is balance in each category. Then, as your energy vibration increases, it will become easier as you move forward with linear momentum. This, in turn, will result in a swiftly moving life path with less effort required. This is because you will not be carrying as heavy a load as when your energy vibration was lower.

Therefore, as you progress with linear momentum on balanced wheels, your natural energy will rise to a higher frequency, which will result in a lighter reality. Life will get easier as you advance and challenges will not have the same effect as before. You will learn to rise above the challenges of life rather than having them drag you down to a lower level.

Spiritual Life – The moment you remember you are a Spiritual Being having a human experience your focus will be on your Inner Self. When this happens, you will be in daily contact with Higher Source Energy. This is the foundation for your life changing from mediocre to magical. This category has a higher natural frequency than the others as it was put into play to give a boost to the other categories when needed. This is one of your core categories; the other core category is Soul Merge.

Emotional Well Being – Emotions are the monitors of your perceived reality. Fearful, negative emotions will drag you down, while light, loving, positive emotions will carry you forward and result in living life light-hearted and happy. These are the monitors that lead the physical body to either health or to disease.

Physical Health – Physical health has a direct correlation with the type of fuel being supplied to it; see Illustration E, *Energy Vibration - Life Fuel Source*. Your body becomes what you fuel it with, both physically and mentally. If you live an easy light-hearted life path fueled with proper toxin-free food, physical exercise and positive emotions, your body will respond to it with ease and vitality. If you live a heavy (self-

66

induced) stressful life fueled with toxic substances (processed foods, excessive alcohol, drugs, etc.), lack of physical exercise and negative emotions, your body will respond to it with disease (dis-ease, out of harmony).

Family Relationship – Part of a healthy, fulfilled life is a balanced family relationship. This means all members of your immediate family as well as your extended family. Your intimate relationship with your mate is the key to providing a healthy relationship with the rest of your immediate family (parents, brothers and sisters) and your extended family (relatives) and whomever else you deem as part of your family.

Soul Merge – When the ego (personality) discovers how to merge with the Soul and receive this higher-energy guidance on a daily basis, solutions to daily life challenges arrive as if by magic. The merging of the ego and Soul is absolutely necessary to achieve the Original Source Agreement intent. Once the energy vibration rises to this level, life becomes a blissful dance in harmony with all perceived reality. It's at this point in The Conscious Energy Process™ that you will be in alignment with Original Source Agreement and start to remember more of that planned path in life. The merging can manifest before you are totally fulfilled in the other categories and will move you forward in quantum leaps once the Soul Merge integrates fully and the *True Personality* surfaces.

Happiness – Being happy is your natural state of being and is easily maintained when you live life in a state of ease, acceptance and compassion. It takes a lot of hard work to place a smokescreen around this natural state of being. Eliminate the stories of the mind and happiness will always be at your doorstep. When you discover how to balance the rest of the categories, the natural frequency of this category will rise automatically from within, powered by joy, to its true intended energy level. This category is the sum total of the other categories of outward expression.

Financial Freedom – Everything is energy, including money. When you are in harmony with your Original Source Agreement, financial freedom (being able to do what you want to without financial concerns) will be your natural state. As your energy vibration increases, so will your financial freedom. Be patient and all that is meant for you to manifest financial freedom in your life will arrive, but you must believe it is on its way for it to happen.

Career – When you are in living your career path based upon the Original Source Agreement you will feel as though your work is pleasurable. It will be something you totally enjoy and will not be perceived as a job based upon survival. It will feel like what you always wanted to do and can be monitored based upon the numerology of your birth date. Personally, I believe everyone should conduct a numerology evaluation for insight into career path. It will provide valuable keys to what is holding you back or moving you forward to financial freedom.

Once your energy vibration begins to increase, the matters of the past that seemed like huge burdens will start to fall away. Life is a process and, like any other processes, it takes time to rise above the challenges. Just be gentle and patient with yourself; the changes will come naturally once you are in alignment with your Original Source Agreement. Remember, you are here for a specific purpose and once that purpose is completed, it will be time to return home. Enjoy your stay while you are here by discovering how to balance your life and live it from a natural state of happiness and joy.

What Happens When the Body Is Gone

Reconnection with Source Energy cannot be described adequately with words. It is a deep Spiritual feeling more than a connection contrived through sensory perception. The knowledge that you are eventually going home where you truly belong, becomes crystal clear once you discover how to reconnect with Source Energy on a daily basis. To try to explain it to anyone that has not had direct connection moments with Source Energy is very difficult. It goes far beyond typical human mass consciousness perception at this point in sequential time. When you discover how to merge ego with the Soul, you will start to understand the magnitude of the feeling. It will be a deep feeling of joy, a bliss which you live every day.

Once you are connecting daily with the Source of all that is, you will no longer have fears, doubts or questions in respect to your daily life path. Although there will be times the ego does not understand why something is physically happening, there will always be the spiritual reasoning or faith guiding you. You will have a deep Knowing that everything that happened is happening or will happen on your life path is in some way part of your Original Source Agreement. You will understand that it is all happening because it is meant to happen and that you scripted many different versions of how things will play out, all based upon your free will choices.

The fact that you are where you are today is always based upon you own conscious connection or lack of connection with Source Energy and your Original Source Agreement. This is important and it is the one truth you must eventually accept if you are to move forward on the actually path you set for yourself. You are in control of your own destiny.

I have been asked, "How do you know what happens after the body is gone?" The answer is simple: prior to returning home or Universe, you will have a brief encounter with God (Highest Source) where you will be asked (not in words) if you are ready to go home. If you are, you will simply leave the form-based body in a state of pure euphoria; if not, you will return back to the form-based body to continue your work on Earth. This is typically called a near-death experience. These experiences have been scientifically documented in numerous studies.

I know this as truth, having been one of the fortunate (or unfortunate) ones to actually survive a near-death experience and this reconnection with Source Energy. Everything changed after that brief surge of energy. This, coupled with deep daily meditative experience, has been a continuing form of serenity that I cannot explain in words; it must be experienced for you to grasp the magnitude of its power. Through the process of deep daily meditation, I have learned to allow energy vibration to rise to I-AM-Ness where this level of energy vibration results in a deeper level of communication. Once you start to experience this level of understanding, you will know the conversations which are being channeled through you are in alignment with the Source Energy Master Plan. You will rarely experience the limiting emotions of doubt or fear and you will simply go with the flow of the life process in acceptance of what is, knowing that whatever happens has a Divine Purpose.

When you know everything is happening in the exact way it is meant to happen, fear dissolves and daily life becomes a blessing. You will live life at a higher-energy vibration where acceptance becomes the normal way of life. Material possessions will no longer have the importance they once did and you will be happy to simply be here continuing the journey of life. You will have the deeply-anchored Knowing that when it is time to finally leave the physical body, you will be at peace with the experience.

Once the physical body is gone, you will return home to reunite with the formless Highest Source. Upon completion of realigning with Source Energy, you will continue to move forward with the Original Source Agreement or you will modify it to the next level. You may return to another form-based body to continue work on Earth or you may choose to stay formless for a period of time. That time period is actually outside the comprehension of physical form (thought), because there really is neither past nor future; everything always happens in the Now moment. Whether it happens in Atomic time or cosmic time is of little consequence as everything is always happening Now in the Present moment. Each of these moments has a significant purpose.

Until you have discovered how to remove the smokescreen covering your Knowing, you will not be in a frame of mind to understand these truths. You will continue to question and be a skeptic. It is very difficult for someone at a lower-energy vibration to see clearly. That's alright; the time will come when you too will see everything with Conscious Clarity. When that time comes, you will simply smile when thinking of the fears you once experienced.

In the next chapter, you will begin understanding there is nothing to fear and you will begin to believe that you are much more than the ego; have patience, as Conscious Clarity cannot be rushed.

Chapter 1 Suggestions - Aligning With True Self

The secret to Knowing that which you really are, a Spiritual Being having a human experience, is within you; in the higher-energy vibration at the core of your Being. Nothing (no thing) of the outside form-based world will bring you closer to your Higher Self recognition than going within.

Most people look to some *thing* or someone outside themselves to teach them how to live a life filled with happiness and contentment. This is typical because that is, in fact, what we are taught since childhood. In truth, there is really nothing to be learned; all the answers are already there within you at the Spiritual Self level.

"Meditation is not some "thing" you do; it is the experience of Being that which you are." – Terry Swejkoski

Suggestions for re-discovering True Self:

- Most importantly, meditate daily, at least once a day (better twice a day, morning and night).

- Live your life based upon Love, not fear.

- Listen closely (meditate) and know that you are a Spiritual Being currently living a human experience.

- Consistently, meditate in silence; recapture the stillness of peaceful connection with God.

- Stop thinking about the past and future; pay close attention to the present moment.

- At the end of the day, journal to discover what you thought about all day.

- Watch for the signs (intuition) that bubble up from within you; it is your true guidance calling out to you.

- Bring your innermost feelings to the surface and let that higher vibration be your guide.

- Know that you are the Conductor of your Train of Life™ and live from that knowledge.

- Integrate the Four Body System together in proper sequence: Spiritual, Mental, Emotional and Physical.

- Let go of unnecessary thoughts and go within for solutions to challenges.

When we align ourselves with our inner Higher Self (Conductor), most words become nothing less than clutter of the mind. The true essence of who we really are is waiting patiently beneath the layers of ego-driven dogma. If you are not willing to meditate daily or find another means to reconnect with Source Energy in which you align with the higher-energy vibrations of the Universe, you will continue to live your life based upon all the outside influences in life situations.

It's up to you to make a choice of whether or not you want to truly understand who you really are. Don't expect anything outside of your Higher Self to provide answers for you. You are the co-creator of the Universe and all the knowledge of that vast extension of you is waiting to be re-discovered from within.

Once you start meditating (reconnecting), you will begin living life in blissful alignment; integrating the Spiritual Body first and flowing with the categories of life situations on *The Train of Life*™, rather than fighting for survival in the material world of confusion and illusion.

Listen to the guidance from within and discover how to truly see the magnitude of your own greatness through the Higher Self connection!

Chapter 2

Conscious Awareness of Your Journey

How Do I Know Where I Come From

We each have the ability to make connections with the powers of Higher Self, which provide all that is necessary for a happy, fulfilled life. The ego does not want this to manifest in its current state. However, there is a deep Knowing hidden inside that will begin to surface once you discover how to reconnect with this power. When you finally do reconnect, you will understand what you have been unclear about in the past. The only way you will ever get reconnected is through an effort on your behalf. One of the best ways to do this is through the practice of daily meditation.

There are also other considerations such as the possibility of contacting a channel to reestablish a connection. However, typically mediums do not provide the Conscious Clarity that you will always receive from your own inner intuition. The feelings that arise through intuition are not a guessing game. The feelings are a sign that you are either in or out of alignment with your Original Source Agreement. Therefore, pay close attention to your feelings as they are the bridge to conscious awareness.

No one can bring you closer to your True Self than you can using the power of meditation. Yes, there are people with higher energy vibrations that can assist you with reconnecting with Higher Self, but when it really comes down to it, you are the only one that will see the signs and only when you are ready discover them. If you believe you can reconnect, you will. If you do not believe, then you simply will not and will continue to live your life in a fog. You will live through experiencing someone else's Train of Life™ other than your own. You will continue to be focused on material-based perceptions of the five human senses and true awareness will be stalled. You will stay stuck in the third dimension with most of the world's population and complain about how tough life is. Acceptance of what is will continue to elude you and victimization illusion will be your mantra. This is all a choice.

Many people today are feeling as though some *thing* is missing in their life. It's possible to find other people that have similar thoughts with whom you can connect to discuss what you are feeling. There are many questions to be asked; meditation and spiritual discussion groups are forming all around the world now that the planet is operating in the fourth dimension. More people are awaking to the beauty of their Higher Self as the mass consciousness of the world increases in energy vibration. However, for most people, it's difficult to believe that what they are living is merely an illusion. Why would you think any different, after all, you have been trained since infancy to only look at life through what you can perceive with the five senses. Can there really be anything more?

In reality, the light at the end of the tunnel does not exist, because the tunnel is an illusion of the mind. However, you can increase conscious awareness when the body is trained to increase energy vibration. When most people gather together in prayer, they believe they are brought together to worship a form-based deity. That worship is usually based upon religion and form-based rules that were set in place at a time of deep fear, contrived through manipulation during past centuries. There's no need to be fearful anymore. No one will burn you at the stake for voicing your Higher Self opinion. Humanity is now in a wonderful age of breaking out of our fear-based shells. Take the time to look around you to see how the world is actually evolving. Old paradigms are being questioned as never before because people are awakening to the essence of who they really are.

In truth, we all come from exactly the same place and the more time you spend with like-minded individuals the clearer that fact will become to you. Once you begin communicating with other individuals that have awakened to higher energy levels of energy vibration, you will begin to release the unnecessary Baggage Cars holding back the momentum of your Train of Life™. It is time to step out of the box and rediscover your true Higher Self. Consider following your instincts more than ever before, because we are on the verge of something really huge taking place in our evolution. The first indication may come based upon a vision you have seen, perhaps as a dream. Do not dismiss the dreams you have, especially the visions that show up just as you are failing asleep. The reality is, at this early stage of perceived sleep is when the highest guidance usually occurs.

When you first begin the reconnection, there will be a period of doubt, then confusion. There will be occurrences of consciousness that cannot be explained with the mind. These periods of confusion are just what is needed to get the energy flowing and the sooner the better. If you feel like you don't belong here in this hectic world, don't give it a second thought because change is on its way. Remember, you are here by choice, based upon the Original Source Agreement, and the life path needed to help heal the world of all its pain and suffering. You have a job to do and feeling like you don't belong is really because you are not of this body. You are the entity within; the rest is just makeup.

Why Do I Feel I Don't Belong Here

When you feel like you don't belong here on this planet, it simply means you are homesick and need a surge of higher energy to get back on track. The truth is you don't belong here, that is in the actual form-based meaning of belong. Never forget you are a Spiritual Being having a human experience; it is imperative for you to accept that reality in order to move forward at an accelerated momentum. When feelings of longing for home arise, just understand that you knew this would happen. Just observe the feelings and ask for guidance in dealing with the way you feel. The feeling of being homesick is there purposely so that you never forget who you really are. It is your Higher Self whispering to you. Once you get further along in the *Conscious Clarity Energy Process™*, it will be easier for you to understand and accept that you are here temporarily. When your mission is complete, you will be going home. That was the hardest truth for me personally, because I allowed my ego to take almost complete control of who I am prior to awakening to truth and merging the Soul and ego together.

We all signed up for this journey knowing there would be challenges along the way. It's all part of your free will to make choices that will carry you forward or set you back a few steps. That's why it's really important to get the Soul merged with the mind. Once that happens, everything changes and the way you go about doing the daily things in this life situation take an amazing turn for the better. I can remember when I felt like I was split in two, not knowing what was reality and what was illusion. The mind will really mess with your lower self to a point where some people are actually not able to function in their life situation or environment. Some wind up in mental institutions and others simply make the choice to check out and return home. Those that do leave early are not fulfilling their mission here completely, because they have allowed mind to overpower their true intention for being here. These people that choose to leave early are making a conscious choice to do so. It has nothing to do with the people surrounding them; it has only to do with their ability to cope with the life situation at the lower energy level until they can increase the vibration to one of higher understanding.

If you are having trouble grasping this whole idea of being here temporarily and then leaving to continue your actual formless life which, of course, is eternal, I can fully understand that at this point. Just be gentle with yourself while you let the energy vibration build. Some of us had to step the vibration down to an extremely low level in order to fit into the situation we were first born into. I remember as a small child, under the age of five, that I felt really out of it, like I didn't belong. I saw what was going on around me and knew there was something better. At that time, I was already mostly brainwashed into ego; however, I knew deep inside, there was something missing. That something turned out to be my direct connection with Higher Self. At that tender young age, I knew I needed to stay connected with my Higher Self to survive growing up in the heart of Detroit's east side. I believe I was more homesick during those times simply because I hadn't been on Earth that long. Even though the life situation world of form was only a few years old for me, from my perception, it was difficult to watch what people did to one another. I knew deep inside we are all One, but the world of form keep trying to hold back my True Self reality.

One of my greatest moments of enlightenment was when an African American friend of mine turned his back on me. I knew we were okay together, but he was hanging with a bunch of his buddies and had to put on a show in front of them. In Detroit, back in the 1950's, it was very racial, especially in the environment I grew up in. In the inner city, you were considered Black, White, Mexican, Indian or whatever other slang words that were used at the time. This was just the way it was and everyone simply accepted it. If possible, everyone lived in their own little, ethnic environment. It went right down to living in an Italian, Polish, German, etc, community. The energy vibration was very low and extremely violent. As a young child, I would watch all the different gangs around me and wonder why they all felt so separated. All I saw was people trying to fit in any way they could.

However, there was always this deep feeling of Oneness inside me, so I was always one to challenge the social norm of the city life. My deep feelings of being connected with all these people was very strong and never really changed that much. I always had a feeling that I was safe, even though the neighborhoods were tough. I somehow knew it was a temporary situation and, someday, I would be moving to a much nicer environment.

Sadly, the same dysfunctional conditions continue to plague many neighborhoods even today, more so in the inner city than in the outside metropolitan areas. I grew up being told if you grow up in the city, you either get tough or you die. That was hard for me to grasp at a young age; unfortunately, some of those same patterns or mistakes are repeated to this day. The vast majority of the planet is still vibrating at a very low level, even with the mass consciousness of the world evolving to a higher energy vibration. I personally believe we are at a tipping-point where we will either raise our collective energy vibration to evolve or we will continue on the current destructive path and become extinct. It all depends on the mass consciousness energy vibration. With the planet now evolved to the fourth dimension, we have every opportunity to make it.

I will explain energy vibration later in detail, but for now just trust that it takes a different amount of input or work from Higher Self to reconnect at various life situation social levels of reality. Even though that may seem unfair to the ego, just always remember you signed up for this journey and the script keeps changing. All of this is based upon your free will to make the changes in the script as you continue on the journey. The ending will be based upon your choices and how you bring your true vision to light.

The most important thing you can do for yourself immediately is get into a daily form of connection with Higher Self through meditation or prayer, such that, you can stay actively connected with your true Higher Self at increased levels each day. As you do so, the Original Source Agreement will become clearer for you to understand each day. Once the mind is quiet and at peace, the reasons for your being here will truly stand out to a point where you will actually start to again "feel" the right direction for you as opposed to only thinking about your life path.

Why Am I Here Now

Learning is not always easy because there is a skeptic (ego) buried within us that questions everything. The fact that you made an Original Source Agreement is probably one of the most challenging forms of acceptance for the ego-skeptic mind to get passed. Accepting this is the basis for all spiritual acceptances. If you are still having difficulty with this reality, I offer that you are not in touch with Highest Self. This is why I continue to stress the importance of finding the right Source connection path for your particular personality. Of all the things you could possibly do for yourself, daily meditation is the first on my list of recommendations. When you are connected with Source, your Higher Self will have actual conversations with Highest Self or Source energy. The teaching at the higher levels of energy does not come from outside of you. It is all an internal reality that is focused on a deep Knowing from within. This Knowing only comes when you have the understanding of faith deeply imbedded in you unconscious Self.

If you really want to know why you are here, and that means know (not speculate), you must get back in touch with Source energy. It's always a challenge for someone that does not accept their true magnificence to believe that they are part of the collective co-creation energy force. There are many references from people of all walks of life that lead to the reality of an Original Source Agreement. One of the best examples I can think of is Neil Donald Walsh and his writings

Conversations with God. This is a story of a man that has lost all hope in life, but then when he thinks all is lost, he hears a voice talking to him. The voice asks him if he has had enough and starts to talk to him from a Source that is far greater than himself or most people's understanding. This is hard for most people to comprehend but is gaining popularly as more of us are opening up to the idea of connection with Highest Self.

I offer you an opportunity to look deep within yourself, past the skeptic and into the heart where all possibilities are there waiting for you to awaken them. If you believe all there is is thought and your life situation experience, you have a long way to go before you will see true reality. If this is the case for you, be gentle with yourself because understanding will come, however, there is no set timing for enlightenment. You will experience brief instances of awareness where you feel truly enlightened, but for the most part until you get the Soul merged with the ego; it will be a tough journey. Don't be surprised if you life makes a turn for the worst before you finally get it. As Emerson stated, "When it's dark enough, you can see all the stars." This statement represents the awakening of oneself to the reality of Source energy or the increased vibration of the Higher Self within. Some people must fall far below ego's manipulations before awakening occurs. The reason for this, in my opinion, is that it's the only path to eliminate thought and just be with acceptance and surrender to what is.

Understanding your Original Source Agreement can only be accomplished by you personally, with an open heart and the proper flow of energy flowing through you. It will become as clear as a cloudless sky. All past doubt will disappear and you will experience a feeling of true bliss and Knowing. This comes in many different forms and only you will know when you are opening your energy path to allow the higher energies to permeate your true higher acceptance of what is.

You must allow the thoughts the day to fall away so that you can experience the peace and tranquility of the moments that Original Source Agreement are made available to you through Conscious Clarity of who you really are. Yes, it is difficult for you to understand that there are conversations with Higher Source waiting for you. I totally get this, as I was one of the skeptics with a deeply embedded set of lies passed down to me throughout my early years. It wasn't until I started to consciously sit in a meditative state that everything became clear. I offer this to you as a reality of "been there, done that". If I had not experienced this miraculous change of heart personally, I would still be living the same life situation based upon the untrue input from others that were also lied to.

You are here for a definite purpose and it is only when you increase your energy vibration that it will be revealed to you clearly. Only you can decide what the next step is for you to awaken. If you want to stay stuck where you are, it's a matter of choice. You set the plan in motion and only you can decide on a straight path to enlightenment or a path of twists and turns that keep you off course and lost in a cloud of smoke.

If you ask me your purpose, I have absolutely no idea; only you and Source energy know for certain. Get in touch with that energy and you will know what to do next. And, the obvious answer to why you are here now is because you are!

Who Decided That I Should Be Here Now

Higher Self controls everything you do when you are not clouded by the smokescreen of fuel that is burning at a very low energy level. During these moments of feeling inspired to do something, is when you are actually in touch with your purpose for being here. It's when thoughts are limited and Spirit angels are allowed to shine through the dogma of the daily life situations that you are the most connected with Highest Self. At these moments, which are the spaces between the thoughts, is when you are connecting with the Universe in ONENESS.

I know it's hard to believe from the ego's point of view that all is well, no matter what the life situation. When we are going through a time of pain, may it be physical or emotional, it's difficult for the mind to accept that this is the way it was planned out. It's important to embrace the knowledge laying dormant in your Highest Self on a daily basis. This is especially true when we are going through a time of hardship. You could call it a test or simply an awakening to the fact that you are not in alignment with your true purpose for being here.

Much of this seems contradictory in nature, but it is exactly the way it is meant to play out. The saying goes, "you reap what you sow", but that is only true when you are doing things based upon the mind. When you are living your life inspired by the creative forces within you, this is when all things are being given to you in harmony with the agreement you made with Source energy. If you believe you are a victim of the circumstances in your life situation, take a close look at those circumstances and evaluate your part of their conception. All that has happened in the past is simply to bring you to the place you are today. Therefore, ask yourself how you arrived at this point in time, that is, from the sequential time viewpoint.

If you are asking "Why am I here now", remember the answer is always you are here now based upon your choice to be here. If your life seems to be out of balance and spinning out of control, sometimes that is exactly what you need to get you back on path. If you feel you are on the path that you planned out for yourself you will feel it deep inside. Even if it's turmoil, there is a reason for it. It may be something you agreed to based upon the Original Source Agreement meeting with all the people in you cast of life. Each person that comes your way is there because you accepted them into your life situation casting membership. The way you utilize them in this life situation is entirely up to you.

If you look at the casual factor of where you are today, you can always get at least a small glimpse of the reality from Original Source Agreement. It may be subtle in the way it shows itself but never the less it will reveal itself if you ask for the guidance. It seems during my lowest times in life that I became the most clear in what I was to do next. When you are feeling emotions that don't feel good, it's a clue that you are off track. When you are feeling emotions that are good, it's a clue you are on track and living your life from a state of inspiration or in alignment with higher Source Energy.

If things are tough for you in your life situation, please do not be discouraged. This is especially true if you are going through a tough time, but are still feeling peaceful with the process. There may be something coming that you are to handle while in this tough situation. It could be something as simple are giving someone else support that is in the same situation as you are. As long as you are taking some form of action toward what you truly believe your Life Plan purpose is, you will come out the other side as a victor. There are no unexplained occurrences in life situation. It's all a process and even though the process can be emotionally painful, it's OKAY.

Now is the time for you to be here; the proof of that is that you are. Remember, you may be in this particular situation to help someone else that has lost their way. There is always a hidden explanation to everything that happens. It's when you are at your highest vibration that the reasons will be clearly present. Look for the signs and be present in each moment so that you do not miss them. Someone or something is coming to guide you, have faith.

Why Don't I Remember Anyone Else

Reality is whatever you make it - that is if you are living your life only based upon the five sensory perception of life. This is typical based upon the living in the illusion of the eight categories of life, but only focusing on the six that are tied more directly to the form-based interpretation of what is.

When you live your life based upon who you really are, a Spiritual Being having a human experience then the illusion takes on a different form. Then you start to see the reality outside of the dream we call life situation. You must always remember you are here to assist in healing the planet from the lower vibration of addictive behavior to bring Conscious Clarity to the reality of the true purpose. We have been in a cloud for so long that it will take a while for this change to happen.

Dreams are described as some form of thinking beyond what the reality of life is. This is so backwards in perception that it is sad to believe most of the world continues this thought pattern which is the real dream! This dream is the manipulation of form-based life's illusion of reality. Anything that came from the form-based reality is the actual dream and that dream has a beginning and an end. What you brought with you when you started this dream is the only thing you will take with you when you leave. When you finally return home, you will be stripped of everything that was co-created in the illusion of life situation.

It's difficult for most people to consider there is something other than what they experience on Earth that they will be returning to at the end of this human life. If that is the case for you, please be patient with me while you read these words, and more importantly, please be patient with yourself. You are not in a position to understand as you have not risen your energy vibration high enough to receive or remember what happened before you came here into this form-based world. Some people would say talking about something that exists beyond what is experienced here on Earth is delusional. Well, I'm here to tell you that kind of perception is what's truly delusional and is lower energy vibration thinking. When you learn to merge the Soul with the mind and ego, you will be able to see what you do not see now.

When you finally experience the Soul Merge part of your awakening to the true reality, you will remember more of what happened before you arrived here. You will also understand that it's not necessary to drag all the train cars of your sequential past time with you as you progress forward in the life situation. The Soul Merge will take you to the next level of understanding.

Until you awaken to the reality of Oneness that you are, you will continue to question any possibility outside your sensory perception of the world. This includes people that come into your life situation to assist you in remembering. We have all met someone that we would swear we knew before but simply can't remember from where. When you feel this type of higher energy interaction, it is because that person is in some way part of the Original Source Agreement process. They may have been a minor part of the meeting you had with Source energy. You may not remember them at your current level of understanding, but they are there for the purpose of helping you to remember your true life path. Just allow them to be with you in whatever small way that is necessary and do not fear what cannot be remembered on the surface.

The increase in energy vibration as you progress through this awakening process will provide you with a glimpse from time to time of the true reality as it was actually intended. Your true purpose will continue to shine forth and you will begin to live the life you were meant to live here on Earth before you lost your way.

What's Life's Purpose Here on Earth

When asking the question "What's life's purpose here on Earth?", consider this a direct question, too. You know you are a Spiritual Being having a human experience. If you have not as yet acknowledged that fact, then it's time for you to stop procrastinating and get in touch with your Higher Self immediately. Start connecting with Highest Source in some way. Each of us has our own best way for doing that, for me, it's through being in a meditative state daily. In meditation, all thought is removed, the mind is emptied and a conscious conversation with Highest Source Energy is possible. If you do not empty your mind of the constant clutter of unnecessary thoughts, you will find it difficult to achieve this sacred connection.

The answers to all questions are found only in the silence between thoughts. It is in this deep space of grace that everything is first created. Looking elsewhere is insanity. If you believe you can find answers or solutions in the same form-based space that created the questions, you are not being true to your Highest Self or the reason you are here. We are all channels of higher energy and are put here on this planet to assist the Universe in evolving to the next higher level of creation. We are all part of the totality of energy vibrated at levels beyond human understanding. When we try to *do* by only using the limiting power of the mind, we place a heavy layer or residue of uncertainty (smoke - created from the fuel of lower energy influence) around our Conscious Clarity. The space where all the answers bubble up is crystal clear because all the outside influences are swept away. When the outside influence is discarded, what remains is a conscious awareness of the deeper realms of knowledge; not knowledge based upon the limited perspective of the mind, but knowledge or a deeper Knowing based upon the unlimited creative power of the Universe.

Each of us has a unique purpose for being here on Earth that is in harmony with the mass purpose of raising the energy vibration level of humanity to be harmonized in Oneness. We are all part of the totality of this Oneness and are here to do a small segment of the co-creative process.

Your part in this Divine Master Plan is clearly available to you if you make the effort to open yourself to it consciously.

Your part of the teaching is hidden deep inside your Higher Self and cannot be accessed unless you remove the form-based uncertainty. When the mind is cleared, the vision or co-creative process is allowed to flow without resistance of any form. In this state of formlessness, you are connected with your Higher Self and your energy vibration begins to attract the higher frequencies or higher teachings from Source energy. When you access these higher vibrations frequently, your core energy vibration increases and your ability to consciously see solutions to life's challenges become clear. When your energy is high, you will find yourself asking better questions and, therefore, solutions to challenges appear as if by magic.

If you are only thinking from a lower vibration level, the answers simply do not arrive with Conscious Clarity. They arrive with mind-limiting doubt and produce more limited questions that do nothing but create confusion. If you are feeling as though this is a cycle that has never-ending circles, you are absolutely correct. This is the typical insane thought process that most people use when attempting to solve a challenge. They don't look to the Higher Self for solutions; they simply stay in the circle of confusion and never really get anywhere. This is totally a choice that is being made based upon the illusion of thought and a limited belief structure.

One of the limiting beliefs most people have that are living strictly from ego is time constraints. If you believe you only have X amount of time to fulfill your destiny, then that's your reality. If you are focused on absolute deadlines, your life will be consumed with going from one issue the next in a chaotic state. All that you can do is your part in the preparation of creating a solution to a challenge. Once your input is received, it's time for you to step away from the issue and allow the Universe to provide a solution in Cosmic time.

If you do not complete your mission during this lifetime, it's OKAY – there will be other lifetimes available to you to do so. Please, remind yourself who you really are each day prior to achieving Soul Merge. Once the merging process is complete, reminders will no longer be necessary, as you will be anchored in your greatness and never question it again.

Where Am I Going After This Life

This is a question that has been asked since the beginning of time as we know it from the ego's perspective. The answer is right in front of you. You will go exactly where you are meant to go based upon how you lived your life situation and how deeply it is in harmony with your Original Source Agreement. This pre-planned agreement has all the detail you could ever ask for; all you need do is stay connected with Source Energy to be clear about your next intended step.

You already know you are a Spiritual Being having a human experience. Therefore, the possibilities of where you are going next are unlimited. The Universe is One and the greater knowledge of that Oneness is interconnected within the Original Source Agreements of all. The intricacies of how these plans all merge together was already pre-planned in the decisions that took place long before you showed up on this planet in human form. Therefore, the question must be opened to a broader perspective which may be beyond your current level of understanding.

If your life on Earth is based upon living the guidance categories at a high level of energy vibration, you will be going to a different place then if you are living at a lower energy vibration. Once you have completed your current intended assignment, you will move on. The where is based totally on the harmony of your current life. You have the opportunity everyday to live a life based on Love or fear. As you grow in your awareness of what is, you will learn to experience the greatness that you are. In that greatness, all things that are fearful will fall away and the divide beauty of a path of Love will shine forth.

When you remember where you came from in the first place, you will know that you will be returning home to Higher Self in some way. How it all works out will not be a surprise for your Spiritual Self. You already know at your Soul level where you are going. For someone living a life of service through Love, you will be going to yet another place of living life through Love at a deeper level.

Each day we are allowed to make choices based upon free will and the understanding of life as we perceive it in the current moment. Therefore, it may be worthwhile to focus on the now and not be concerned with what the future will bring. In reality, all time is form based and has no reference in the Universal Divine Master Plan. There is no past; no future and all there ever will be is Now. Stop here and ponder that for awhile. If you can learn to wrap your arms around that concept, you will not require an answer to the question "Where am I going after this life?"

A life filled in deep presence of the current moment will lead to the next now moment in harmony and Love without question. It will be the blessed place you are meant to be at in that exact moment and you will realize the more you can ground yourself into that moment, the better off you and everyone around you will be. Where you are going next, will no longer matter.

What's the Purpose of Grounding

To fully understand the purpose of grounding, you must first understand what grounding is. When someone is said to be grounded, it means that they are actually living a life in sync with the Earth by having the Earth Star chakra solidly planted in reality. The Earth Star chakra is a sub-set of the eighth chakra which is the Soul Star. They are located approximately one foot below the feet and one foot above the head, respectively. There is a constant flow of energy that moves through the body chakras called Kundalini energy, which is regulated and anchored to the Earth consciousness through this systematic flow. (See Illustration F for a general visualization of this flow.)

Source Energy is so powerful in amplitude that it requires a stepping down process or transformation into the lower energy vibration prior to its entrance into the physical body. If this stepping down process was not conduced first through the chakras, the lower self body would simply burn up. Because we are multidimensional beings, we have the power to step down Source Energy to assist in the process of transformation to the lower levels of understanding. Therefore, when it is said that you are grounded, it means you are living life on Earth based upon having that higher energy stepped down to a level of power that is in harmony with your current level of Knowing. This may seem a bit confusing on the surface or to the lower self level; however, it becomes clearer as your energy vibration is stepped back up through opening the chakras to allow the higher energy to flow through your body effectively.

This is why it is important for you to first realize "who you really are" during the awakening process I am slowly assisting you with. The awakening is not a physical occurrence, but consists exclusively of a development in consciousness. Kundalini awakening brings increased perception of cosmic vibrations and radiant energy and understanding of the connections and laws within the universe deepens.

You could relate the whole process of energy to that of a high tension wire which flows thousands of volts of electricity to a transformer that then steps down that higher voltage to a usable rate. Typically, that is either 240 volts or 120 volts depending on the way the receiving device is wired. If the transformer was not there to step down the electrical energy, the receiving device would be fried immediately.

We all have the ability to step down Source Energy and, conversely, we all have the power to step up grounded energy back up to a higher vibration by opening the chakras. The way you live your life here on Earth is based upon how high you choose to transform the original energy back up to a greater level of connection with Source. This all relates to the discussion earlier in the *Conscious Clarity Energy Process™* and can be better understood by reviewing Illustration C, *Energy Transformation*. In this diagram, you can clearly see how the energy from Highest Source level is stepped down through the Life Plan Categories and eventually grounds to Earth through the wheels of *The Train of Life™* analogy.

Therefore, if you are living a balanced life and are in harmony with your Original Source Agreement, you will feel grounded and in harmony with the energy levels flowing through the human body. These energy levels are channeled through at higher levels through your Higher Self which is in constant contact with Source.

Once you discover how to unblock the chakra energy system, you will merge the Higher Self (True Self) with the ego. When this Soul Merge is completed, you will then be able to channel higher energy understanding. Until the Soul Merge is completed, most of this information will be perceived by your ego as meaningless or "way out there". This deeper understanding will not happen all at one time, but it will happen exactly when you are ready for it to happen. That means when the student is ready, the teacher will show up. That teacher is your Higher Self or could be another person vibrating at a higher energy level (already clearly receiving the higher energy messages) and will channel the higher energy information to you.

Can All People Channel

Channeling is nothing more than stepping energy down to a lower level of understanding, such that it can be used as a teaching experience. Everyone can channel without exception; channeling is enhanced through meditation. The way we all teach is based upon our own life experiences, what we think and what we believe. This is typically viewed from an egoist perspective as something that is hard to do or something that requires some special talent or savant nature. Well, the truth is we are all savants (learned person) in our own respect. We all are really good at something. That something is your true higher power and is a gift to share with the world through teaching.

Your true talents rest deeply buried within yourself and only you can bring them into the light of the higher energy levels of teaching. On the inside, we are all the same. We are all Spiritual Beings having a human experience. It's the outside labels and distractions of daily life situation that place a smokescreen over our true Higher Self. Part of the smokescreen or untruth is that we are different. Therefore, it is necessary for the ego to place labels on our outward appearance. These labels separate us from our true Higher Self and will be there until you decide to take back control of your life situation. You can do this by practicing the act of meditation.

Meditation is some "*thing*" the ego wants you to think you can't do. The keyword here is "thing", because if you are thinking in the form-based sense of the word, you are not vibrating at a high enough energy to connect with Higher Self directly. It is in the silence between the thoughts that meditation occurs. Meditation is nothing more than consciously connecting with Higher Self by eliminating the constant clutter of egoist thought. Once you mastered the natural state of meditation, the channeling capabilities increase in energy and you will have conversations at a higher level of awareness. This is where all the solutions are to every perceived challenge you have in the daily life situation reality.

One of the best ways to begin the perceived practice of meditation is by simply sitting in a quiet room without any attempt to do any*thing*. The keyword here, again, is "thing", which includes thought (thoughts are form-based – therefore a "thing"). One of the recurring questions people ask is "How can you not think?" The answer is simply by Being. When you are Being, all thought is gone. That means you are Being that which you are. The Spiritual Higher Self does not require thought. When you are sitting in this state of non-thought, simply Being, the messages received are beyond thought. This higher energy vibration is uncommon to the vast majority of the planet, because the mass consciousness understanding is too busy trying to figure every*thing* out. During meditation, there is nothing to figure out because there is no thought. It's amazing what bubbles up once you learn to empty the mind.

When the body learns to relax and just be with the present moment, all stress and self-limiting thought is gone, you are at peace. This is your natural state of Being; it is the peace and silence of conscious connection with Higher Self or the greater energy vibration Self which is still you, but the you of the Universal One. You are not here to separate; you are here to connect at a higher level of understanding. You will vibrate at a higher energy each day you actively participate in meditation.

"Meditation is not some "thing" you do; it is the experience of Being that which you are." – Terry Swejkoski

Your energy level was stepped down when you arrived on Earth, such that you could blend into your physical body without burning up. When you meditate, you increase this energy a little at a time and are in contact with other entities vibrating at the higher levels of reality. Meditation should be an essential part of your daily life. If not, it makes it difficult to actively channel your true gifts to the people around you for the benefit of all. You may not realize it now, but we all have a greater purpose for being here, one that is far greater than what is usually seen on the surface. Meditation will reconnect you with that greater purpose and allow you to teach that which is misunderstood by most of humanity.

Is There a Greater Purpose

Purpose is an open-ended word based upon one's beliefs, both spiritually and humanly. Each of us has our own perception of reality, totally dependent on our current energy vibration level. The Spiritual Self has an advantage over the ego self as it knows the true purpose for you being here on Earth. The Higher Self has the capability to see the Original Source Agreement clearly without all of the outside influences of life situation. Prior to the Soul Merge process being achieved, it will be difficult for you to see the true purpose of your life here. This is mainly because the ego (mind) will have already been manipulating you for so long that you have forgotten your true purpose.

The coming home or Soul Merge with the Spiritual Higher Self is a slow process. It takes time to remove all of the layers of doubt and fear. You must learn to be patient while the *Conscious Clarity Energy Process*™ moves forward with focused intention. Please understand that once you get the Kundalini energy flowing freely through the body without the typical blockages caused by fear, everything will change for you. You may not see the changes in immediate sensory perception; however, you will feel them as the energy flows through you and makes cosmic connection with Source energy.

Your particular part in the Universal greater purpose of life will become consciously clearer to you each day that you spend in silence once you have learned Soul Merge. Right now, it is impossible for you understand the higher purpose you have because your energy is still blocked. The best way to unblock that flow of energy is through daily meditation focused on the Divine good of all. It is time for you to purge the thoughts of self-centeredness from your mind and start to look at life from the higher perspective of the Universal plan for all of mankind and the Cosmic levels of reality. There is much more to your purpose than what you are capable of perceiving through the typical sensory level of awareness. It is a beautiful place to behold once you have experienced Soul Merge.

To explain further, so you may understand with increased clarity, consider the Universal Plan as the entire movie. Your role is simply a small portion of the script, almost as a walk-on in the total picture. Yes, each one of us is an important part of each scene and we each have our own greatness. The most important part to remember is that you are part of the whole; without you, there is no totality or Oneness. Just as each drop of water makes up the entire ocean, you are an important part of the Universal Oneness.

The human mind is not capable of understanding the Universal Plan which is why you must go far beyond thought to experience the big picture. There are multiple levels of awareness that you will step through as you progress through the *Conscious Clarity Energy Process™*. You must be patient and allow your energy level to build at a rate that is compatible with your level of awareness.

If you have doubt or fear, your energy will block again and you will lose momentum on *The Train of Life™*. This is nothing to be concerned with at this time; it is a natural process until the Soul Merge occurs. You may not realize it now, but soon you will understand that you are the creator of your own reality. However, once the Soul Merge does occur, you will no longer be controlled by the mind. You will see yourself as that which you are - a Spiritual Being participating in a human experience which is a miraculous opportunity for spiritual growth.

What Does Human Being Mean

To live a life of happiness and abundance, it is imperative that you rise above the level of ego's dominance over you. You were never intended to live life based upon simple survival mode. You are far greater than your ego will allow you to believe you are. Therefore, it is in your best interest to regain control of your life situation, but at a higher level of awareness if you are to achieve what you have pre-programmed for your life in your Original Source Agreement.

The Universe is a combination of form and non-form entities which are in the process of coming into conscious alignment or ascension. Source energy (God) created human beings for the purpose of interaction at the lower levels of energy vibration (See Illustration C, *Energy Transformation*) based upon starting the Life Plan journey at the current level of mass consciousness. However, Source energy never intended form-based human beings to interact only at the form-based (ego) level of understanding. Source energy's intention was to allow human beings to begin human-life form at the lower levels of vibration and then, utilizing the categories of Life Plan Balance, sensate or sensory perception and free will to slowly raise their energy levels back up to a Universal level of understanding.

At the Universal level of the *Conscious Clarity Process™*, the human being is guided completely by the Spiritual Higher Self. This is possible because at this level of energy vibration the Soul Merge process is complete. Therefore, the level of understanding is above that of ego, due to ego merging with Higher Self energy. At the Universal level, the chakras are open and Kundalini energy guides your life situation. Once you reach the Universal level of reality, everything transforms to yet another quantum leap in awareness. At this level of awareness (energy vibration) the *True Personality* is revealed (always guided by Spirit) and the mind is no longer lead by old ego perspective.

Please review Illustration E, *Energy Vibration - Life Fuel Source* to gain a better understanding of how energy vibration is associated with your actual life situation experiences and outside influences (fuel source). In the diagram, you will see three different columns which explain energy vibration, life fuel source and resultant reality. Study the diagram and see where you may fit in at the current moment.

Energy Vibration – You came from Source energy which may be beyond your current level of ego's understanding. That energy level was gradually stepped down (Illustration C, *Energy Transformation*) until it reached the level of current human mass consciousness. This transformation process was necessary to allow you to enter the human body without burning it up upon merging within it. Remember, you are a Spiritual Being having a human experience; you are that which is within, not simply that which is experienced through sensate perception.

Life Fuel Source – The outside influences (fuel source), which you allow to feed the human body, will determine your level of energy vibration at any given moment. It is important for you to understand that you have been giving an amazing gift, the Life Plan Balance categories (guided by ego), which allows you to experience human life form from the sensate perception level of awareness, as well as, the spiritual level.

Resultant Reality – The resultant reality of your life situation is a direct reflection of the fuel source you choose to power *The Train of Life*™ based upon the free will choices made daily. Your life path will be in direct proportion and response to these free will choices and the energy vibration of the fuel source absorbed will be your *perceived* reality in life.

The lower part of Illustration E represents the linear momentum of *The Train of Life*™ analogy based upon Original Source Agreement and the *Conscious Clarity Energy Process*™ level of understanding. Once the ego and Higher Self merge together (Soul Merge), the ego's smokescreen disappears and higher consciousness is achieved. Then you are vibrating at a higher energy level and direct contact with Source energy is restored while lower level ego is absorbed. At this level of understanding, you begin to consciously assist in the healing of the world at a greater level of awareness, because you have learned to live life beyond old ego's dominance. At this level, you allow Source to guide your every move and you check in before making any decisions.

How Do I Stay Connected With Where I Came From

When the reality of Knowing you are a Spiritual Being currently having a human experience becomes part of your belief system, you will understand you are always connected with Source energy. The feelings surrounding your belief system will change and you will be living a life based upon the wisdom anchored deeply within the human body. Once the fog of the egoist mind is lifted through Soul Merge, it becomes easier to receive the messages coming from Highest Source which in reality guides your Higher Self.

When acceptance comes from the Higher Spiritual Self, daily life situation becomes a precious joy. The way you think about situations surrounding you will change and you will see the greater good in every situation. Even though challenges of daily life will still come and go, your perception and reactions will be based upon the Higher Self awareness of acceptance of what is. You will continue to live life on the surface as part of typical humanity; however, your inner reality will be in alignment with the Original Source Agreement and *True Personality*.

Some would say it's impossible to feel at peace within if there are challenges all around you. Well, to a certain extent is true. That is if you allow the mind's truth which is based mostly upon fantasy stories that the mind tells us when a challenge comes along. The mind is a major influence on every part of the Four Body System. Therefore, if we allow the mind to be in the forefront controlling the body, it has influence over how we react to any given situation. However, when the Higher Self or Spiritual Self is in the forefront controlling what the body perceives, the outcome changes.

We all consist of a Four Body System and how deeply we are integrated into the various parts of that system determines how we approach our life situation on a daily basis. If you could discover how to simply acknowledge that you do indeed have these multiple aspects of the body without allowing them to control you, your life would be a lot happier. Through meditation, you can consciously stay connected with the highest power of this system, the Spiritual Body.

The actual sequence of the Four Body System is of the utmost importance with respect to our perceived level of happiness. Therefore, it is naturally aligned when in the sequence below.

The natural Four Body System alignment consists of the:

1. Spiritual Body
2. Mental Body
3. Emotional Body
4. Physical Body

Example – Typically Out of Alignment:

The vast majority of humankind lives their life based upon having the Four Body System reversed, where control is perceived at the Physical Body first.

- Physical Body - When the Physical Body is first, it identifies as situations happening to me (identity) or a physical reality.

- Emotional Body – This, in turn, excites the Emotional Body, whereas, now a feeling is generated due to what is perceived as having been done to my physical identity.

- Mental Body - These emotions then excite the Mental Body into thinking about what has happened to me (my story), usually based upon thoughts of the past and false beliefs that then lead to some type of reaction to the life situation experienced.

- Spiritual Body - Then finally, after much self-inflicted torment, the Spiritual Body sends a message that perhaps you may be overreacting to the situation at hand. At that point, an inner dialog or discussion within lower self begins and a decision is consciously made to either build on the story (which the Mental Body created) or to drop the issue in acceptance of what is.

The difficulty with this type of pattern is it usually leads to fear-based action, unless you have learned to catch yourself when you see this destructive pattern emerging.

Example – Naturally in Alignment:

If we analyze the same situation and reverse the control mechanisms of our Four Body System, there is a completely different result.

- Spiritual Body - When the Spiritual Body is in control and a life situation occurs, it is first acknowledged as what is and acceptance is immediately allowed. The

112

perception is merely "this happened", it did not happen to me, it simply happened.

- Mental Body - Then the Mental Body activates to confirm; yes, this happened and some type of action may be required.

- Emotional Body - Next, the Emotional Body ignites with a feeling of empowerment to the challenge; it creates positive, solution-based emotions and provides action to resolve the issue, rather than focusing on the challenge as a perceived problem.

- Physical Body - The result is the Physical Body feels peaceful and excited that there is a challenge to resolve. The Physical Body remains stress-free and the solutions appear from a higher knowledge base.

The beauty of this type of pattern is the Four Body System then works in harmony without fear and feels peaceful Knowing that Love through Divine power and wisdom can bring light to any life situation.

In each of the above examples, the resultant actions will vary dramatically depending on whether you are living your life in a state of Love or fear. This may sound rather idealistic to some of you; however, if you make a focused effort to realign yourself with the Spiritual Body (through meditation), your life will be more balanced and in alignment with the higher level of understanding which is experienced through Love, Peace and Light.

The best way to stay connected with your Spiritual Body in the forefront of life situation is through the practice of daily meditation. When you discover how to keep the Spiritual Body in the forefront of your life, your level of awareness in any given situation will have a higher energy level and Conscious Clarity will be the result. When the mind is quiet and Kundalini energy is flowing unrestricted, the highest level of Spiritual communication is possible. It is in that clarity of mind that your true purpose is revealed.

Is There an Alternate Plan

The most difficult part for the mind to understand is the concept of multiple endings or variations to the Original Source Agreement written prior to human birth, because the mind wants to put limits on everything. If you are living your life based upon false limits induced by a belief system of scarcity, then it will be impossible for you comprehend the concept of multiple variations to the Original Source Agreement.

Every possible ending and variation to the Original Source Agreement was written in every detail, including all the various major events, people and constant changing situations of daily life, prior to your first breath. When you learn to become still and purge lower self-limiting beliefs from your body, then and only then, will you be able to fully comprehend the unlimited possibilities available to you in your life situation. You must first be open to the fact that anything is possible. Every thought, action and reaction has already been written. Each possible ending for each life situation has been scripted and it is your free will to choose which actions take place at any given moment.

You do, in fact, create your own reality. Picture yourself living in a movie where you are in total control of everything that is part of that movie. You can change the script, do a re-shoot of a scene or change the actors at anytime. Once you get past the belief system limits that you have set for yourself, the greater possible outcomes will evolve as if by magic. It's the mind and it's limiting ifs and buts that cause all difficulty in life. The really amazing and sometimes confusing part of those limits is the fact that you also wrote those limits into your Original Source Agreement.

Mankind wanted to have free will choices to keep life interesting, exciting and ever-changing. The only way to evolve is to have choices. The whole idea of being here is to evolve to your highest possible Self while experiencing the joys of form-based life situation. The physical aspect of being here is all part of this amazing journey into deeper understanding. Once you merge the Soul and Body together, you will better understand how this whole process of evolution works. You must take small steps at first to open your mind to new possibilities and then you will be ready to take quantum leaps in evolution. Once your understanding is clearly coming from your Higher Self in the forefront, then you will be in a position to grasp the higher levels of understanding.

As you grow older in human form, the wisdom you have will bubble up and you will bring forth the necessary language to teach others with clarity. If you feel as though you are disconnected with all of this – it's OKAY – it's difficult for the mind to accept that it is not in charge of your reality. The mind (ego) will always try to control every life situation as that's how it was taught early on in life. Accept what is in the present moment and you will start to see things with greater clarity. Once the cluttered stories of the mind are put to rest, the evolution of your higher Spiritual Self will bubble up to greet you. Just be patient and live as if today is always the best day of your life. The truth is all you ever have is the present moment, for each past and future moment can only be lived in the present time. Open your eyes to what is in front of you now and let your energy grow into the next level of understanding with faith.

There is always an alternate plan to everything you can possibly imagine - it's the mind's comprehension that causes the doubt. Therefore, to close the mind simply means to eliminate the doubt and open up to the unlimited possibilities of your purpose for being here. Enjoy it! You are the one that wrote it anyway.

Who Decides My Purpose

It's so hard for most people to grasp the fact that you personally are in charge of your own destiny. When you are constantly overwhelmed with outside influence coming primarily from other people's egos, it's hard to see the light at the end of the tunnel. Well, it's really not that you cannot see the light (Spiritual Self); it's just that you have had a layer of fog or uncertainty around you for so long, it simply makes it hard to see that there is another possibility.

Life was never meant to be hard. The mind can play havoc with your normal higher spiritual sense of being that which you really are. To put aside all thought is, in fact, possible. Whether you believe that or not is a matter of how far you have allowed yourself to reconnect with your higher spiritual side. The Higher Self has nothing to do with ego's judgment of higher or lower; Higher Self or lower self only has to do with energy vibration level. The ego will attempt to manipulate you into judgmental patterns, including saying that you are judging if you say Higher Self or lower self. Please do not allow ego to trick you into believing this falsity, the ego does not know any better.

We are all equal and we all have the same ability to raise our vibration level to a natural higher level of energy vibration. We all came from the same place. No one is greater than anyone else. However, when it comes to energy vibration level, it's true that someone may be vibrating at a higher energy level than you are currently. This does not matter as all it means is they are consciously clearer about what is real and what illusion is. Once you finally break through the smokescreen of mind controlling your life situation, all of this will become crystal clear. I understand the difficulties which are encountered along the path to Spiritual awareness. There will be times when your energy vibration falls off a little, this is totally normal, especially when you consider the current mass consciousness level of the planet. Simply be patient because there will be a moment when you finally get it, all will be completely clear.

Your purpose was defined with you during the Original Source Agreement phase of your eternal existence. Once you finally remember who you really are, you will understand the secrets of the Universe. They are all within you and cannot be found outside of you. The mind simply cannot comprehend the possibility that all form-based time is merely an illusion and part of a greater Master Plan. It is so far out there for the ego to understand and the mind will do whatever it can to trick you into thinking the physical body is all there is. It will tell you that you were born and you will die; when, in fact, it is only the body that was born and will die. This only means the physical functions of the body will stop, however, it does not mean the Spiritual True Self will cease to function. You will go on forever. There is really no end to the energy and depth of your true Higher Self. It is simply beyond your comprehension at this time.

The magnitude of the Universe is far beyond that of lower vibration comprehension. Therefore, you owe it to your Higher

Self to consciously work on raising your energy vibration level daily. You are only here for a short period of form-based time and, in this physical lifetime, there is much to be accomplished. Remember, you have a purpose which was written in collaboration with Source energy, co-creators and in alignment with the greater Master Plan which ultimately is all the same energy. Just as an ocean is a combination of many droplets of water, you too are a droplet of energy which is part of the whole Universe. Your purpose is hidden deep within you; do not expect to have it revealed by searching outside of you. Journey deep within and you will be amazed at what you find. Once your energy is flowing with Conscious Clarity, all doubt will be erased, your ego will merge with the Soul and you will live life at a new level of awareness. Outside influences will no longer control you.

When Do I Return

The mind would like you to believe there is actually some place you will return to once the body dies. The truth is that you are already there in that which is deemed as home. When you are living from the deep Knowing of observing life from the Spiritual Self, you will begin to realize the present moment is all there actually is. Each present moment is home at that given moment. To seek something other than what already is confuses the mind; however, the Spiritual Self understands completely.

There is an old saying "home is where the heart is". In reality, what that really means is home is where the Soul is. And, from a spiritual perspective, the Soul is everywhere at once. As being part of the Universal Oneness implies, all that is is in each present moment. There is no thing better than what is and there is no thing in the future that will give more of Spirit. When we awaken to our true Higher Self, we see the present moment as being that which is blessed with the grace of Source energy. Please, remember you have not reached the energy vibration to understand all that is being presented at this level. However, it is important to provide you with the necessary steps in sequence so that you know the layers of ego are being stripped away. This is not to say that the ego will be gone in the true sense of the mind meaning. It means the dogma of the ego's control mechanism will be stripped away such that you will have Conscious Clarity of the truth.

As Spiritual Beings, we are capable of much more than the mind could ever comprehend fully. Once you move to the Monadic level, you will begin to see that the mind will always place limitations on all matter. The Spiritual Self will witnesses these limits as the simple control mechanisms of the ego and dismisses them at the higher energy vibration levels.

The whole concept of going home after death means the death of the ego and the ascension into the higher energy vibration of the Universe. Yes, it could also mean the death of the body and the merging of the Universal Oneness. However, at this point, I doubt the Conscious Clarity has surfaced to the point of that higher energy vibration

120

understanding. Please, realize the current moment is happening now and now is all there every will be. Each present moment was once the future and will also be the past, but only from the mind's perspective. The Spirit does not assign "sequential time", it only knows the present moment. Therefore, if the present moment is all there is or ever will be, does it not make sense to live each moment in sequential time as if it is the only time available to you? If you do so, you will begin to see the greatness of each moment and the absolute power you as a Spiritual Being has enjoy and cherish each moment.

Human beings from an egoist point of view are always looking for something better in the future. When in reality by doing so, they miss out on what is actually here now. If your mind is wondering off someplace in the future, or worse, staying focused on the past, what is is lost in the thought process. When you finally truly understand the present moment is all there is, then and only then will you begin to see the magnitude of the great power you possess within you. You will then realize that each moment is part of an overall Master Plan. of which, you have already agreed to in the Original Source Agreement. You will also realize that each entity agreed to Original Source Agreements in the exact same present moment. When you see this clearly, you will be home.

Chapter 2 Suggestions - Conscious Awareness of Your Journey

There are many stories contrived by the mind everyday which can have a strong influence on you current life situation. The key is staying in alignment with the Spiritual reality of who you real are and not to allow the mind to influence you in a negative way.

Always remember, we all came from the same place before we arrived here on Earth school and we will be returning to the same place without any of the material items acquired here. The Physical Body with fade away and dissolve back into the Earth, but the Spiritual Body will live on for eternity.

The following suggestions may help you to fulfill your Original Source Agreement in an easy and relaxed manner:

- Bring the Spiritual Body to the forefront of daily life.

- The mind will wonder - simply allow it to do so.

- Live each present moment to its fullest by minimizing thoughts of past and future.

- Life is "meditation" *which is not some "thing" you do. It is the experience of Being that which you are!*

- Allow Love to guide you by listening to the guidance that comes from the inner intuitive messages.

- Your purpose is predetermined by the Original Source Agreement you co-created with Source Energy.

- Sit in silence as much as possible so that you can hear the Spirit guides that are assisting you daily to remember your Original Source Agreement.

- Remember that we all came from the same place, are equal and part of the total Oneness of the Universe.

Make it an everyday practice to be conscious of whether or not you have the Spiritual Body in the forefront of everything you experience. The most important aspect of living a life filled with Love, Peace and Light is through consciously living life from a Spiritual Body perspective. By allowing life to unfold in this manner, you will always feel connected to Source Energy and live a fulfilled life situation while co-creating everything from a Higher Self perspective, where your Conscious Clarity realization knows that Love conquers all.

Chapter 3

Write Your Own Script

Is Free Will Really Free

Love is the answer to all unrest in the world. The more you align your True Self with the power of Love, the greater your chances will be to eliminate fear and eventually always live at the higher levels of energy vibration, which God intended you to enjoy.

By now, you are starting to understand the greater possibilities you have in this life situation. The more you increase your energy vibration, the more you will see that you have free will to change your reality in a heartbeat. Only you can make the choices available to you. You are the author of your own story, the script is already written and, now, it is up to you to decide which lines are brought into the playbook of life.

Whenever a situation presents itself in life, we always have at least two choices or directions we can choose. This is when we must be alert and ready to process the necessary inputs being made available to us from a higher level of awareness. If you eliminate all the unnecessary thought patterns in your mind, it will always be easier to answer life's challenges with Conscious Clarity.

If you want to have a better life, you can for it is totally up to you and you alone. Your current life situation is now the sum total of all the choices you have made thus far and can change dramatically in the blink of an eye. I know this is true because I have experienced this many times throughout my personal lifetime. Once you become consciously aware of the signals coming to you from deep within you, that God-like power, you will truly understand there is a Conductor guiding every moment. You are never alone. When this realization (at the mind level) hits home from deeply within, through acceptance of what is and the power of Love, you will begin to see the true possibilities you established for yourself long ago.

As your energy vibration increases, the messages coming from the Conductor of your Train of Life will become very clear. It may still be hard for you to believe that you actually have this wonderful loving energy within you guiding every moment of life situation. However, you will experience the Soul Merge in subtle ways as you step through the *Conscious Clarity Energy Process™*. These small steps will gradually increase your energy until you are ready to fully Soul Merge your personality with your Higher Self. After the Soul Merge enlightenment occurs, it will feel as though a heavy weight has been lifted from your shoulders. You will walk through life's challenges as if you are walking on a cloud and the feeling of peace, tranquility, and yes, utopia will be present most of the time.

Yes, even after Soul Merge, there will still be times when ego's influence will make an attempt to control you. However, when this happens, the Higher Self will see this for what it really is and encourage you to become even more alert. It's at these times, when you are preparing to make quantum leaps in faith, that the ego makes its last attempts to overpower the Higher Self. This will come in the form of some basic fear tactic. This is natural because ego knows it is being overpowered by Higher Self and it also knows that as your energy vibration increases, the chances of ego's manipulations regaining control of your life situation is reduced. The ego does not realize that it will not actual die, it will merely be joined with Higher Self in the glorious Soul Merging process of Faith, Love and Compassion for that which is.

When you learn to open all of the chakras (energy flow centers) and allow the path of Kundalini energy to flow naturally through the body, then you will be fully vested in understanding the truth of the Four Body System. At the exact moment of experiencing a fully open energy system, where ego no longer controls you, you will begin living life at the Universal level of the *Conscious Clarity Energy Process™*. When you reach that level of awareness, each day on Earth will be experienced in a new light and you will understand your part of the Original Source Agreement at a greater level. Then, you will understand what it truly means to have free will guided by the higher energy of the Conductor through daily presence.

127

How Can I Make a Difference

Teaching is something we all do every day; however, most people don't realize they are doing it. Each one of us is really good at doing something special. And that special gift is what we should be doing with our time here on Earth while enjoying this human experience. When we vibrate at a frequency in harmony with our purpose for being here, there is an unexplainable peace and understanding that we will make a difference in this world.

It's not a secret that there are times when everything we touch seems to turn to gold and we feel as though everything is in its proper alignment. At these times, our intuition seems to be providing guidance at an accelerated level. That instinct is your Higher Self, the Conductor of your Train of Life™, stepping into your awareness to assist you with making the best choices. When you experience this higher energy vibration assistance, it feels natural and the end result is always in alignment with Original Source Agreement.

A proven method to ensure you are making the most of your life in harmony with what is best for you is to meditate daily. Most people do not realize the power of meditation, simply because they have never attempted it or they give up on it after one or two attempts. This is part of human nature, to give up if something is beyond our level of understanding or perceived attainment possibility. Therefore, if you have tried to meditate in the past, but became frustrated because of the constant chatter of thought interfering, please understand that this is a normal human reaction. Meditation is all about harmony with Higher Self. Therefore, if you are used to living life at a lower energy level, it will take some readjustment to increase your energy vibration. Simply be patient and you will experience gradual increases over a period of time.

Remember, the ego does not want you to stay connected with your Higher Self. If there is a way for ego to manipulate and control you, it will attempt to do so. However, as you continue meditation daily, over a period of time, you will become consciously aware of ego's attempts to control you. You will discover that you can quickly dismiss the constant clutter of unnecessary thought.

It is a scientific fact that a complete shift in habit can be achieved in as little as twenty to thirty days. Once you start meditating consistently, the Universal powers will know you are serious about making contact with higher energy vibration communication. Then, you will experience an increase in your intuitive guidance system to align yourself with a higher energy vibration and ultimately your Original Source Agreement. The higher your energy vibration is, the more clearly the intuitive guidance will become.

It is important to always remember, you already wrote the script for your entire life and the choices you make in life determine the perceived reality in any given moment. When you listen to the guidance coming from Higher Self through intuition, your life will change and align with the higher energy vibration of the Universe. This is hard for most people to accept due to the current low mass consciousness of the world. However, once you discover how easy it is to increase your energy vibration in alignment with Higher Self, your level of understanding increases exponentially, too.

It is at the higher level of energy vibration where all the secrets to living a happy and fulfilled life exist. This higher guidance is there for you to use, but you must first do your part in showing the Universe you are ready and serious about making this choice. You have the power to move forward and achieve all of your dreams and manifest all that is required to assist you on your journey. Pay attention and guidance will show up exactly when it is needed.

Does Everyone Have Say In the Outcome

Confusion is a normal part of discovering the actual power you have over the end result of your life situation. When the mind is searching for an answer to a challenge, it simply means there is some level of uncertainty associated with the outcome. However, if you realize you rewrite your own script in each moment of your life situation, it becomes easier to make decisions when uncertainty arises. It's the uncertainty of life that actual makes it exciting and provides the adrenaline rush for discovering the end result of your life script or story in any given moment.

Remember, you are the author of your Original Source Agreement and have the power to override all influence from the many people you have brought with you in the boxcars on your Train of Life™. Each day, more people are added to the list of influences, but you are ultimately the one to make the choices of life based upon your own free will. This is an incredible power that has been given to you as a gift. It is of the utmost importance that you take full responsibility for all your decisions in life. Yes, you are influenced by many factors as there are many people offering advice for any given situation. Some of the advice serves you well, but some also provides negative influences which you need to filter out.

One of the best ways to filter out the negative influences in life is to meditate on what was said. Sit in stillness and you will feel the energy of the advice given. Use what resonates with you and leave the rest behind. The Higher Self always knows what is best, without exception. When you connect with Higher Self, even if it is for a brief moment, when a decision is necessary, it will come to you as if by magic. Your intuition will guide you as it comes from a higher Source Energy that overpowers any fear or doubt you may be experiencing. Always pay attention to that gut instinct; it will never fail you as it is always pure.

When you are connecting in harmony with the Original Source Agreement, you will always feel good about the decisions you make in life. The knowledge carried with you since its creation will always be there as your inner guide when challenges arise. It's in the deeper Higher Self that you can tap into this knowledge base for answers when confusion comes. You will discover all the answers are there simply waiting for you to place them into the script of life at just the

131

right moment. Listen to the inner guidance and your life will flow in harmony and peace. You are in control of building your own reality; therefore, when confusion comes, understand that guidance is on your doorstep waiting for you to feel its spiritual power.

You will always feel good about the decisions you make when they are in alignment with your higher purpose for being here. Trust your inner guidance system and be free from the burden of negative outside influences.

How Do I Know I Am Living My Purpose

The most perplexing questions of all time are "Why am I here? What is my purpose?" The answer is really rather simple, however, most of us have a tendency to complicate and confuse Life Purpose with Life Plan.

Once you have adequately investigated the discovery process pertaining to who you really are, you will realize you're a Spiritual Being having a human experience. And that ultimately means you are actually the God-Self having an Earthly experience. You are simply looking out through the eyes of the body to see the life situation in front of you. This experience, which is ultimately the perception of what is to the mind, is merely an illusion or nothing more than a dream state. From the perception of the form-based self, this dream state is identified as reality by the mind and can easily be identified as all there is. The reason for this limited perspective is because of the energy vibration being reduced to a level where you no longer see the true God-Self of which you are.

The first step to grasping the enormity of the God-Self and why you are truly here is to understanding the concept of Oneness. There is only One God and we are all part of that Oneness. Therefore, if God is the Ocean of all life, then we are all droplets of that same ocean. No matter how many times the Ocean is divided into additional droplets, it remains the same Ocean. Therefore, by using a form-based body to house the droplet (ourselves), we can each experience the totality of the Oneness as an observer of all that is.

Consequently, the ultimate purpose for being here is the same for everyone. We are here to discover the true essence of which we are, the Oneness of all that is. We are here to awaken from the limited experience of humankind and discover with Conscious Clarity how to relate as ONE. Accordingly, everything is actually God-Self or consciousness looking out and we must endeavor to awaken from the dream state if we are to fully understand Self.

Therefore, our only purpose is to explore Self and to align in harmony with the Oneness of the Universe.

Our Life Plan is merely the methodology used to align with the consciousness of the Universe. And this is meant to enhance Love, happiness and a peaceful experience here on Earth. If we are fully aware or cognizant of the dream state of life situation, it is easier to explore the unlimited possibilities of Self and, then, life flows with little effort.

Can I Have More Than One Life Plan

Life Plan is often confused with career and life path. If we are to explore Higher Self at a level of understanding, which will consistently raise our energy vibration, it is important to be aligned with a Life Plan that is in harmony with Original Source Agreement.

When we live rooted in Love, Peace and Light, the energy flowing through us is aligned with Divine Source Energy and can take us on an unlimited number of form-based lifetime journeys. Each of these lifetimes can further be broken down into smaller segments or form based mini-life paths. However, they are also an integral part of the Original Source Agreement made prior to physical birth.

An example of this mini-life may be multiple career paths where increasing energy vibration is the main rooted purpose, but it is accomplished through various careers that continually move a person forward toward their ultimate goal. The careers may start out at a lower level of service and then progress to higher levels as the person is awakened to the Higher Self purpose. However, the hierarchy is only observed by form-based, lower self, not the Spiritual Higher Self. This rooting is typically used as a means to integrate with the mass consciousness of the world at the present moment vibration. At the Higher Self level of awareness, there is no hierarchy, all is equal in every way without separation at all times.

There are many ways to determine if your work is in alignment with your Original Source Agreement. The best measurement of whether or not you working in harmony with your agreement is the level of happiness experienced through your chosen work. If you feel energized about going to work when you get up, it is a good sign that you are doing your real life work and not just going to a job for survival. Most people are still spending their days in survival mode, mainly because the mass consciousness has not risen to level of understanding where they can clearly see truth. However, as more people awaken to Higher Self reality, they will instinctively teach their children to do what is available to them at the higher levels of Conscious Clarity.

Therefore, if you change career paths multiple times, it is not a sign that you are out of alignment with Original Source Agreement. It may only mean you are progressing at your own rate of awakening unique to the life situations you chose in each current moment.

Who Creates

Everyone co-creates in every moment based upon their own unique life situation; however, we should always remember that the creation process itself is all part of the totality of Oneness. Therefore, what we co-create has an affect on everything else in the Universe, both form and formless. Separation is only in the mind. Therefore, we are all part of the same Source, constantly changing to meet the current life situation from a standpoint of Oneness.

As we mature in our perceived unique awareness, we begin to understand the true meaning of the power we have over the creation of our own circumstances. We are all exactly where we are meant to be at any given moment and are constantly co-creating each moment in real-time or each *present moment*. This is hard for some people to accept as fact, especially if they are currently experiencing some level of pain. When we feel pain, it's hard to imagine that we brought it to ourselves in the co-creation process. It's far easier to place blame someplace else. However, if we are living with Spiritual Self in the forefront of our daily life, we then understand what this actually means at a much deeper level of awareness.

As the body ages, typically the mind is awakening to some new awareness in each moment. This includes the manifestation of thought, which in turn becomes our visualized reality in the life situation illusion. It can be very confusing to the mind as it only understands the lower energy vibrations, at least at first. Conversely, the true Spiritual Self understands the full meaning behind co-creation and creator level of awareness.

As energy vibration increases, the expectations of the mind become less relevant to our happiness in each perceived moment in time. We discover that there are no victims in life situations because everything that is taking place *in the present moment* is in harmony with personal energy vibration at that exact moment. In other words, there is a distinctive match or alignment with the circumstance. Therefore, whoever enters that harmonic match is brought to us by the match of the frequency being projected by each person. Yes, as difficult as it may seem, we actually project an energy that draws more of what we current align ourselves with directly to us, like a magnet.

Therefore, if you want to manifest more of what you *really* want in life, the first step is to raise you energy vibration such that it is in harmony with that which is visualized or what you *truly* want. Do not merely ask for a change; see yourself as being the change you want to manifest. Carry out the necessary due diligence, see the outcome in the forefront your mind's eye, align your belief system and then allow the Universe to provide what is necessary to achieve it.

Ask yourself this question: Do you share what you *really* want in meditation or prayer and then have faith that all will manifest from within the Divine wisdom of the Universe? If the results are not what you actually visualize, then some part of you is out of harmony with what you *really* want.

How Does Ego Fit In

Until you discover the secret of merging the ego and Soul together, it will be difficult to accept faith as a guiding light to whatever it is you want to accomplish in life. The ego by itself will attempt to control you by making up stories that simply are not true. This occurs when you live your life rooted in fear and denial. The most powerful negative "what-ifs" will always come from a place of lower energy vibration and fear. The ego will hold you prisoner to its stories through manipulation, using jealousy, uncertainty, control dramas and whatever form of negativity it can in an attempt to hold you back from re-discovering your true Higher Self.

Anchoring your thoughts into an identity is one of ego's favorite tactics to hold you back from being your true Spiritual Self. This is to be expected as most of us grow up in some manner of control drama, which of course has a significant impact on daily life situations. When living a life filled with false identities, it is very confusing to see what is actually readily available or within our reach. The secret is to go within where you can discover the true essence of being here.

When discovering what is real, or conversely illusion, some teachers make the mistake of attempting to bring awareness to light prematurely with words, prior to the student's energy vibration being raised to a level of higher understanding or perceived capability. However, it also offers the possibility that there is something going on in the background of our life situation, which we simply do not understand as yet. That's the challenge with most conventional teaching, Knowing when the time is right for bringing to light the next step in the discovery process. And, to further complicate the issue, not everyone discovers/learns in the same way.

The mind/ego has three root methods for discovering truth - visual, auditory or kinesthetic:

- Visual Discovery – When a student is enlightened through observation or watching a process.

- Auditory Discovery – When a student is enlightened through listening to words being spoken or written.

- Kinesthetic Discovery – When a student is enlightened through actually physically touching and feeling.

In truth, we all use each of the three discovery tools daily. However, in general, only one stands out as our peak or key potential learning strength. This is why so many people have difficulty discovering something that may seem new to them; if they are being taught using the wrong method, it produces confusion rather than understanding.

This is the main reason or explanation as to why some people test poorly, because the typical testing system is not setup to compliment each method. For example, if you ask a kinesthetic person to describe in words or draw a picture of putting together a mechanical item, they may be lost. However, if you give them the components, they can construct the mechanical item easily because their strength is in doing or physically touching, a hands-on approach.

Therefore, the next time you feel as though you do not quite understand a test/lesson that is being presented, simply understand that the teacher may not be reaching your core strength of learning potential attribute.

What Is the Purpose of Ego

The purpose of the ego is to think and analyze life situations through free will choices and to pilot us forward on our Life Path intentionally in peace with Higher Self guidance in the forefront - that is it in a nutshell. However, somewhere along the evolution of humankind, the ego has lost its natural course and has taken on the role of controller.

The purpose of the Soul Merge level of the *Conscious Clarity Energy Process*™ is to re-align the ego with the Higher Self (Soul) such that it is in harmony with the original intention Source Energy (God) had planned for it.

The ego is merely the workhorse of the body, the engineer or the locomotive pulling us along life's path. Its main focus is always on free will choice which either keeps us on track or moves us through life in a series of never-ending detours. This can be very confusing especially when a person is deeply rooted in role identity beliefs and fear. Once someone is anchored in fear (as their perceived normal way of living), it is very challenging to break away from this dysfunctional way of thinking. Fear is like a snowball that keeps growing the more it moves down a certain negative path. However, this negative momentum can be overcome easily through meditation which connects us directly with Higher Self and eliminates dysfunctional thought for a few moments while ego is controlling our beliefs.

Following is an example of a person living life situation, based upon role identity and separation in the mind from true reality:

Michael is an executive that is now middle-aged and has spent most of his life focusing on only one category of life – his career. Therefore, he has been very successful in his role identity and being in charge at the office. However, this superficially allows him (his ego) to feel superior to others due to his responsibilities and stature. The rest of his life situation has been very unbalanced which has caused a great deal of pain and suffering for those around him due to his egoist need to control. He works in an environment that was established back in the Industrial Age, which has not evolved to fit in with the current Information Age and forthcoming Spiritual Age. Michael feels most comfortable when he is at work, because at work he is the boss and can actively control most situations.

Michael's life is lived based upon a constant state of focusing on the worst that could happen, rather than being optimistic about what life has in store for him and those surrounding him. This dysfunctional way of living causes endless fear-based stories in his daily life situations, especially outside of the office. Outside of work Michael feels lost and out of control. Therefore, he is known to have a short fuse on the home front. This fear causes him to see life outside of work as a never-ending challenge filled with drama and disappointments, which in turn makes everyone around him feel like they are walking on egg shells.

The ego is meant to be the piloting form-based life-force, guided by Higher Self for the betterment of humanity. However, when negative role identity enters the story, it becomes extremely difficult for the ego to overcome the temptations of the mind. If an imbalance occurs due to living life based solely on role identity, the ego will do what is best for only lower self. This is commonly known as living life based upon being totally self-centered, without considering the effects on others.

When someone lives strictly from egoist beliefs, the body becomes inundated with fear and the whole base of existence becomes survival; this, in turn, results in self-induced stress and a prolonged feeling of victimization. For this type of person, it seems as though the world is out to get them. In their mind, no one else can do anything right based upon their limited perspective. If they are not happy, it is their subconscious goal to make everyone around them as unhappy as they are - misery loves company. This eventually results in self-sabotage of each new relationship and, of course, someone else is always blamed for the relationship breakdown. This pattern will continue until something takes place to awaken this individual to the truth.

One of the best ways to awaken from this type of scenario is by simply spending a few moments each day in peaceful, silent meditation. The intent is to minimize the negativity brought on by self-indulgent thoughts and allow the inner peace to bubble up to the surface in the present moment. By increasing the energy vibration in this way, it provides a glimpse of awareness that would otherwise be lost in the smokescreen of non-truth and outside influence. This minor glimpse of merging the Soul with the ego can be the catalyst for moving forward in life situation.

By re-discovering acceptance of what is during these periods of meditative silence, it provides understanding and also allows the ego to move from fear to Love - its true natural state of Being. These brief glimpses of awareness can be the very rewarding in a relatively short period of perceived time.

How Do I Stay Out of Ego's Control

The key to staying out of ego's control drama is to live life from a Spiritual perspective, rather than from the mind (ego). The alignment of the Four Body System is critical to living a happy life from the Higher Self. If you are living from the mind as the primary alignment factor, then the challenges of life will be blown out of proportion based upon the stories the mind (ego) creates, influenced by emotions, which are typically misinterpreted by the ego.

To better understand the Four Body System, it is critical to live life from a Spiritual perspective. You should remember this from previous chapters; however, it is so very important, I will review it here again now.

The actual sequence of the Four Body System is of the utmost importance with respect to our perceived level of happiness. Therefore, it is naturally aligned when in the sequence below.

The natural Four Body System alignment consists of the:

1. Spiritual Body
2. Mental Body
3. Emotional Body
4. Physical Body

Example – Typically Out of Alignment:

The vast majority of humankind lives their life based upon having the Four Body System reversed where control is perceived at the Physical Body first.

- Physical Body - When the Physical Body is first, it identifies as situations happening to me (identity) or a physical reality.

- Emotional Body – This, in turn, excites the Emotional Body, whereas, now a feeling is generated due to what is perceived as having been done to my physical identity.

- Mental Body - These emotions then excite the Mental Body into thinking about what has happened to me (my story), usually based upon thoughts of the past and false beliefs that then lead to some type of reaction to the life situation experienced.

- Spiritual Body - Then finally, after much self-inflicted torment, the Spiritual Body sends a message that perhaps you may be overreacting to the situation at hand. At that point, an inner dialog or discussion within lower self begins and a decision is consciously made to either build on the story (which the Mental Body created) or to drop the issue in acceptance of what is.

The difficulty with this type of pattern is it usually leads to fear based action, unless you have learned to catch yourself when you see this destructive pattern emerging.

Example – Naturally in Alignment:

If we analyze the same situation and reverse the control mechanisms of our Four Body System, there is a completely different result.

- Spiritual Body - With the Spiritual Body in control, when a life situation occurs, it is first acknowledged as what is and acceptance is immediately allowed. The perception is merely "this happened", it did not happen to me, it simply happened.

- Mental Body – Then, the Mental Body activates to confirm; yes, this happened and some type of action may be required.

- Emotional Body - Next, the Emotional Body ignites with a feeling of empowerment to the challenge; it creates positive, solution-based emotions and provides action to resolve the issue, rather than focusing on the perceived problem.

- Physical Body - The result is the Physical Body feels peaceful and excited that there is a challenge to resolve. The Physical Body remains stress-free and the solutions appear from a higher knowledge base. The beauty of this type of pattern is the Four Body System then works in harmony, without fear, and feels peaceful Knowing that Love through Divine power and wisdom will bring light to any life situation.

In each of the above examples, the resultant actions will vary dramatically, depending on whether you are living your life in a state of Love or fear. This may sound rather idealistic to some of you. However, if you make a focused effort to realign yourself (through meditation) with the Spiritual Body, your life will be more balanced and in alignment with the higher level of understanding which is experienced through Love, Peace and Light.

One of the keys to understanding this system of alignment is to keep in mind that the only purpose for feelings (emotions) is to provide a measurement tool to let us know whether or not we are in alignment with our Original Source Agreement. If feelings are positive, our alignment is typically correct. However, if feelings are negative, we know we are out of alignment and need to alter our life path in some way.

Is There a Way To Maintain High Energy

Energy vibration is the key to living a happy fulfilled life. When energy frequency is high, we are connected with the invisible Source of All That Is to a much greater degree. Therefore, we actually experience contact with others vibrating at like frequencies, which we would otherwise miss if our energy vibration were low. In other words, like attracts like. The key to keeping energy vibration at a higher level is mainly by living life aligned with the Spiritual Body in the forefront of our daily experiences based upon Love rather than fear.

In our current culture, it is very challenging to stay aligned with Spiritual Body first. This is simply due the fact that we are taught by most of society, including our school systems, to live life from a mind (egoist) standpoint. This is obviously unfortunate; however, as we move out of the Information Age and into the Spiritual Age, more schools will be standardizing Spiritual Body stimulation. This does not mean religious stimulation which is based upon human-based rules; it will be purely spiritual – beyond most typical current religious understanding. This will be challenging for some people, as they now follow some of the more authoritarian standard religions, which mostly teach separation and fear, rather than unity with everything or Oneness.

In Spiritual teaching, separation is abolished, through the belief that we are all One and realizing that there is only one God which we are all part of in true reality. Consequently, with Spirituality, unity of all religions is the normal state of belief. There is no right or wrong religious belief. God in infinite wisdom provides many different avenues for connection with Higher Self (God-Self), but the intention was never intended to separate any one religion from another. People are simply people, it does not matter what geographic area you live in and we are all still One Humanity. Love has no boundary; it is beyond control and does not even understand fear-based thought.

It is the fear-based dogma of the ego that separates and manipulates humankind into the false belief that one religion is better than another. It's this type of separation that causes all alienation from Higher Self and is ultimately the cause of all wars and the insanity that a war can be deemed a holy war. God never intended for humankind to shed a single life in his name; it's simply illogical to believe he did.

If you truly want daily high energy, do all things through Love, Peace and Gratitude, while allowing the light of the Higher Self to be the beckon of light guiding your daily life path. Meditate daily to consciously connect with Source energy (God) and understand that you have emotional stimulation to use as a tool to monitor your current energy level. Use the emotion tool as it was intended to be a monitor, not a decision maker. To put it simply, if you feel emotions in alignment with Love, you are on your true path; conversely, if you feel emotions aligned with fear, you have taken a detour off your intended path and need to take action to get back on track.

We all make free will choices and it's those choices that have put each of us exactly where we are now. It is our individual responsibility to pilot our life based upon what we agreed upon prior to being born into the human body.

When Do I Write My Own Script

Life is a wonderful journey mixed with ups, downs and multiple detours. This makes it exciting and fills the journey with a mixer of endless possibilities. What most people do not realize is that the journey is a complete creation of their own, written far before taking the first breath in the human form.

We each write our own script for life's journey, including all the possible variables, both positive and negative, to facilitate every encounter we may have as a human being. If you can, for just a few moments each day, step up to the possibility that you are in charge of your own life, it may become easier for you to experience the down times. There is a greater purpose for everything that happens to you in life. It may come as subtle clue you are meant to receive, but you must be ready for it living in awareness to experience it in its true form. If you live life based upon knowing that each moment is special and created especially for your own giving life situation at the time, life becomes a little easier. However, at times, this can be difficult to do, especially if you are not feeling as though your current experience is something you would have mapped out for yourself.

When you blend your actual life experiences with a feeling of acceptance for all that is happening, it makes it possible for you to open up to possibilities that you would miss if you were feeling as though you are being victimized in some way. Many times people will say, "Why me? Why is this happening to me instead of someone else?" The truth is, it is meant to happen in exactly the way it is. How do you know this, because it is happening!

It's not always best to attempt to figure out why something is happening, sometimes it's better to simply allow what is and go with the flow to see what else happens as a result.

If you are not yet living from the Spiritual Body in the forefront of everyday occurrences, maybe it's time you try a little harder to realign yourself from the dogma of living as if everything seems to be happening to you. I'm not saying it's easy to make the change, because it's not, especially if you are older and are set in your egoist way of living life. However, it's never too late to make a change for the better. And, knowing that you write your own script for the journey of life situation, you have in store for you may just be the exact catalyst you need to get out of our own way. The mind (ego) can really play tricks on you to convince you that you are only the Physical Body, and therefore, vulnerable to everyone else's input to what your life journey should be. Nothing could be further from the truth; you wrote your own script a long time ago. Maybe it's time for you to get in touch with your true purpose if life is not what you believe it should be.

The key to moving forward in life is to have faith in yourself and the unlimited power of the Universe to assist you in any endeavor, truly Knowing in your heart what is right for you. Only you can decide which track you want to be on in any given moment.

Ride your own Train!

How Do I Get It Done In One Lifetime

The vast majority of Western culture believes that life is short. While this may be true from the standpoint of typical calendar time, it is further from the truth than the mind can fathom. If you still think of yourself as a Human Being rather than a Spiritual Being, then you probably fall into the egoist category nicely. However, when you finally understand that you are in fact a Spiritual Being having a human experience, everything changes and you begin to realize that your Original Source Agreement may take multiple lifetimes to achieve the final outcome.

It's difficult for most of humanity to accept the possibility of reincarnation; to actually return to Earth in another body is way too far out there for most people to even contemplate. However, for the sake of attempting to grow and expand your horizons, let's take a quantum leap and assume that reincarnation is truth. If you are beginning to believe you are a Spiritual Being, then it should be easy to understand that you are eternal and therefore only use a body as a vehicle to accomplish what you as a Spirit have planned for yourself long before arriving on Earth the first time.

How long and how many reincarnations it will require for you to actually fulfill your mission is totally dependent on the choices you make in your life situation experiences and the guidance you choose to follow on your journey. Keeping that in mind, it may be easier for you to understand that calendar time is of little relevance to a Spiritual Being. The truth is it really doesn't matter how many times you need to return to fulfill your planned destiny. Life is about self-discovery, not the amount of things you can acquire while you are here on this planet. You will be here for as long as it takes to fulfill your responsibility of achieving the goals of your Original Source Agreement or until you decide not to return home because you are fully awake.

As long as there is a need to heal the planet of its insanity, people will continue to return to Earth in human form and life situations will continue to evolve based upon what accepted by the mass consciousness at any given moment. Unless you are living someplace totally isolated from the rest of the world, where communication is cutoff with the exception of your local community, it would be hard to imagine that the world will awaken any time soon. Although the mass conscious of the world is rising, it will require another tipping point for us to evolve to the level of understanding that we must either wakeup or watch ourselves self-destruct.

The best way to consciously raise the energy vibration of the world is to become the peace that you want the world to be. If each person could awaken the Spiritual Self to their natural state of being, the planet would be a much better place to live; imagine what it would be like if people abolished killing one another and simply lived life from a state of conscious peace.

Our journey on this planet is meant to be fun, loving and peaceful. The people you spend most of your time with are a reflection of your current energy vibration and how far you have to go to achieve your full awakening into the Divine entity of which you truly are.

Do I Need Everyone That Comes To Me

Every person that comes into your life does so because you are in harmony with them in some way and because they were selected during the Original Source Agreement as being an important part of your life. This can be very difficult to accept if you try to analyze the reasons in the mind. One could certainly argue that a particular random life situation which brings a complete stranger into your life that you believe (in your mind) is not anyone you would even associate with does not make sense. However, the truth of the matter is, if they were not meant to be part of your life experience, they would not have showed up at that time. The simple fact that they showed up is the proof that they were meant to be there.

If you consciously discover within yourself, the power of acceptance as a prevailing trait that is deeply imbedded into your Higher Self belief system, you will begin to see life situations with increased clarity. The script is already written, it is simply up to you to determine which part unfolds in each exact moment. The choices you make will be determined by the actual energy vibration you are transmitting at that time and how it aligns with the Master Plan of the Universe. Don't be too quick to brush off chance encounters that may seem irrelevant to your current life situation. Be very aware of your surroundings and who crosses your path, especially if you find yourself in a challenge where you were just asking for help or clarity with a decision you need to make. It's possible that a messenger is right in front of you just waiting to say the right thing to put all the pieces together.

There are many levels to your existence and how each moment unfolds is always based upon your conscious awareness and which direction you take due to your free will choices. In reality, there are only two choices to make at any given moment. You can choose decisions that empower you to higher vibrations and move you forward in life or, conversely, you can choose decisions that diminish you and hold you back from your true greatness. Never give up on something that you truly believe is coming from your Higher

Self guidance. It is the intuitive messages coming from within that will empower you towards your truth, listen and be ready for the messengers that you manifest through the power of focused attention.

Chance encounters are all part of the synchronistic life process, therefore, the next time someone holds eye contact with you for what seems to be a longer time than you think is necessary, start a conversation with them and see what unfolds. Life is full of empowering surprises which in many cases go unattained simply because we use our minds more than our hearts. Sometimes a simple smile is all that is necessary to increase your energy vibration to a point that it is in harmony with what you are looking for in the first place.

Every new beginning is part of some other new beginnings end - just go for it!

Do Others Challenge Your Script

Interactions with others is as natural as breathing, however, how you choose to allow that interaction to affect what actions you take is totally up to you. We each have our own Original Source Agreement (script) to fulfill while we are here. The people that come into our life each moment have something valuable to share with us; it may only be a small input into our awareness, but none-the-less, it is all important.

Life can be very confusing at times and how a person finds their way on our path can be one of the most confusing times. When this occurs, our mind (ego) can always find a way to make up a story as to why an interaction happened. Sometimes an interaction with a stranger is only you fulfilling an agreement made to assist them in some small way. It could simply be a smile offered as you walked past them to trigger their memory to just be nice. Just go with the flow and know everyone shows up for a reason - you don't really need to know what it is. Always remember, if an interaction with someone is meant to be significant, your Higher Self will let you know through the intuitive feeling that arises from within. If that little voice inside you is telling you to interact at a greater level - do so without question.

The life process will place many challenges in front of you, people are no exception and it's all part of the process. New people will come into your life every day, but it is a choice to bring them with you on your train or to leave them behind. If someone is meant to stay around for a while, it will usually come naturally with comfort and peace to assist mutual growth. Some will come for a particular reason and then be gone almost as fast as they came; others will linger, even when it seems like you want them out of your life. There are lessons to be learned from everyone, just go with the flow and allow you inner Higher Self to be your guide. When the lesson is over, you will feel the urge to release the relationship, this is a natural progression.

If you are not moving forward while in a relationship, it may be best for you to move on, however, do so from a feeling of Love. Life is too short to hold yourself back from your natural evolution. There will be those that follow and those that are left behind. If you are growing and they are not, a decision needs to be made as to whether or not they will continue on your life path with you. Communicate your feelings in a loving compassionate way and ask for understanding of those feelings. You may just resolve the challenge at hand by having that conversation before you make your final decision.

One of my favorite authors, Les Brown said, "I make it my job to be happy." If someone in your life is dragging you down, put a stop to it immediately. It may only take the word "no" to let the person know you are not sticking around to live whatever drama they feel they need in their life. Don't ever be afraid to send a direct message to someone that is not part of your intended happy life. People will challenge you daily with their own stories; however, you need not be part of their drama. Just move on after your role is complete.

Does Your Script Alienate You or Blend You

There can be no alienate of scripts, any more than there can be alienation of Oneness. We are all One and the same from the Spiritual realm of understanding. Although there may seemly be division in the Physical Body, the truth is that they are no more than a different vibration level being perceived at multiple levels of vibration.

All scripts were written at once, therefore, there is overlap of scripts and roles played out in life. The consciousness of each personality is based upon the required harmony and level of Knowing necessary at any given moment to play out the roles in each entity's script. Just as in a novel of great value, there are multiple characters and scenarios being played out. Therefore, the author uses chapter separations to bring about the complete picture of the story. It may require multiple chapters to describe what is happening to six main characters in one given moment. To each of these characters, what the other is doing is at that exact moment is of little importance to them at that time as they are busy with their own role.

Once the story continues to a level where the scripts become synchronized, the roles begin to blend together at a more conscious level. The harmony eventually becomes a reality to all characters at the same time and they begin to interact at a different level of awareness. This is also true for every script written, whereas, the members of the cast are brought together behind the scenes in the play of life situation based upon their energy vibration. An example of this unfolds when two cast members in a movie actually fall in Love in true reality of their actual life. They no longer are playing a part or character; they are becoming the true reality in their perception of what is at the moment.

There will always be people coming and going in and out of your current life situation. How long they actually stay in the scene of the script will depend on the higher understanding or Knowing of each person. Even if someone were to step away for a few years, there is no guarantee that they will not return at some later time to fulfill some part that is not yet played out to the end. Just allow what is to transpire and know that there is a higher Divine Purpose for everything. Focus on your current part of the play and always be prepared to accept changes as they come.

The Life Plan evolves at its own level of vibration; all you need do is see to it that you balance your life such that you are ready for the next act to unfold with greater level awareness of what is at that moment.

Chapter 3 Suggestions - Write Your Own Script

All of the scripts are already written with every ending you could imagine. Allow yourself to play the role you are destined to play in each moment to its fullest. And, always be aware of your surroundings as you never know when a change is coming. Life is an amazing journey, and using the analogy of *The Train of Life*™ to assist you, the mapping makes it easy to understand how ego could mislead you into thinking life is something it is not.

- Keep Illustration B handy to assist your visualization of the triad of *The Train of Life*™ analogy.

- You have free will choice each time you come to a fork on the tracks of your life journey, choose which direction to take from a Spiritual Body perspective.

159

- You can make a difference in the world; never underestimate the power of which you are here. We are all equal and have unique gifts to use to assist us in raising the mass consciousness of the world. Make a list of what you Love to do and then write down your strengths that allow you to stand out in that field.

- Never allow other people to make choices for you; always stay true to yourself and realize you are ultimately the only one responsible for the path you take on life's journey. Practice saying "no" in a pleasing, compassionate manner. It will serve you well.

- Try not to confuse your Life Purpose with your Life Plan. Everyone has the same purpose, to explore Self and to align in harmony with the Oneness of the Universe. Our Life Plan is merely the methodology used to align with the consciousness of the Universe. Your role on this journey is to use your unique gifts or talents to empower you in making the journey peaceful and filled with abundance.

- We each have only one Life Plan, but can have many roles to its ultimate fulfillment. Play each role from a spiritual perspective and stay in harmony with the power of the Universe through daily meditation.

- Practice living life situations with the Spiritual Body in the forefront of every decision you make and every action you take, always moving forward in each present moment.

- You are the creator of your own reality. If you feel out of harmony with peace, Love and happiness close your eyes, take a few deep breaths and stop thinking for a few moments. This mini meditation will realign you will a higher energy vibration and will allow a solution to bubble up from your Higher Self.

- Be patient with yourself and those around you as everyone is doing the best they can based upon their energy vibration in the present moment. Acceptance is the key to all peace and harmony, simply allow everything to be what it is without feeling responsible to change it.

- Everyone that comes into your life is there for a specific purpose to assist you in some way. Simply feel their energy vibration and be alert so that you can receive the message they have to offer.

- Ride your own Train!

When you pay attention to your own business, it keeps you on track and allows others to follow their own path without your interference due to your agenda. Blend your life path with others, but never allow your script to be changed by someone else that is trying to control or manipulate you. You are in control of your own destiny - no one else is.

Chapter 4

Live a Balanced Life

How Do I Map a Balanced Life

As stated in previous chapters, your entire script for your life has already been written by you personally during your Original Source Agreement meeting with Source (God). Remember, this includes all the possible scenarios you could possible imagine in the mind. However, the way your script unfolds is totally up to you based upon the choices you make in each moment.

The key to living a happy life in alignment with highest purpose is to live a balanced life. When the Spiritual Body is in the forefront of your daily effort, it becomes easy to flow in harmony with the Universe. You have the ability to live an easy relaxed life where you can accomplish anything you set out to do. If you follow the emotions that are there to assist in determining whether or not you are on the right track, it will be easy to flow with your highest purpose.

As you progress with increasing your energy vibration, you will have opportunities to make quantum leaps in your level of understanding. Through Conscious Clarity of Self, you will experience an outstanding life that will endeavor to provide you with an abundance of everything you need to fulfill your ultimate purpose. Never settle for little when you are pre-programmed to live a life of magnitude. By aligning yourself with other people with the same intentions of fulfilling a higher purpose, you will see an increase in energy vibration and you will be provided with opportunities that arrive at just the right moments.

As you make your choices of the friends you select, keep in mind that you are a Spiritual Being having a human experience. If you align with others that understand this core fundamental of understanding, you will continue to do greater things than most will ever experience in today's society. This does not make you better than anyone else, it simply means your energy vibration is higher at the moment and you see clearly what others do not due to their lower energy vibration. The ego will continue to test you. Therefore, it is imperative that you stay alert until you have fully integrated Soul Merge into your life. Once you are living with an open heart on a daily basis, you will see when ego is attempting to manipulate you and you will live with Conscious Clarity of purpose.

You have the power to balance your life in accordance with your true higher purpose and by consciously monitoring your daily activities you will be able to see quickly if you are off track. Take a few moments each night to meditate on your actions from the day to determine whether or not have fulfilled your true intentions for that day. The emotions that bubble up will be your guide to determine whether or not you lived that day with Higher Self consciousness.

If you find that your energy chakras are blocked in anyway, simply go deeper inside and ask yourself for clarity. You will be amazed at how much you discover by following this simple exercise. If you feel you are playing the role of victim in any way, ask yourself what you are afraid of. Dig deeply into the root cause for you fear and you will discover in most cases that which you fear is out of your control. Simply allow the feelings to bubble up and then dismiss them for what they are and practice opening fully to the beauty inside your Higher Self intentions.

By intending to BE happy you will experience a new outlook on your surroundings and realize any pain you may be experiencing emotionally is all induced by lower self. In some manner, you will discover that you are out of Spiritual Balance.

What Is a Balanced Life

The life we have lived so far is based upon our decisions made up to the current moment in our life situation here on Earth. We have all been given the opportunity to live a life filled with harmony, bliss and the deepest Love for all beings and life itself. This is our natural state of Being as a Spiritual Entity having a human experience. The challenge is to stay on track with our Original Source Agreement and to ensure that our Higher Self always controls our life path. A balanced life is one that follows the guidance from within our Higher Self in harmony with the abundance of the Universe.

Please review the Life Plan Categories in Illustration D again to bring to light any energy blockages you may be experiencing at this moment. If you have not been consciously observing each of these categories and analyzing where you stand in each one based upon your energy vibration, it is an excellent time to start now - this is extremely important.

Our overall happiness in this life situation is determined by how we live daily and how aligned we are with our core purpose for being here. When you are in harmony with the gifts provided to you before birth, you will find it easy to balance each Life Plan Category to its full potential. And, to be redundant for a moment, the best way to do this is to live a life guided through daily meditation, so that you stay in constant direct conscious connection with Source (God) energy. This will ensure that you keep the Spiritual Body in the forefront of what you take action on daily.

Once the transition has been made to live life from a Spiritual standpoint through Love, patience, understanding and acceptance, you will feel the ultimate blissful feeling of contentment in everything you do. It will then be possible for you to experience a balanced life, because you will have released the ego's control over you. By living through daily conscious observation of how each action has an impact on each category, you will begin to understand why it is so important to live in the present moment. When we are alert in the present moment, we actually witness opportunities that arise which would otherwise be invisible to us at lower energy vibration levels in this illusionary world.

A balanced life will be rewarded with abundance in every Life Plan Category, whereas there is only Love without the presence of fear controlling any of your actions. This level of Being is all based upon our level of acceptance to what is currently taking place in our life situation. Please, always remember that everything is taking place in the now moment and that there are valuable lessons to be discovered through Conscious Clarity of that knowledge.

Once you are living a balanced life through spiritual awareness, you will see how secondary drama is ego's attempt to control you and how detrimental that drama is to your overall life balance. By living in a conscious state of spiritual awareness, you will arrive at the tipping point of consciousness where everything you do becomes easier, more peaceful and very relaxed.

Is My Life Balanced

Living a balanced life is more than just excelling at the roles we play on a daily basis to survive in this world. It is more about how we feel when we perform the duties we all encompass by using our God-given gifts to thrive through living a life filled with purposeful Love and attention to sharing those gifts for the benefit of everyone that comes our way.

Once you discover the secret to a happy, fulfilled life is daily service to others your priorities will change and you will start to think about how you can use your talents for a greater purpose than just your own satisfaction. When was the last time you did something for someone else without expecting to get something in return? Some would say it's impossible to do that arguing that even if you benefited by feeling good in some way it's still self-centered because you still benefit from the gesture by feeling good. From an egoist standpoint that would be a rational argument, however, what if you lived your life daily without seeking out feeling good. What would it be like if you simply naturally only focused on good things all the time? Would you feel less prone to expecting to feel good for a worthy gesture? If your life was always lived from a deep sense of Love and devotion to those around you, do you believe it would shift your perspective?

To truly live a balanced life, it would mean taking into account the outcome of each of your actions and how it affects those around you. If every action was balanced in the respect that it would benefit everyone, would it change the way you did things? A balanced life is a lot more than simply selecting a category of life and working hard on it to raise your energy vibration while attempting to better only yourself. When your perspective changes from *me* to *us* the abundance of the Universe begins to flow through you with every action. When you do all things for the benefit of everyone associated with the action it changes the amplitude of the energy vibration. It allows the flow of energy to reach out and touch more people from the greater perspective of Oneness.

So, if your life is filled with scarcity and drama and it is a big chore to get anything accomplished, maybe it's time for you to re-access what's important to you. If you can discover within yourself how to move beyond the ego's need to do for yourself first, then you may begin understanding that life can be a blessing, one that can flow through Love, Peace and Light. If you are not feeling balanced in life, it's not because the Universe is working against you, it is because you are not flowing through life with the assistance of faith and Love guiding your way.

It will become easier for you to raise your energy vibration, so that you are in harmony with the Universe, once you discover how faith and Love play an important part in your life balance. Rather than working hard at playing out your role in each daily life situation, why not attempt getting out of your head and into the power of the Universe. When you daily do everything with an open heart, expecting nothing in return, it will become natural to feel good all the time. And, the result will be a natural higher energy vibration which will ultimately lead to a fully balanced life.

How Does Energy Play Its Role

Everything that exists, both form and formless, has a defined energy vibration frequency. Each form-based entity is vibrating at a much lower frequency that formless Spiritual energy. We are all Spiritual Beings (formless) having a human experience while housed in a form-based vessel labeled the body. How the two interact pertaining to energy vibration or resonance frequency plays a significant role in how successful we are in living a balanced life that is in alignment with our Higher Self intentions.

Our Original Source Agreement always allows us to experience many diverse scenarios in life situation which can either increase or decrease the vessel (form-based body) energy vibration; while the Spiritual Body or true Higher Self always vibrates at a much higher frequency in harmony with the Universe. This is why it is important to frequently connect with the lower vibrating Mental Body (ego), Emotional Body and Physical Body, as well as, with the Spiritual Body. The best way to do this is by connecting directly through meditation and Conscious Clarity of how the lower vibration aspects of the lower-self body can be brought in harmony with the Higher Self.

Since all things both form and formless are vibrating at their own frequency, it is imperative that we discover how to keep our vessel vibration high in order to receive or resonate with those things that are vibrating at a higher frequency which we are oblivious to at lower energy vibration levels. In other words, like attracts like. Therefore, if you are to live a life of abundance, you must increase your energy vibration to that which you desire to align with at the higher levels of vibration frequency.

Here is an example that will help you to understand how important it is to increase your energy vibration to a higher frequency:

If you would like to attract a person in your life that is fully vested in living a life focused on Love and abundance, it is necessary for you to increase your own energy vibration such that it resonates with that higher energy frequency. Conversely, if your own form-based vessel is vibrating at a lower energy vibration, you will not "naturally attract" a person that is vibrating at a higher level. Therefore, you need to become that which you are intending to attract into your life situation. However, if you do not maintain this harmonious energy vibration, it is likely that the relationship will not last. This is commonly seen in people that increase their energy vibration temporarily to attract someone, then after a period of time the true sustained energy level shows through and the false personality is revealed. This is commonly known as putting your best foot forward at the beginning of a relationship and eventually the relationship falters.

This is also experienced in a relationship whereas one person is growing (increasing energy vibration) and the other person is not. In these cases, if conscious, open communication is not part of the relationship, it will become difficult to continue that relationship based upon its intended future. Through open communication, a discussion can be had to explain the out of balance condition of the relationship and a joint decision can be made as to what steps can be taken to save the integrity of the relationship. In some situations, this decision reveals that the relationship is completing it natural cycle. This can be very difficult for the ego to accept.

Our natural state of Being is a state of peace, Love and acceptance to all that is, which is an extremely high Spiritual energy vibration. However, until the Soul Merge process is complete, the chance of falling back into a lower energy vibration is high, because of the power the Mental Body has over us when we are vibrating at a lower level. The ego will consistently manipulate every life situation by using past negative experiences as a catalyst to build fear into every life situation we encounter. However, there is a way to balance this negative and self-destructive manipulation, which will be explained in the next section of this book.

Can Anyone Help Me to Move Forward in Life

We each have a spirit guide and mentors to assist us in raising our energy vibration and to watch over us when times are troublesome. However, it is necessary for us to be alert and ready to receive the assistance when it is offered.

You are never alone, even when you may feel as though the world has been tough on you. Always remember, there are lessons to be had in every life situation and many of them come from circumstances that may seem unfair or as though you have been wronged in some way. Each life situation has value, even when you feel you do not deserve the harsh reality of a challenging event in your life.

If you feel as though life is being too hard on you, instead of asking yourself, "why is this happening to me?", ask yourself, "what is my energy vibration right now and what was I thinking just before this occurred?" Those questions may be all that is necessary for you to regain harmony with the Universe and your Original Source Agreement. Remember, if you are falling out of alignment with your true purpose for being here on this planet, the Universe will step in to provide a nudge to get you back on track and sometimes the nudge may be a bit harder than you appreciate in the moment.

Each person that comes into your life does so for a purpose. There are no accidents in the synergistic events that unfold in your life. Every person that comes into your life shows up at the exact time they are meant to and they will attempt to communicate their message to you in some specific way which will have an impact on your energy vibration. Each person is meant to "get your attention" and move you back on track with your Original Source Agreement intention. When you begin living your life in acceptance of the reality that each and every occurrence in your life happens for a specific purpose, you will begin to understand the power of your thoughts.

We always bring to us what is in harmony or balance with our current energy vibration. Therefore, if we require a particular lesson in life to move us forward, it will show up at exactly the right time to bring the full lesson to the forefront of our perceived reality. Jesus said, "Ask and you shall receive", this is true for all matters, even the ones you do not want. If you are a person that is constantly dwelling on the unpleasant matters in life, you will continue to receive the same, because your focused thoughts are on what you do not want. Therefore, you are resonating at that frequency and the Universe will always provide that which is equal to your current thoughts and energy vibration.

This is *very important* - never forget the Universe cannot distinguish between what is good or bad for you, it can only provide more of what you are directly and indirectly asking for. You are in control of everything that comes into your life and the sooner you realize this to its full extent, the sooner you will begin to discover how to align your thoughts with what you do want. And, you will no longer play the part of victim when something happens around you that is not to your liking.

When you are off track, there will be a little voice that will gently ask, "How did I get myself into this mess?" The true answer will always be, by asking for it, either directly or indirectly. Only YOU have the power to change your thoughts and when you do so, you will change your reality in life. When you begin to vibrate at the higher frequencies of abundance, you will clearly see how your thoughts equal your own manifested reality in life and you will no longer self-sabotage your life situations or hold others accountable for your reality.

Who Decides If I Am Balanced

The simple truth is only YOU know if your life is truly balanced which really means that you are truly living life in harmony with the Universe!

When we are in alignment with our Original Source Agreement, life seems to flow effortlessly. It is not that we no longer experience challenges in life. However, the challenges that do come are a simple reminder that we are here to discover yet another portion of ourselves that may require some attention. Or a challenge may present itself because we need it to assist someone else on their life path that has gone off track. It's all part of the script and acceptance of what comes our way is the first step in moving forward at an accelerated rate. Never under estimate the power of the Spiritual Self to step in at exactly the right moment. Be sure to look closely at what shows up because there is always an important message, even though it may be masked by what seems to be an unwanted challenge at the time. Go deeper within Self and find the possible hidden reason for the challenge at hand. Remember, you are here to serve others, not just self-centered objectives.

The mind is a complex tool to be used for the benefit of mankind and not just for the ego's own self-indulgent purpose. It is important that you travel beyond mind consistently in order to dig deeper into the wonders of the true Higher Self where you will understand what you are actual capable of doing while you are here. Your mission (Original Source

Agreement) will unfold in the deep resources (gaps) available to you between thoughts. You can and will understand this once you allow yourself to accept that you are capable of far more than the mind alone is capable of taking you. You are not simply a limited physical form that is only here to do what the five sensory experiences can understand. You must always remember that you are a Spiritual Being having a human experience and that part of you is capable of far more than the current conscious mind will allow you to experience. This is why it is so very important for you to continually increase your energy vibration so that you can travel deeper within to consciously visualize your true intentions in life.

You have the power within you to see with a second set of eyes which is commonly known as third eye focus. This chakra center (third eye) located at the center of the forehead is capable of showing you a path that the form-based sensory eye is unable to see. When you live life with the chakra system open and operating at its true full potential, another world opens up to you.

That which is invisible to you now (in your lower state of energy vibration) will gradually become consciously clearer as you discover the power that is patiently waiting within. If you are still not meditating at least once per day, you are only experiencing a limited amount of your true potential. And, if you are only experiencing a limited amount of your true potential, it stands to reason that your life balance will be out of alignment with the Universe.

If you are still locked into the limited Physical Body mode of experiencing life, you are out of alignment and should not expect too much from life. Only you can make the choice to move past your current limited belief system. Once you do finally accept your true calling, you will start to expand to the limitless potential of the Universe. You always deserve conscious clear awareness; it could be the subconscious mind that is holding you back from your Divine alignment with Source Energy.

What Does a Balanced Life Feel Like

In the general sense of the word "balanced", one would be lead to believe that you must be completely balanced and at the higher vibration levels to be truly happy. This is a myth as we are constantly increasing our level of energy vibration beginning the day of conception. When we arrive in this form-based world, we are completely in balance with the Universe. However, we arrive at a lower energy vibration to allow us to enter the life situation illusion at the level of mass consciousness/awareness. Therefore, we have not experienced life situation categories as yet. We have absolutely no need for the categories of life situation at conception.

At birth, we are pure Love, living a blissful existence while everyone around us baths in the beauty of that innocence and happiness. In fact, the left hemisphere of the human brain does not begin development until approximately four years of age. We have no need for it; we are in a "pure state of Being", because we have not been influenced at that point by society where the left brain is even necessary. We are still pure creativity in the beautiful form of the innocence God had intended for us.

As we progress in life situation, we grow in academic wisdom through form-based schooling. Spiritually, we grow through life situation experiences and ultimately through our focused attention on staying in direct contact with Source Energy. This is also known as maintaining Spiritual awareness. How balanced we remain is based upon our life situation circumstances and how we perceive the influences around us. We could remain completely balanced as we progress through life on Earth, even if we have few material things. An example of this is a person living within a small tribe in a jungle. They could be perfectly balanced, but not have the same possessions someone in the advanced social cultures deems necessary for happiness. The human form is only as happy as the mind allows us to perceive in each moment. Once we discover how to live beyond the perceived limited confines of the mind by putting our spiritual Well Being in the forefront of our education, we will regain our natural state of bliss or utopia only experienced at the higher levels of energy vibration.

Our level of energy vibration is determined by the significance we apply to outside influences, may they be societal, tribe or personal. As infants, we are vulnerable to outside influences; we simple take everything presented to us as truth. We have a purity and deep trust that we will be taken care of by our parents and those that our parents choose to bring into our lives for form-based guidance. We have no need for comparison to what actual truth is, because we are totally innocent and believe only good things come to us. To balance the equation such that we better understand the opposite of positive experiences, we receive challenges/problems to solve during our form-based life on Earth. How we deal with these tests is the essence of our discover process and how we begin to understand and ultimately appreciate the positive or perceived good that comes our way.

As we age physically, our belief structures (mind's perception of what is) continuously changes and most of us begin to place judgments on life situations and the people surrounding us. This is typical for most people because of the power of influence we allow other people to have over us. We allow this because we do not know that our teachers are placing their own judgments on what they are teaching us, which of course is based upon their limited beliefs and their own life situation experiences and judgments. This becomes a vicious circle whereas belief structures influence the next generations to come. However, in the new current fourth dimension planet we are now experiencing, less of these influences are being taken seriously by the younger generation, especially by those that are naturally retaining more of their natural state of Spiritual Being Awareness.

These children are known as Indigo Children and can consciously see through the false dogma of the mind.

When we live life from our Higher Self and take responsibility for our own decisions in life, it is possible for us to begin to see the true balance of our natural state. When we strip away the outside influences and make our choices based upon truth rather than speculation. We begin to see a conscious clear picture of what is. When we move past the self-imposed judgments of others and stop blaming others for our life situation, we begin experiencing life through different eyes. When we consciously bring awareness to the surface of our everyday life situations, we begin to experience life in a more balanced manner by living a life situation based upon acceptance of what is naturally unfolding in our daily life. Then, we allow ourselves to bask in the beauty of our Higher Self perspective of life's energy and begin to experience a different understanding of actual truth. Then from this perspective as we age physically, the level of energy vibration surrounding us seems to increase naturally. This is due to the wisdom we obtain through life's challenging lessons. We discover what is really important and what matters not.

If you are living your life based only on academic study and what is pumped into you daily by others living from a limited state of perspective, you are truly missing the mark. When life is experienced from a "Spiritual Being" perspective, true balance is realized and the importance of form-based reality is minimized.

How Many Categories Should I Target at Once

When consciously working at balancing your life, the general practice of overall balancing is very important. However, it stands to reason that you can only focus on one category at a time if you are expecting to move forward quickly. Just like anything else in life, what you focus on mostly is what expands the most in the present moment.

The typical mind-based approach to a balanced life is to simultaneously work on all the categories at once to achieve balance. The mind believes a blend is considered to be a more balanced process. However, because we are Spiritual Beings having a human experience, the better approach is to build the energy in one category at a time - strategically. This will actually raise the energy level at a much faster rate, because when your Spiritual Life is in harmony with your Original Source Agreement, you will find that it becomes easy to focus on the other areas that require the most attention.

First, concentrated effort should always be placed on Spiritual Life, because by raising your energy in this category, you will be bringing the Higher Self into play at the beginning of the process. This will quiet the mind and allow you to consciously focus from a higher state of awareness when it comes to the ego's objections and attempts to manipulate you into falling backward into old patterns of unconscious rebellion to truth. Because the Higher Self has the power to overcome the ego's most stringent tactics, you will not fall victim to egoistic tricks which attempt to hold you back from focused attention on your true purpose in life.

The ego does not want you to be happy and fulfilled. It wants control over you and will do whatever is necessary to maintain that control. Therefore, the second most important step is to consciously focus attention on the Soul Merge category. Once the mind begins merging with the heart, the process of allowing the Higher Self to provide guidance in the forefront of your daily life situations will become the natural flow of all your actions. You will no longer listen to the dark little voice trying to move you in the opposite direction you truly want to travel.

When the heart is open, the experiences in life are viewed differently, with a sense of deep Knowing that whatever is occurring in each moment is due to a specific reason or has a unique intention. This form of acceptance allows you to move past the limited perspective of the mind into a new realm of understanding. This will allow the Kundalini energy to flow through you in an un-obstructed manner and your perspective of what is happening in the moment will be viewed with consciously clarity rather than the clutter of the mind.

Once you have the basic building blocks of higher energy flowing through your energy system by first focusing on the Spiritual and Soul Merge categories, the rest will fall into place naturally. You will then be vibrating at an energy frequency to experience what may be considered a quantum leap in awareness. Then, you can focus on the next category that requires the most attention based upon a higher level of understanding of the Oneness of Self. You may actually find it very useful to document a strategic plan with specific goals where you focus on a targeted outcome each week. Then, once you achieve the intended outcome for a particular category, you simply move on to the next category, which, of course, you have prioritized as being the next most important area to concentrate your efforts.

The optimized goal for any endeavor should always be to experience whatever is flowing onto your life path with an open heart or also known as an open chakra energy flow. When the Kundalini energy is flowing freely without blockage, life becomes a blessing and miracles appear as if by magic on a daily basis. Without this Spiritual opening of Self, life will continue to be a never-ending challenge based upon the form-based limitations of the mind. When you begin to understand that any limitations you are experiencing are all self-induced, you will start to look deeper into what is manifesting through you.

How Do I Know I'm Balanced

You will know when you are balanced when the outside influences of life no longer have a negative effect on your inner peace and acceptance of life. When you discover the secret to happiness is living in acceptance of what is in each moment, then you will be balanced and your energy will grow exponentially with little effort on your behalf. You will then be in harmony with life situations as they come and will experience an inner state of peace that most people will never achieve in one lifetime.

It does not take an abundance of worldly possessions to balance the categories of life situation. You can be completely balanced while building your energy frequency to higher and higher levels of awareness. Inner peace is the secret to all of the limitless possibilities in life. When you finally allow that truth to bubble up from the inner regions of your reality, you will then begin to see life from a totally different perspective. You will find yourself doing more for others naturally without worrying about whether or not your own life is completely balanced. We must always remember, until we reach the Soul Merge level of Spiritual growth, the ego will always play its tricks on our perceived reality.

When the little things in life begin to have more meaning to you, then you will discover the true blessings that are really most important. And rest assured, none of what is really most important has anything to do with form-based accumulation of objects. You came into this world pure and will leave to return home in the same state you arrived. All that is truly important will go with you when you leave and all that is meaningless (in truth) will stay behind to be re-circulated by others. If you believe only monetary wealth is what matters while you are here having this human experience, you have missed the mark and should consider rethinking your priorities. A simple smile or someone acknowledging your Higher Self will always be worth more than all the dollars in a bank account.

The intention of the categories of life is simply to provide a tool to measure whether or not you are living your true purpose for being here. They allow you to see a well-rounded view of how you are using your God-given gifts for the betterment of humanity, as well as your own personal growth. Life can be very challenging at times, but the rewards on the other side of the challenge can be a wonderful experience. When you see yourself as being balanced, you will understand your Divine Purpose. You will be living your life in a state of gratitude for what is ultimately the reason for waking up every morning.

Think about what is most important to you and then ask yourself if you are thinking clearly or have you been fooling yourself into a false state of perceived balance. If you were to die tomorrow, would you have left the world a better place than when you first arrived here? If the answer is no, it's never too late to change your daily actions such that they are in harmony with your true purpose.

When you no longer have a need to ask yourself whether or not you are in balance that is when you will truly *be* balanced!

How Does Spirituality Fit Into Daily Life

Spirituality is the practice of living life from the Divine power of the Universe, from the God-Self or greater power than your human form alone. When you are living in-Spirit (inspired), you begin to tap into the awesome power and limitless potential of all that is - the Universal power of Oneness.

Your thoughts, words and deeds are a direct reflection of the spiritual life you live each day. When the power of the Spiritual Higher Self is in the forefront of your daily life, it flows effortlessly, because acceptance is the natural belief you bring to every life situation moment. Everything that is taking place in this exact moment is meant to unfold in the precise manner it is currently taking place. The proof of this is very simple, it is happening *now* at this exact moment. Each life situation is experienced in a "now moment", nothing happens in the past or the future. Therefore, if it was not meant to happen now, it simply would not.

The Spiritual Higher Self understands the power of now and acknowledges the presence of the unseen power of Spirituality. This limitless spiritual understanding (faith) is what aligns us with the Divine power of the Universe and guides us directly to the greater possibilities of life. By allowing yourself to flow with the universal energy of all that is, you will live a life of abundance. All that is necessary for you to live from this higher perspective of endless possibility is faith. When you know deep within you that you are being watched over and guided by this Highest Energy Source, you become willing to accept whatever manifests into your life. Your thought patterns change and you begin to realize that all you need do is ask for guidance.

When you put Spirituality in control of your daily life, you begin to establish a direct communication link with God. This does not mean a one-way link (prayer) where you ask and never receive direct guidance. You have the power to connect directly with God daily, because you are part of the Universal Oneness of all that Is. This direct connection is experienced at a level of understanding which is in harmony with your personal energy vibration in each current moment of your life.

If you truly want to experience direct contact with the Divine power of all that is, all you need do is set aside a few minutes each day to begin a two way conversation that is guaranteed to resonate with your current energy level. This direct connection is meditation.

"Meditation is not some "thing" you do; it is the experience of Being that which you are." – Terry Swejkoski

When you choose to have direct connection with God through meditation, you will begin to experience his guidance with Conscious Clarity and unquestionable certainty as to what you should do next during your current human experience. *"Ask and you shall receive"* exactly what you focus on with Conscious Clarity of Spiritual Self.

How Does Love Fit Into Daily Life

Love is the Spiritual equivalent of living a life based upon the limitless power of the Universe. God has intended great things for you in your life and you are the pilot of how these limitless possibilities unfold on a daily basis. When you live your life with an open heart based on Love as the root driving force behind all you do, it aligns you with the higher energy vibrations of the Universe which are in harmony with God's Divine intentions.

There are two base emotions that drive *The Train of Life*™; they are Love and fear. All others emotions are derivative of those two base emotions. Absolute truth comes from Love which provides all the possibilities available to you if you live your life from an open heart (open chakra energy flow) perspective. When this limitless energy vibration is in the forefront of your life, you are capable of experiencing a harmonious lifestyle filled with abundance in all categories of your life.

How your life unfolds is ultimately all about your belief system and the alignment you have with Source Energy. When you are in alignment with Source Energy, the challenges (tests) of human life are minimal. The reason for this is because your energy vibration only brings to you that which you are aligned with at any given moment. Therefore, if you are consistently in alignment with the Divine power of Love within you, it will stand to reason that you will only bring to you those things that are vibrating at a like frequency. God does not understand lack or scarcity; these are all form-based manifestations of the mind (ego). If you are living in scarcity in any category of your life, it is an indication that you are out of alignment with God's Divine power.

The natural flow of energy within you is in alignment with Source Energy through your Higher Self. It is the Higher Self or Love-based Self that has the driving power of faith to support every portion of your daily life. When you live life from the perspective of spiritual alignment with the spiritual knowledge that we are all interconnected to each other as One, life is experienced from a higher state of awareness. You no longer simply live life for you own basic needs; you begin to see the larger picture of life and see the ripple effect of your actions on the entire world and each person you are connected with either directly or indirectly.

When you live your life based upon Love, you become a direct messenger for Source Energy and your attention on the true intention for all of humanity.

How Does Career Fit Into Daily Life

Each of us has a unique set of talents/gifts given to us to develop to their peak potential. These gifts are not something you should take for granted, but something you should pay close attention to because if you follow you true spiritual gifts, you will have a life filled with peace, Love, happiness and fulfillment. These gifts are part of your destiny to develop not just for yourself but for all of humanity. You are here to serve for the benefit of all that cross your path.

Whatever lessons that are perceived as too tough by you will have the hidden meaning revealed to your Higher Self once you finally decide to live a Purpose Driven Life. You

189

have already agreed to your assignments in this life situation based upon your Original Source Agreement. You must pay close attention to the signals you are receiving from Higher Self if you are to develop your gifts at an early age. The sooner you begin living your life situation with the Spiritual Body in the forefront of your daily life, the sooner it will be that you connect with those you are here to teach.

As you develop your God-given talents to fit into a specific career, you will become increasingly aware of the ease at which the lessons unfold for you. Keep in mind that you are a Spiritual Being having a human experience and nothing is limited in the spiritual realm of possibility. Do not allow ego or other people's influence to dissuade you from refining your ultimate role in this life situation that you are currently playing out. You are the master of your True Self and are without limitation. The only limits that could possibly stop you from moving forward in the career or careers you are intended to fulfill are the limiting beliefs of the mind (ego).

You have a choice to be a messenger of Source Energy or an ego-controlled puppet manipulated by the limited perceptions of the mind. Let go and let God! Be the co-creator of a life filled with abundance and happiness. And then, teach others how to realign their Four Body System with the harmonious abundance of the Universe.

You may find yourself looking into the future as a messenger for the betterment of all of humanity or you may allow the power of the Higher Self to guide your journey such that you seek out a career path that is in harmony with the higher aspects of what is truly in store for you. You will receive guidance from within your Higher Self. You will receive a clear message from within as to whether or not you are moving in the proper direction. Listen to your intuition and never be afraid of taking what appears to be a risk on the surface. Look at the bigger picture from a spiritual standpoint and keep the mind at bay as much as possible. The longer you focus on the spiritual aspects of a situation, the sooner you will be assured of success in everything you do.

You are not alone on this journey, but you must watch closely for the signs as they may appear as subtle feelings within you that you may not understand on the surface. If you feel as though something is right for you, the chances of it being true are exponentially feasible if you allow Higher Self to guide your path. Your career will unfold for you quickly when you focus on the things you are naturally good at doing and Love to do. Forget about how much money you will make, focus on service first and then the money will arrive as if by magic.

How Does Financial True Potential Fit Into Daily Life

There is a natural energy vibration for every form-based thing, this includes money. Spiritually speaking, money is nothing more than green energy. Therefore, if you are in spiritual alignment with the higher energy vibration of financial wealth, you will have more money than you know what to do with. Conversely, if you are in alignment with scarcity and limitation, you will live a poor or mediocre life filled with financial problems and lack.

Energy vibration only knows that with which it is in harmony with. If you believe you will never succeed in life from a financial standpoint, you will get exactly what you believe. To reverse this self-limiting belief, all you need do is reprogram your mind to see all possibilities from the spiritual standpoint of abundance and wealth. Change your thoughts and your outcome will align with your new thoughts. Be patient and allow the power of the Universe to flow through you, instead of you working against the natural flow of abundance.

Life is really quite simple. You get what you think about most. Whether it is abundance or scarcity, it does not matter. You will always manifest what is closely in harmony with your thoughts in each moment. Therefore, be careful what you think about because it will begin to manifest even before your thought is complete. The Universe has an amazing capacity to align the miracle of balance with your thought process. Ask and you shall receive. The best way to do this is through focused meditations where you are in conscious contact with Source Energy. You will receive specific direction as to what you should do next, so long as you are truly coming from a position of faith rather than fear.

Monitor your emotions as they are there to alert you when you are out of harmony with your Original Source Agreement. It is human nature to align with the mind (ego), however, you do not need to be the prisoner of the mind when you believe in the spiritual truth. Do not allow the ego to fabricate stories in the mind that are not true. These are only tricks to keep you living the lie of scarcity and struggle. You are much better than that and if you are willing to build trust in the spiritual practices of abundance, you can turn any situation around for the better. Never underestimate the power of Love.

Financial security and monetary abundance are simply a reflection of what is going on inside the energy vibration you are transmitting to the Universe. Therefore, the Universe can only supply what is in harmony with your own personal energy vibration. If you believe you are broke and not able to achieve the financial goals necessary for financial abundance, you will stay stuck in your current financial situation. When you change your thoughts/beliefs about money and what it does for you, it will be the beginning of the new you. Always think in abundance and then simply allow the power of the Universe to fulfill your ever desire in alignment with your natural state of creation.

How Does Relationship Fit Into Daily Life

Relationships are no different than any other category of life. You are always co-creating the relationships you are in alignment with based upon energy vibration. This is why it is so important to choose an intimate partner (spouse) based upon spiritual energy vibration rather than physical attraction or worldly thought based reasons for material gain.

A Spiritual partnership is based upon equals assisting one another in spiritual growth. This is a Universal law based upon all of us being Spiritual Beings having a human experience. Therefore, when you are moving forward, but your spouse or significant other is stagnant or non-responsive to building a life filled with spiritual abundance, it begins to damage the relationship balance. If you are with someone that is not in alignment with you spiritually, your relationship will be limited and less than what is available to you. This can be uncomfortable at best and can be a tipping point in the relationship; the relationship grows in acceptance and patience or it comes to an end where both agree it is time to move on.

What is best for every relationship will be brought to light during your daily meditations. Through this direct connection with Source Energy you will be guided into the light of the correct choice to make concerning the relationship. This is an excellent time to discuss this dilemma with your partner, prior to making the final decision of which path to choose. At this junction, your intimate relationship will either take a quantum leap in spiritual development or the discussion will simply fall on deaf ears. Contemplate on the reasons for beginning the relationship in the first place, was it spiritual or was it merely physical attraction for material gain?

All relationships, whether intimate or friendship, come into existence for a specific purpose. Some will be based upon a particular short term focused reason, some for a longer partnership and others for a lifetime. Whatever the case may be, it is imperative that you begin to understand the differences as soon as possible. When your heart is open, it will be easy for you to feel the energy vibration of each relationship and you will better understand its progress or decline. Simply allow what is to transform based upon what feels right for you in your heart. As you continue to grow in spiritual wisdom, it will be easier for you to consciously accept each relationship for what it is ultimately meant to be.

Always remember, Source Energy has a Master Plan for every moment in life situation and will never bring anyone into your life that is not meant to be there at that exact moment. Your Original Source Agreement is destined for flourishing to its optimum level of attainment and the people you co-manifest onto your life path in each moment are meant to be there. Learn as much as you can from each person that shows up as they each have a particular message for you that will let you know if you are in alignment with Source Energy or are being manipulated by the ego. Pay close attention to the relationships that come your way and cultivate them to the fullest. Also remember, we are here to be of service to one another, therefore, the purpose for someone manifesting may have nothing to do with you and everything to do with their spiritual development.

Pay close attention to those people that continuously show up in your dreams and during your meditations. These people have a significant reason for being there. They will be there for you for an extended period of time without exception. If you were not in harmony with their energy vibration, they would not be popping into your life as frequently as they currently are. The reason will eventually reveal itself to both of you and the spiritual partnership will continue to grow in harmony with Source Energy.

Never fear releasing someone from a relationship for it may be the best for both of you when you ultimately begin understanding the reason you are truly here having this human experience. You may be a stepping stone for one another in moving forward through your Original Source Agreement purpose.

How Does Personal Growth Fit Into Daily Life

Most people live their life from a limited perspective based upon what society dictates as personal growth which is all related to the mind, worldly performance and acceptability. This is the greatest scam ever perpetuated on humankind. If you are living your life based upon outward influences, you are being deceived by those that simply want to control every aspect of your life. The relationships you build each day will determine your path as you progress or stagnate in personal growth. You are far more than what is seen on the surface which is typically based on the ego's perception of the relationships developed with others or roles being played that also have a limited perspective on lives which are typically judged by other egos.

Personal growth starts from within without exception - not from outwardly insignificant influences and half-truths of what society dictates as truth. There is only one truth - the truth of Source Energy providing all that is necessary for a happy, fulfilled and peaceful existence on this temporal journey we are all on as humankind. Most of the world is so focused on being human, they forget, in fact – we are not human at all. The simple truth is we are all Spiritual Beings having a temporal human body experience. The body is simply a vessel that is playing host to our True Self which is limitless and eternal. Therefore, anything that can be perceived without limitation can be manifest into reality by our true Higher Self with the assistance of Source Energy providing Divine power. The limited mind cannot even begin to grasp the limitless possibilities available to each person. All we need do is simply place our Spiritual Self in the forefront of our daily life situations to receive the limitless rewards.

The vast majority of humankind is taught to go to school, get a job and work for someone else. This is not what Source Energy had in mind for us to prosper to our fullest true potential. We are all meant to discover our Higher Self first and then develop a career path based upon our unique gifts/talents given to us during our Original Source Agreement meeting with Source Energy. The Spiritual discovery is by far more important than the academic studies that are there to awaken our Mental Body intellect. Humankind has had this backwards since the beginning of time as we know it based upon our outward perception of who we are.

Right now, before you read anything thing else, as yourself one question and be completely honest when you answer, "Who do you think you really are, right now, in this moment?" The answer will be in direct correlation with the current fulfillment of your human perception of life possibilities. Your outward world will be a direct reflection of your inner world and my belief is that you are living life far below your true potential.

Human life was never meant to be lived in scarcity or mediocrity, meaning limited conscious awareness of Higher Self and only through worldly perceptions of abundance. However, humankind has been mislead into believing that life on Earth is all there is. This limited belief is based upon the illusion of materialism and seeing only what can be seen through sensate human-form perception. This has been the downfall of human evolution, until now. We are now evolving into the Spiritual Age and are living on a fourth dimension planet where more and more people are awakening to true reality of Knowing they are Spiritual Beings having a human experience. Therefore, spiritual ignorance is now being slowly awakened and many leaders of the new Spiritual Age are being recognized as such.

We are now ready to free ourselves from the bondage of the ego (mind) and move forward based upon spiritual knowledge that has been lying dormant within us. Each person has the opportunity to seek the spiritual truth and release themselves from the grips of the old third dimensional illusionary reality of who they think they are. It is now time to step up to the limitless Divine power within and acknowledge our true calling in life. The spiritual seekers know there is something far more than what they have been lead to believe and are now questioning the religious beliefs more than ever.

The secret to personal growth is located within each one of us and is readily accessible to everyone in the spaces between mind-based thought. There is a higher power of communication available to everyone in the silence within where you can participate in a direct conversation with Source Energy (God). Only those whose energy vibration has evolved to these higher levels of understand can actual carry on a two-way conversation with Source Energy. Those that are still living in the old third dimensional paradigm do not hear the messages being conveyed at this higher level of awareness. To them, the conversation is one-sided and they do not believe because of their spiritual ignorance. This is the reason it is imperative that you discover a method that is right for you to raise your energy vibration. If you stay where you are today, you will continue to live the lies of the past and stay within the bondage of the manipulating ego.

The choice is yours to move forward in spiritual growth which in turn will automatically accelerate your human personal growth or you can continue to live a life of mediocrity and pain.

Chapter 4 Suggestions - Live a Balanced Life

Everyone has the resources available to them to rediscover the truth about living life from a higher level of awareness. To connect and join in the direct conversation with Source Energy (God), you must first commit to placing spiritual growth in the forefront of your daily existence. You can do so by simply aligning yourself with each category of your life situation in harmony with the Divine power of the Universe.

By far, this is the most important suggestion of all - REALIGN THE FOUR BODY SYSTEM!

1. Spiritual Body
2. Mental Body
3. Emotional Body
4. Physical Body

By realigning your system in this manner and living a life of Conscious Clarity, you will experience a life of Love, Peace and Light bringing abundance to every category of your life.

If you change nothing else, change this alignment and you will begin to experience daily miracles in your life!

Chapter 5

Choose Happiness or Sadness

Is It Really That Simple

Source Energy (God) provided us with a wonderful freedom to assist ourselves in determining whether or not we are following our Original Source Agreement or have in some way taken a detour. This freedom is the ability to make choices based upon free will without the need for someone else to make them for us. Yes, the exception to this is when we are newborn, we must first fully rely on our caregivers to make choices for us until we have learned enough about the world to start making choices for ourselves. Therefore, we are initially limited in our perception of the world by the beliefs of our caregivers and other outside influences, such as TV, radio, Internet, etc. These are all influences which are constantly bombarding us with half-truths and, in many cases, complete fabrication based purely on the self-limiting beliefs and manipulations of others.

These lessons (meaning academic and influencing beliefs of others) in most cases shape our ego (mind) into a belief system that is at best out of harmony with our true Higher Self awareness. Because of the amount of time we spend being bombarded by these outside influences, they become very real to us and we form beliefs (opinions) about what is true and what is false. We believe what we hear from others during infancy because we have not been around long enough to question what is being presented to us as fact or fiction.

We do, however, have an inborn inner balance system to assist us in determining what is actually best for us. This system is called the Chakra Energy System, also known as Kundalini energy. (See Illustration F for a visualization.) It flows within us and is the core spiritual guidance mechanism to all truth. When Kundalini energy is flowing through us properly without blockages, we naturally feel happy and at peace. When this energy path is blocked, we feel an innate sense of sadness, which is unexplainable by the mind because it is far beyond what the mind can comprehend. We all have the capability to connect directly with this Higher Self guidance system which is always available to us at higher levels of consciousness. Tapping into this energy source is one of the keys to a life filled with abundance and happiness.

The mind can be an amazing gift when in alignment with Kundalini energy and Original Source Agreement, but it can also be an unbelievable burden if it is out of alignment causing blockages in our natural flow of energy. The goal for us as Spiritual Beings is to break past the limiting behaviors of the mind. Once we discover how to eliminate the blockages in the Kundalini energy system, we simply flow through life situations in acceptance of what is and allow our Higher Self to guide us down the path of right thinking. The Higher Self will always endeavor to move us in a favorable direction no matter what situation arises in daily life. However, if we are to live a life of true happiness and prosperity, we need to be alert and ready to receive the guidance that is being sent from Source Energy through our chakra system.

When your energy vibration is high and in harmony with Source Energy, miraculous things will happen in your life. That is, for the general mass consciousness, it will seem miraculous; however, for those that live a life in daily spiritual awareness of the God-Self, it will be understood as the normal flow of life. We do have a choice to live a life filled with happiness rather than sadness. It really is that simple.

What Are the Steps to Happiness

The secret to happiness is not found in the daily dramas unfolding around the roles played in the illusion of life situations. Happiness is found deep within, in the uncluttered peace and tranquility of the silent moments, shared with our highest creative Self. Once you bridge the gap between thoughts and the dogma surrounding your daily activities, you will gain a new perspective of how to consciously connect to your natural state of being which was always intended to be happy.

Most people are so wrapped up in the roles they play in daily life they forget why they came here in the first place. We all have a mission in life and that mission is clearly visible to each one of us in the silence of meditation. When you take the time to silence the mind and get in touch with your true Higher Self, you discover all the reasons you are here. They will unfold in the manner they were intended. Remembering your purpose is easy once you begin removing the cluttered thoughts of everyday life situations and open yourself up to reconnected with your Original Source Agreement.

The steps to happiness are all a matter of your perspective on life and your acceptance of what is while living life focused on what is truly important. Example: During a tribal meeting in Fiji, with guests present, a village chief was asked by one of the guests, "What is the purpose of life?" This question brought a smile to the faces of the villagers sitting in the circle for discussion, as the chief answered, "Why the purpose of life is to be happy mun." It is really that simple. You are not meant to be anything other than happy; it is truly your natural state of Being. In this particular village in Fiji, the members of the tribe did not work outside of the village (in a job) if it diminished their happiness. It was understood that happiness was the main purpose for living life and to take away from that happiness in any manner was not in alignment with core purpose. Those that choose to stay within the compound only participated in activities that were necessary for them to sustain life based upon using their natural talents. They live a life filled with Love, Peace and Light with happiness being their main priority. Life can be just that easy.

Prior to being born into this world, we are provided gifts/talents based upon our Original Source Agreement. Those gifts are meant to be cultivated as we age. We will always have a feeling of happiness if we pay close attention to what seems to come naturally to us. If we utilize our natural gifts to their fullest intention (based upon our Original Source Agreement) we will be in natural harmony with Higher Self purpose.

Most people spend their life seeking a career that will bring them the most money, instead of focusing on what brings them the most happiness. When happiness becomes the forefront purpose of your existence, you will be in alignment with your true Higher Self and money will no longer be the driving force for the career choices made. When you live life with your natural talents guiding your existence, money will natural flow to you as if by magic in the exact amount necessary to fulfill your true purpose in life.

The most important step you can take in moving forward with a happy blissful life is to reconnect with the gifts you were provided before birth. You can do this through meditation where you become naturally connected with your Original Source Agreement. The smokescreen of role playing is not who you really are - you are far more than your mind will ever allow you to be. You are an infinite Divine power simply waiting to blossom into your greatness. Only you know what your true gifts are and they are available to you with every breath you take on this miraculous journey called life. Pay close attention and they will be revealed to you.

No one can tell you what will maintain your state of happiness - as it is a discovery only you can cultivate.

What Are the Steps to Sadness

We already know deep within us that our natural state of Being is happy. So what is it that seems to drive us down the unnatural path of sadness so often? The answer - Self-limiting beliefs and a fear of the unknown.

It actually takes a lot of hard work to perceive life from a standpoint of sadness. There is an enormous amount of thinking that goes into manifesting a negative reality. However, we also know from past experiences that the ego will do whatever it takes to maintain control over us. The easiest way for the ego to control us is through negative emotions and perceiving outside occurrences as more than what they actually are. The ego will even go so far as to take past stories and manipulate them into anchors that are triggered by a past event or statement of words.

I like to use a particular occurrence to describe a trigger which took place in my home one evening during an informal gathering. A friend of mine (call him Jack) brought his new girlfriend (call her Jill) to the party. I learned later that "what people thought of her" was very important to Jill and she wanted to make a positive first impression.

See if you can quickly identify the trigger/anchor:

During the course of an evening party, we were all standing around a kitchen island counter having a great time talking about various topics. We all found that Jill was quite intelligent and worldly wise. Therefore, she added a lot to the discussions during the course of the evening and was having a great time getting to know my guests. Everyone was in a positive uplifted mood simply enjoying the evening without a care in the world. Then, there was a sudden crash on the kitchen floor; Jill had knocked over her glass of red wine. The kitchen floor made of tile caused the glass to shatter sending fragments of glass and red wine everywhere.

I quickly responded to the incident by asking everyone to step into another room so that I could clean up the broken glass and wine spill. Everyone followed my lead and went off into the other room to continue their conversations as if nothing had happened; that is, everyone except for Jill. She stayed back to help with the clean up. Jill seemed overly upset about the whole incident and began to degrade herself all the while we were cleaning the spill. I simply let it go and continued with the task at hand while looking forward to getting back to my guests. However, Jill's demeanor continued to shift even further into a negative story she seemed to be telling herself. I explained it was no big deal, accidents happen and continued with the cleanup, believing that was the end of it.

Following the accident cleanup, I poured Jill a fresh glass of wine and figured we would continue our conversation where we left off before the incident. To my surprise, Jill refused the wine glass and asked for a plastic cup instead of the glass. She said she did not want to chance breaking another glass due to her clumsiness and became very firm in her stance pertaining to the matter. I simply provided her with what she asked for and proceeded on with my evening enjoying my guests and never thought anymore about the whole incident. Jill never rejoined the conversation and secluded herself with my friend Jack for the remainder of the evening. They left the party early and I could tell something wasn't quite right with them.

A couple weeks later, I was talking with Jack and asked how he and Jill were doing. He chuckled a little and said, "Jill broke up with me shortly after the party." He told me Jill simply could not get past being so embarrassed about breaking a glass of wine at the party and did not want to see any of those people ever again. He explained that her statement lead to a passionate discussion between them on the drive home. Jack learned that Jill's father constantly told her she was clumsy as a child. As it turns out, Jill has a pattern of breaking things due to a false belief which was deeply embedded (anchored) into her mind as a child that she is clumsy.

That night of my party, in Jill's mind, she made up a story in her head about how someone would hurt themselves because she broke the glass. She assumed it would lead to someone cutting their foot and eventually winding up in the hospital to get stitches and possibly die from an infection. All of this was very real for Jill in her perceived storybook reality. And therefore, her father's anchor from years ago, associated with clumsiness, continues to haunt Jill to this day. Even though she is a highly intelligent, worldly wise person, she still allows her past and people's opinions to falsely control her life all because of fear of the unknown and negative input from her father.

The truth is sometimes accidents happen in life; so simply clean up the fragments as best you can and move on to the next moment. In the big picture, most people do not care about what happened in the past. The reality is, it's not our responsibly to even care about their opinions in the first place. However, if you continue to judge yourself based upon other people's opinions, you will sadly live in stagnation of your higher purpose in life.

Our mind is a powerful tool to be used to cultivate our given gifts, not to tear down our greatness due to embellished negative stories. Therefore, never make anything out to be more than what it is. It will not serve you well and will only lead to self-induced sadness.

How Do Emotions Control Us

Emotions will affect you in one of two ways and it all depends on the alignment of your Four Body System. You can choose to be a prisoner of your mind or a master of the universal spiritual power within you.

Now you will clearly begin to see how your false beliefs about yourself and identifying with only the role you are current playing can either raise or lower your energy vibration. Your energy vibration will provide you with the emotional feedback needed to decide which path to choose.

Emotions are only a tool to alert you as to whether or not you are in harmony with your true purpose for being here. However, the majority of the population does not understand this fact because their Four Body System is wired backwards.

There is a secret to overcoming this self-limiting dilemma. Consider following this recipe to success which is worth studying multiple times during this process.

The actual sequence of the Four Body System is of the utmost importance with respect to our perceived level of happiness. Therefore, it is naturally aligned when in the sequence below.

<u>The natural Four Body System alignment consists of the</u>:

1. Spiritual Body
2. Mental Body
3. Emotional Body
4. Physical Body

<u>Example 1 – Typically Out of Alignment:</u>

The vast majority of humankind lives their life based upon having the Four Body System reversed, where control is perceived at the Physical Body first.

- Physical Body - When the Physical Body is first, it identifies as situations happening to me (identity) or a physical reality.

- Emotional Body - This in turn excites the Emotional Body whereas now a feeling is generated due to what is perceived as having been done to my physical identity.

- Mental Body - These emotions then excite the Mental Body into thinking about what has happened to me (my story), usually based upon thoughts of the past and false beliefs that then lead to some type of reaction to the life situation experienced.

- Spiritual Body - Then finally, after much self-inflicted torment, the Spiritual Body sends a message that perhaps you may be over-reacting to the situation at hand. At that point, an inner dialog or discussion within lower self begins and a decision is consciously made to either build on the story (which the Mental Body created) or to drop the issue in acceptance of what is.

The difficulty with this type of pattern is it usually leads to fear-based action, unless you have learned to catch yourself when you see this destructive pattern emerging.

Example 2 – Naturally in Alignment:

If we analyze the same situation and reverse the control mechanisms of our Four Body System, there is a completely different result.

- Spiritual Body - When the Spiritual Body is in control, when a life situation occurs - it is first acknowledged as what is and acceptance is immediately allowed. The perception is merely "this happened", it did not happen to me, it simply happened.

- Mental Body - Then the Mental Body activates to confirm; yes, this happened and some type of action may be required.

- Emotional Body - Next, the Emotional Body ignites with a feeling of empowerment to the challenge; it creates positive solution based emotions and provides action to resolve the issue, rather than focusing on the perceived problem.

- Physical Body - The result is the Physical Body feels peaceful and excited that there is a challenge to resolve. The Physical Body remains stress free and the solutions appear from a higher knowledge base. The beauty of this type of pattern is the Four Body System then works in harmony without fear and feels peaceful Knowing that Love through Divine power and wisdom can bring light to any life situation.

In each of the above examples, the resultant actions will vary dramatically depending on whether you are living your life in a state of Love or fear. This may sound rather idealistic to some of you, however, if you make a focused effort to realign yourself with the Spiritual Body (through meditation), your life will be more balanced and in alignment with the higher level of understanding which is experienced through Love, Peace and Light.

Therefore, when emotions are monitored with the Spiritual Body in the forefront of our life, miracles always shine through and overpower the limited perception of lower-self energy.

How Does the Ego Manipulate

The ego's main purpose is to hold you prisoner to your thoughts rather than allowing you to flow freely with your Spiritual Higher Self in control of your life. The ego will use the various roles played in life as a way to manipulate you into believing you are those roles. The truth is the roles are only stage performances based upon a story that is fabricated by the ego using drama as its main form of influence. The ego

213

will always do whatever it can to control your free will choices in life by using false beliefs about you based upon past mistakes made in a never-ending circle of drama.

The ego uses time as its prime manipulator of your perceived life. It will use the stories made up in the mind about your experiences in life to hold you back from enjoying each present moment to its maximum potential. These stories are typically formulated by thoughts of the past and future, rather than simply allowing what is to unfold in the present moment. By going back to yesterday, the ego is pulling you out of the present moment and manipulating you into believing the past will equal your future. When in reality, the past never equals the future if you live your life without resistance to the present moment.

Take a few present moments to review your thought patterns. It's best to actually journal about what you think about most. It will provide you with an insight that may be very interesting. You will discover how you perceive your life from a higher understanding. Not only will it enlighten you to the realities of your deepest thoughts, it will also show you whether you are a prisoner to your mind or a free flowing Spirit that allows life to be lived to its fullest potential. When you simply allow life to be what it is in each present moment, you will begin to experience the ease of living life as it was always meant to be lived … happy!

Whenever there is a sense of drama in your daily life, it is the ego causing this perceived reality. In truth, if drama is present, it is nothing more than a story you are telling yourself. Drama is never a natural state of being. It is always a form of manipulation by the ego in an attempt to hold you back from living your highest purpose in life. When you discover the difference between living a happy, balanced life based upon acceptance of the present moment rather than the story the ego forms from past experiences, you will be amazed at the changes in what actually manifests in your life.

The power of the present moment is always greater than whatever illusion the ego can manipulate into perceived reality. When you are truly living your life in the present moment, the ego dissolves and you begin to experience the happiness that is your true natural state of being. It is impossible for the ego to manipulate any given situation if you are living in the present moment. The present moment is always the death of the ego and it will do whatever it can to manipulate you for its survival. Remember this when you are feeling down. Ask yourself if you are living fully in the present moment or if you have slipped to the past or are thinking about what the future will bring.

The power of your Higher Self will always shine through the manipulations of the ego if you are being present. Even reading these words, you have a choice to simply allow them to flow through you or your mind will hold on to the ones that will serve the ego. Never underestimate the amazing power of living life in the present moment. You will be truly mesmerized by the differences in your perceived reality when you simply live your life in a state of nonresistance to what is in each present moment. Acceptance of what is provides the key to all spiritual growth.

How Do We Live With Ego

The ego can be very clever and can manipulate in more ways than you could ever imagine. That in itself is the secret to living with the ego. What is presented by the ego is always imagined and never true reality. The stories contrived by the ego will always be focused on past or future moments, but never the present moment. The ego knows that if you are living your life based upon the present moment, it will lose control over you.

Ego will come and go in your daily thinking, however, the sooner you convert your Four Body System to align with the power of the Universe, whereas the Spiritual Body is in the forefront of your daily life, the sooner you will be able to identify the times the ego is manipulating you. The key is to merge the ego into your true Higher Self by staying in constant communication with your Higher Self guidance system.

When the ego interrupts your natural Higher Self state of being in daily life, simply smile and acknowledge what is happening. Allow the ego to have its fun and then get back to true reality in the present moment. Until you have fully merged the ego into a higher state of energy vibration, it will always crop up to disrupt your right thinking and attempt to manipulate your choices in life to the advantage of lower self

216

or role placement thinking. You are much better than that and can easily dismiss the constant interruptions of the ego's need to be in control of your life situations.

Whenever discussions surface based upon fear-generated dogma, allow your feelings to guide you back to the true essence of your Higher Self perspective of the situation at hand. You will know when you are thinking correctly and when you are wrong thinking. The feelings you sense are the triggers to knowing if you are in harmony with the Universe. If you find yourself feeling anything other than happy, joyful and at peace, it is a surely a sign that you are out of harmony with your Original Source Agreement.

Always remember, you are here for the purpose of advancing the energy vibration of the world as we know it. Your gifts are the tools you brought with you to assist humanity in the next step of evolution. When you are living from this higher state of awareness, you will always do what is best for everyone, instead of being focused on what is best only for your false personality. If the personality is standing in the way of doing what you know in your heart to be correct, there may be ego-dominated consequences to pay for your actions. Let this be whatever it is for it matters not whether or not you get what you "think" you want. What really matters is what is best for the collective Oneness.

You are not the false personality (ego) or the role being played in life situations; you are the Universal embodiment of the greater whole as seen through the eyes of a Spiritual Being having a human experience. Your greatness will always shine through when you are in alignment with this higher level of energy vibration. Have faith that you will endure any ego-based situations that have been placed in front of you on your journey. There will always be times that the ego will attempt to sabotage that greatness. However, if you allow the Higher Self to guide you, it will always overpower the limited thoughts the ego contrives to control you life situation.

The ego will always dissolve when you are focused on the present moment and, only you can decide, based upon your free will choices, to live as captive to the ego or in harmony with all that is limitless. There are always ways to put ego in its proper place and you will discover them as you progress in your self-discovery process.

Remember, all of life is a self-discovery process and only you have the power to manifest a change for yourself. Know your true Higher Self and the ego will dissolve.

One Simple Step to Eliminate Ego

Recruit the mind to serve the heart and then prepare to be amazed by the miracles created. Once the ego is merged with the heart, it will no longer find it necessary to manipulate you with the stories of the past or future.

The ego believes it is necessary to manipulate you with stories contrived to show its dominance. This is always based on fear and must be modified if you are to evolve to a higher state of Being. There is nothing to fear as the true reasons for fear are contrived by the part of the mind which the ego does not understand. The ego at its lower-energy vibration is totally oblivious to the fact that it can serve the heart as well as itself. It is simply ignorant to the unlimited power embodied in service to your Spiritual Higher Self and others.

Higher Self discovery is a process achieved through trust, faith and a deeper understanding of the true meaning of free will. The power of merging the mind into service of the heart brings with it all the creative juices flowing from a deeper realm of reality. When the heart is open and alert that which was once thought of as limited by the ego alone becomes limitless and life becomes a daily blessing or better known as heaven on earth. We can each discover how to live in this utopian state of being here on Earth by simply allowing our heart to guide us.

Living life with an open heart means living through Spirit which is truly the essence of which you are on the greater scale of reality. When the Spiritual Higher Self is in the forefront of your daily life activities, challenges become learning tools to move you forward in the evolution of Oneness. When the greater power of an open heart is activated compared to only using the mind (ego) alone, then you will begin to understand the limitless possibilities open to you when challenges arrive. You will no longer focus on challenges as problems. In contrast, you will learn to welcome challenges as a means to grow and, in doing so, your energy vibration will increase to a level where solutions to the challenges in life appear as if by magic.

The dance of life becomes a beautiful harmony when the mind (ego) and heart (Soul) are in alignment. Fears dissolve and a greater state of understanding is realized. As the mind merges together with the Spiritual Higher Self, it will discover that this same Oneness can be experienced by all. This Higher Self awareness will build as you surrender to the higher vibrations of Universal Harmony and you will flow with all that comes your way on a daily basis.

Imagine what your life would be like if you truly understood that everything comes to you based upon your energy vibration in each moment. Would you then strive to increase your energy vibration to a greater level each day? Ponder that for a few moments and then ask yourself honestly – What would it be like to live life from this higher state of awareness and acceptance that you are filled with limitless possibilities? What would it feel like to have inner peace even during times of worldly unrest?

Sit with that for a while in silence and visualize that a new life is well within your grasp providing you stay consciously connected with Spirit/Higher Self.

How Do I Stay In-Spirit

The type of energy you portray to the world is based upon whether your life is in alignment with egoistic thought or inspired thinking. The difference between those two levels of energy vibration can mean the difference between living a life filled with sadness or happiness.

Perception is the key to all manifestation of form-based choices as they are made from one of two places, lower self or Higher Self energy vibration. Your feelings are the key to knowing your vibration level at any given moment and will always provide you with accurate feedback. Therefore, pay close attention to the way you feel in each moment as it will determine your next action in every life situation.

You have a choice to be reactive to life situations or to use them as messages informing you of what you are bringing into your life based upon vibration harmony with that which is being brought forth. This is confusing for the ego if you have not yet discovered how to align the Four Body System in its proper order with the Spiritual Body in the forefront of your daily life. If Physical Body is still in the forefront, you will continue to be reactive to life situations and miss the actual important points being presented to you at a higher energy vibration level.

All form-based thought is centered on a role you are playing in the game of life. If you are locked into this limited perception of life, you will simply live a life going around in circles being under the influence of others around you. This is not the life that was intended for you. In the bigger picture, you were meant for greatness. The Original Source Agreement you made prior to your arrival on Earth is filled with Peace, Love and Happiness. It is the true essence of which you are. It is the natural intention of the Universe for you to discover your greatness based upon sharing the unique gifts (talents) you brought with you into this world.

Once you are in alignment with the energy vibration of those talents, your life will change from mediocre to magical. You will begin to see yourself in a different light and you will begin to participate in life at a higher level of awareness that is in alignment with your Original Source Agreement.

By bringing your Spiritual Body to the forefront of your daily activities, you will begin to discover your true purpose and will use your gifts to their fullest potential. This is where you belong and it is where you will feel the most comfortable. When you are in alignment with your true higher purpose, you will be at peace with your surroundings and you will allow the free acceptance of what is in each given moment. You will begin to understand what it means to simply acknowledge the events unfolding around you for what they are actually meant to be rather than what your mind/ego's perception manipulates events to be.

If you are still confused, it is a sign that you are out of alignment with the Higher Self and need to sit in silence to hear the inner guidance that is available to you in every moment of form-based time. When confused, simply meditate and allow the clarity to bubble up from within by eliminating thought which provides Conscious Clarity of Higher Self guidance, and always remember to be patient with yourself.

What About Opposites

We all have heard the statement "like begets like" at some time in our life. This has a great deal to do with what is perceived by the mind as similar or *"like-minded"*. This natural harmony is anticipated, such as a child acquiring certain traits from a parent as *"the apple does not fall far from the tree."* Many would say, we pick up a lot of our personality from the DNA of our ancestors and are locked into this DNA for life. However, in the broad spectrum of life, this can be modified by using the greater power of our Higher Self to create adjustments in our DNA. Do you believe that is possible? Maybe the better question is: Are you willing to accept the possibility that we can restructure part of our DNA by using more of our limitless capabilities beyond our current level of understanding?

The mind/ego is limited in its perception; therefore, it is difficult for it to comprehend the likelihood that changes can be made in DNA. Most people truly believe they are stuck with what they get and change at this core level is not possible. However, science is now learning this is not true. DNA can be modified primarily by utilizing Higher Self energy vibration and co-creation through higher levels of consciousness. The study of opposites/polarity or Yin/Yang, male/female, light/dark, up/down are bringing new discoveries to old school false beliefs.

We are no longer living on a third-dimensional planet, but mass consciousness and the subconscious mind do not understand that fact. Ever since the Harmonic Convergence of our planet, which began integration on August 15-16, 1987, a major shift happened and our galaxy started to vibrate at a finer energy vibration. This moved us into a fourth dimensional planet vibration. This shift provided a higher level of connection with the unity of the Universe and many people have discovered how to tap into this higher Source Energy through meditation. By opening ourselves up to the unlimited possibilities of the Universe, we can discover what the mind refuses to accept as reality. This requires some dedicated "thinking outside of the box" and deeper connection with Higher Self at a level that was not possible in third-dimensional reality.

The DNA of our galaxy is evolving to a new level of awareness which will continue to bring new discoveries to us as we increase our energy vibration. There is never just one way to look at anything. There are limitless ways to view our lesson plans for life and, quite frankly, the scriptures have been misinterpreted for far too long. Religions take the scriptures far too literally and have missed the discovery of the intended higher energy vibration messages.

Denial of one one's divinity is a false belief that comes from an unrealistic sense of unworthiness. When we tap into the limitless discoveries of Source Energy available to us in unity through meditation, a new perspective is uncovered that is unseen on the surface of old school third dimensional thinking. This is known as the Spiritual movement or connection with Higher Self.

"Within Source, all is unity – there is no polarity. There is actually no up and down, in and out – it simply is EVERYTHING. Pure Energy (which you are), in its ultimate sense, is simply energy, and then it is stepped down into

224

realms of duality so that the limited mind/ego can grasp a small portion of its true potential. And down at the lower levels of energy vibration or the realm of duality, it expresses into the polarities – the positive/negative, the male/female, Yin/Yang, good/evil, etc." – Brain Grattan

If we are to survive as humanity, we must leave behind the old paradigm of opposites/duality and merge the mind/ego with the Soul or our Higher Self. By doing this, we will evolve past the unrealistic limited beliefs found in today's mass consciousness and the separation of True Self will cease to exist.

What Is Spiritual Light

Spin a Yin/Yang symbol and what do you see? The natural energy of all that is – the Higher Self energy of light over darkness. If that doesn't tell you something, then you are vibrating lower than you may believe. And, in the reality of the bigger picture, it's all OKAY. It simply means you were not aware of the power of light in your life until now. Each one of us is exactly where we are supposed to be at any given moment on our life journey. How do we know that? Because we are here in that exact moment NOW, what greater proof do you need?

Did you know there are scientific studies which made an attempt to remove light completely, but it is simply impossible to do so? Even under the most optimized conditions there is always a flicker of light that overpowers darkness. If that is the case, what does this say about opposites like light/dark, good/evil and happiness/sadness? Do they really exist or are they only elements of duality that are needed for the mind/ego to use to manipulate us in an attempt to separate us from the essence of which we really are – pure radiant energy or Spiritual Light.

Our natural state of being is meant to be happy and full of reverence for life. We were meant to view life from this perspective, not from the crippling effects of negativity which of course is brought on by the mind's manipulation of our nature state. Have you ever had someone tell you to "lighten up", because you were making more out of a situation than what it really was? The stories the mind conceives are meant to deceive you and hold you prisoner to misinterpretations and are cluttered with unnecessary thought. The more you think about any given situation, the more you will turn off the radiant light by focusing on what is unreal or fantasy in the mind's illusion.

In a nutshell, Spiritual Light is TRUTH! No further explanation is necessary. The true power of Spiritual Light can be found through meditation, for "*Silence is to the Soul – what Oxygen is to the Brain!*" Without oxygen, the brain will discontinue functioning. Therefore, without silence, the Soul will be cluttered with unnecessary and confusing thought. Believe it or not, all the answers to any question the mind can conceive are easily found in the silence of meditation. The mind/ego does not want you to be aware of this miraculous truth. The ego would much prefer that you stay its prisoner in darkness, separated from the limitless possibilities of the power of Spiritual Light found in silence.

Spiritual Light is always with you. It is available in each moment of everyday. All you need do to access its miraculous power is BE SILENT.

What Is Darkness

Darkness is nothing more than the limited perspective of the mind or the absence of Spiritual Light as perceived by the ego. The mind needs to have duality in order to accept certain "things" as being possible. Whereas, the power of Spiritual Light acknowledges the "truth" that all is possible in Oneness.

Once you discover how to break through to the unlimited power of Spiritual Light, you will begin to understand that darkness is nothing more than a lower level of light. Science has proven that no matter how dark some things may seem, there is always a small factor of light that cannot be removed for light is eternal.

Most people perceive darkness as some form of negative or limiting belief that is brought forth by some defining opposite. The truth is the ego is what drives darkness to that perspective. A Course In Miracles states, "be not content with littleness." This is actually seen by the sensory perception as a measurable form of separation. The ego thrives on this type of manipulation and does not want you to fulfill your true mission in life. Therefore, the more you allow the limited perspective of ego to control you, the longer you will remain in darkness.

If you allow yourself to live in the state of bliss that is actually meant for you, it will become easy for you to recognize the truth that darkness does not exist. It is merely a fragmented perception of the mind which is meant to confuse you. By discovering the greater power of Spiritual Light hidden within you, you will learn to overpower the negative stories when the mind/ego distorts truth.

You are more powerful than the mind would ever allow you to believe. It is time for you to come into the Spiritual Light and claim the rewards that are waiting for you in the truth of each silent Spiritual Higher Self realized moment. Jesus said, "Be still and see!"

Can you feel the power of that truth as absolute light?

How Do I Stay Light

Most people walk through life's situations with the Physical Body (which is the lowest level of the Four Body System) in the forefront of their perceived reality. Which means, they are living their life playing out many different roles throughout the day that are all focused on ego or what is being done to them personally. By doing this, they are typically focused on a life filled with drama which holds them prisoners to the perceived problems of life.

The very first part of changing this dysfunctional course is to align oneself with the Spiritual Body in the forefront of daily life. By doing so, you no longer play out the role as having something done to you. You simply become the Witness to what is happening in daily life situations and, therefore, problems dissolved and are seen at a higher energy level or as challenges. One of my favorite quotations from Albert Einstein is, "I didn't arrive at my understanding of the fundamental laws of the Universe through my rational mind." By placing the mind in the proper alignment of the Four Body System, you begin to receive the added benefits of this higher energy vibration.

Once you learn to live life as the Witness and observe well, your heart will always answer with solutions to the challenges of perceived life. You will be open to what is happening and emotional ego-based reaction will be replaced with spiritual awareness which in turn will allow you to see the Truth of each situation with Conscious Clarity.

Ask yourself what it would be like to live life everyday without drama? Do you believe it's possible to step into this new way of living? That is the first step to staying in the light of each moment. The Spiritual Body has the ability to see far beyond that of rational mind. The rational mind has limitations because it is of the ego and cannot see past limitations.

Once you discover the power of living life through the proper alignment of the Four Body System, you will discover the secrets to eliminating all of the minds perceived drama.

Then you will begin to see the Truth in what is meant by living in the Light. Unburdened by the drama of the ego, you will see the daily events unfold as they are meant to be experienced, in the loving state of Grace.

Is There a Reason for Light and Dark

Harmony is the goal for living life in touch with feelings, rather than separation of the ego which is based upon drama or darkness. Our perception of our feelings can either lead us into darkness or Light. If you believe the Physical Body is in charge of your Train of Life™, the chances are good that your lower vibration emotions (Emotional Body) will run your life based upon whatever stories the ego contrives. However, once you are in touch with your Spiritual Self guidance and live each day by placing the Spiritual Body in the forefront of your daily life situations, you will understand that nothing ever happens to you. It just happens around you.

In truth, there is no difference between Light and Dark - one is simply less than the other in energy vibration. The reason for Light and dark comes from the ego and the duality that it needs to separate us from the unity or Divine understanding of Oneness. This duality has been deeply embedded in us for many reasons that seem very logical to the ego. It's all about the control drama; the ego needs to stay on top of life situations. Once you discover the secret to living life from a spiritual viewpoint, you will have a much easier acceptance response to all that comes on a daily basis.

The underlying reason for all control drama is the ego needs to be in the forefront of life situations and will do whatever it takes to maintain its control over us. The major control tool the ego uses is fear. It uses this fear to manipulate us into believing there is a right or wrong, Ying and Yang, good and evil, heaven and hell, and then, of course, Light and dark.

In reality, there are only varying shades of LIGHT. And always remember, in Light there is always Love and Love is the answer to all unrest in the world. Never forgetting this truth is essential to your spiritual growth.

Why Do My Feelings Confuse Me

Emotions or feelings cannot confuse you; it is the ego/mind that perpetually fabricates stories that actually confuse you. If we are to live a life filled with Peace, Light and Happiness, it's imperative that we get the ego under control and blend it with our heart. This is a formative task, but definitely very possible. The key is to get the Spiritual Body in the forefront of the daily life situation and to focus attention on the intention of living for miracles every day.

There comes a time in life when you really start to review where you are and how you arrived at this exact   moment in time. If you allow the ego to develop the story for you, it will probably be filled with many regrets and what ifs. However, if you take the mind out of the review and simply open your heart, you experience an unbelievable feeling of gratitude for

231

every moment of your life. Even the moments that seemed as though they were extremely painful, you will soon discover that those were the moments you learned from the most.

Choices made in life are determined by your level of consciousness you are living at each and every moment. There is a famous quote that I just love, "You don't know what you don't know," (author unknown) that is, until you discover it. In truth, you actually know everything there is to know, it's simply been clouded by living your life with the Physical Body in the forefront of your life situation.

I realize I keep bringing this spiritual alignment up – that's because it is probably the most important part of this book. If you walk away after experiencing this process in its entirety with the Spiritual Body in the forefront of your daily life situation, then I have been successful as your current coach. There is a limitless amount of Love, Peace and Understanding for each of you to enjoy in this lifetime; don't waste it on the dogma of the ego's manipulations.

As we flow (dance) through life, there are always choices to make. This is part of the blessing of "free will" that has been given to us. In our mind's eye, we arrive at a fork in the road of life just before each choice. The direction we take is totally determined by the perspective based upon our discoveries, beliefs and past choices. When ego is in control, all decisions are of the mind. However, when Spirit is in control, all decisions are of the heart. The key is to discover how to blend the two together so that they overlap allowing us to make a decision logically from an open heart perspective which is based on Oneness, rather than simply doing what's best only for the ego's limited perception of lower-self desires.

What's in a Question

Guidance can always be felt from within you, with respect to the questions that arise out of life situations. All you need do is to stay consciously alert and the Divine answers (guidance) or solutions to every life situation will be presented to you. This is a rule of the Universe and will never fail you.

Never dismiss a message that is coming to you from within as it is the guidance needed at that exact moment in time. Questions are meant to bring you to a new understanding of yourself and the surroundings you are currently involved in during each present moment. By staying alert and bringing this guidance to the forefront of your life situations, you will be positioned to do miraculous things in the world.

All questions are important. They are a means of communicating from a higher level of understanding. If you are asking questions, you are always learning and experiencing life to its fullest potential. If you simply sit back and let life slip past you, living unconsciously without asking questions about areas that seem unclear, you will be partially living your life in the fog of uncertainty and will not focus in the present moment. If you are not asking questions, you create a void between communications with higher power.

Jesus said, "Ask and you shall receive." When you do this, you empower yourself to the level or vibration of a higher magnitude of Universal understanding.

Be like a child, ask questions. And, if the answer does not satisfy your feeling of understanding, ask a better question. For the magnitude or power of the question is equally proportional to the answer and the amount of higher understanding you will receive. We are all meant to do great things while we are here and the power of questions is an incredible resource which should be experienced daily if we are to live our true life potential.

Also, surround yourself with people that seem to resonate with solution-based mentalities. They will assist you with strengthening your weaknesses and will provide you with the answers that are truly for the betterment of humanity as ONE.

Chapter 5 Suggestions - Choose Happiness or Sadness

Our free will provides us an opportunity to make choices and take complete responsibility for those choices. No one else is responsible for those choices and, therefore, the life we live is a direct result of our own choices. And, since there are no victims in a Spiritual Body alignment, we know that as long as we stay in that alignment, we will always be in harmony with our Original Source Agreement.

Here are a few suggestions for maintaining happiness and living a life of pure joy:

- Realize everything that happens around you is happening to either show you that you are in alignment with your Original Source Agreement or you are not.

- Monitoring your emotions is the best way to feel whether or not you are in Spiritual Body alignment.

- Your internal Chakra Energy System is comprised of seven root chakras, strategically located within the body to alert you of any misalignment which is triggered by emotions. Pay attention to blockages and clear those blockages as soon as you bring them into awareness.

- Live your life in the present moment so you live based upon your core happiness and joy showing through in every action.

- Remove negativity from your life by accepting what comes and not judging others for their mistakes (mis-steps).

- Recruit the mind to serve the heart and then prepare to be amazed by the miracles created.

Once the ego is merged with the Soul, it will no longer find it necessary to manipulate you with the stories of past or future.

- The *new ego*, which is a blend of mind and Spirit merged and existing in harmony, allows you to stay fully aware of each moment. By living in that full awareness, you will have Conscious Clarity of what is happening around you and how you can use that information to help others. This is the *True Personality* shining through in pure Light!

- Spiritual Light is the only Truth. Darkness is merely an illusion brought on by the perception of the senses. In reality, darkness is merely an absence of bright light. Therefore, when you feel some form (form-based reality) of dualities blocking your energy system remember that it is merely a lower vibration of light confused by stories of the mind.

- Above all, live your life from a position of Love and eliminate fear by staying in the present moment with your Spiritual Body in the forefront of each decision (free will choice) you make.

- Never hold back from asking questions. They manifest from the mind to assist you in understanding the reasons for being here. Jesus said, "Ask and you shall receive." When you do this, you empower yourself to the level or vibration of a higher magnitude of Universal understanding.

- Remember to surround yourself with people that resonate with solution-based mentalities and harmony. They will assist you with strengthening your weaknesses and will provide you with the answers that are truly for the betterment of humanity as ONE.

You are now ready to move into Section Two of the Conscious Clarity Energy Process – Soul Merge Level. In Section Two, you will be guided by actual steps to create a life based upon new ego merged with the Soul.

This is a pivotal moment for you as you will soon discover how to:

- Get in Touch with Feelings

- Discover Simple Steps for Staying on Track

- Take the Path of Least Resistance

- Discover Your Life Purpose

- Stay Out of Old Ego

Until then, please review each of the Soul Merge summary pages from Part One, so that you will be sure to anchor in what you have already discovered. Sit in silence and let your Higher Self express your inner most feelings. Feel where your energy vibration or awareness is now resonating and prepare to manifest a quantum leap in fourth dimension reality.

Part Two

Soul Merge Transition

Chapter 6

Get In Touch With Feelings

Is It Easier Said Than Done

You discovered in Part One of this program that all it takes to complete the Soul Merge Process is to keep the Spiritual Body in the forefront of everything you experience in life. And one of the best ways to achieve this is through sitting in silence at least once each day communicating with the Highest Self (God-Self). By sitting in a state of meditation you have a direct connection with Source Energy, where you actual hear the guidance of the Universe. There is no greater power than the Divine Universe!

Now that you understand what it takes, it's important for you to anchor that awareness into your daily life situations. It's time for a quantum leap of faith, time to step up the energy vibration into the next dimension of understanding. For illustration purposes, I call this the Universal Level of Awareness. At this juncture, you will begin seeing the manifestation of your visions coming into you daily life situations very clearly. You will experience co-creating with God-Self at a higher level of vibration which will be in harmony with your true purpose for being here.

The Highest Self (God-Self) wants you to observe your true peaceful Self through feelings. Therefore, you will always receive limitless messages brought to you throughout each day. It's up to you to be alert and pay attention to them and bring them into deeper awareness. The ego will do the opposite; it will attempt to control you for some time by using fear as a tool to keep you a prisoner to its demands. Ego will still attempt to lead you to a life filled with half-true stories. However, there will come a time when ego will fully merge with the Soul. Once the ego is merged with the Soul, it will no longer have the same affect on how you feel about life situations. Soul Merge is a wonderful state of Being that brings out emotional joy as never before.

It is imperative at this juncture that you maintain the Spiritual Body in the forefront of all that you experience. I promise you it will become easier everyday and you will discover many ways to confirm that you are in alignment with the Spiritual Body. The greatest understanding will come when you continue to feel a deep inner peace even in the face of severe life situation challenges. There will be a calm feeling radiating through your body while others are becoming agitated by outside interferences. The old ego control dynamics will disappear replaced by a higher sense of harmony.

Old ego attempts to control situations, whereas Higher Self simply allows every aspect of your life to simply BE based upon your free will choices. You are now far enough along in the *Conscious Clarity Energy Process*™ to understand that you have a free will choice to blend the ego and Higher Self together in every life situation. There is nothing to fear, because Love always overpowers all fear in every situation. When we are locked in the old ego control drama of fear, we feel as though everything in life situations is happening to us. This was explained earlier in the Four Body System examples. But now, we know clearly, there are no victims in reality.

In truth, we know when old ego is attempting to manipulate us when our energy feels blocked. By paying close attention to our feelings, we can monitor ourselves to ensure we are not slipping back into fear-based thoughts. Our feelings allow us to integrate that which is best for us. And it becomes easy to simply dismiss negative thoughts if they arise. We now know it is easy to just smile and walk away from that which we do not want in our life. By making the choice to change our thoughts, it changes the outcome.

The Divine wisdom of God-Self is always guiding us. Through that wisdom, we can choose to always experience a life filled with Love, Peace and Light. It's our choice, all we need do is listen to the inner guidance and all solutions to every challenge in life will be revealed. It's actually that simple.

Pay attention to your feelings. They are there to serve you at your highest level of awareness. God-Self brings you to a level of energy balance that far exceeds anything experienced before Soul Merge. Enjoy the new you!

What Is Good About Feelings

The balance we can experience in life is equally proportionate to the way we monitor our feelings and how in touch we are with them. Our feelings are a mapping system for the body to alert us of where we stand in our energy vibration. If you did nothing else but pay close attention to the feelings you are experiencing and which part of the body you may feel an energy blockage, your life would always be in balance.

All feelings are energy, so each feeling has its own energy vibration level. The more you focus on your feelings, the more you will understand the level of Conscious Clarity or present moment awareness. Conscious Clarity is stepping into the greatness you so deserve in life and taking massive action in the direction of that greatness.

When you are consciously making decisions based upon "what is" as opposed to the story made up by the mind, clarity results in each present moment. If you feel out of sorts with any given life situation that is happening around you, simply ask yourself this important question "Is the Spiritual Body in the forefront of what I believe in this moment?" If not, simply change your perception by getting out of your story and get back to reality.

If you determine your feelings are resonating at a low-energy vibration, look closely at the results of your thinking. You may find you have been living the moment in a story -

one that does not serve you well. Simply re-adjust your story to what is actually happening. This will increase your vibration and you will see that your feelings adjust in alignment with what you believe to be truth in each present moment.

By taking a few moments to simply be present, it will take you to a place of conscious awareness of what IS. The past never equals the future and the future can only be created based upon what your perception is of the present moment. Therefore, by being in touch with your feelings you can actually map out how balanced you are in each moment.

If you choose to write down your feelings throughout the day, let's say in the morning when you first get out of bed, in the middle of your day and, then finally, just before you go to sleep, you may be amazed at how useful the mapping becomes in adjusting your daily balance. There's no need for an elaborate essay here, simply choose three or four core (one word) feelings you are experiencing in each part of the day and document them for review at the end of the day.

What Is Bad About Feelings

The simple answer to the question, "What is bad about feelings?" - NOTHING! Feelings are merely a roadmap to assist you in what you believe to be truth, which thereby increases or decreases your energy vibration. The only way a feeling can be determined as "bad" is if you allow your old ego to place judgment on what you are feeling. All feelings are meant to assist you with healing that which may be challenging your current beliefs.

If you feel sadness, that feeling can be replaced by one of happiness. For example, if you are feeling sadness about someone you Love that has died, you can easily replace that sadness by thinking of something you experienced with that person when you were laughing and enjoying one another's company. Only the body dies the true Spiritual Self lives on for all of eternity. When the body dies, the Spirit merely transitions to a higher level of energy vibration and returns home for its next assignment.

We must always remember that all sadness is a resultant of the story we are telling ourselves in any given moment. Joy/happiness is our *natural state of Being*. Therefore, we must actively do sadness or bring sadness to our life situation to experience it. That means we must create a story in our mind to make ourselves unhappy.

By staying alert and checking in on our feelings, we can quickly determine whether we are in our *natural state of Being* (joy/happiness) or have slipped into a story (sadness) which will either strengthen us or diminish us respectively. By doing (actively participating in) sadness, we bring our energy vibration down and create a story that is typically in alignment with some form of negativity. The good news is we always have the opportunity to change our thinking (in a heartbeat) and simply accept that for a moment we brought ourselves to a state of sadness. Sadness will come and go; however, we do not have to live there for extended periods of time. Allow yourself to feel the sadness, but then let it pass through you rather than anchor into you.

One of the most difficult tasks for the old ego to achieve is acceptance that everything happens exactly at the right moment which is always based upon our Original Source Agreement. We never agree to anything that will harm us in the big picture of life. What may seem like a setback at the time can evolve into a wonderful blessing in the future. One of my favorite statements is "This is a blessing in disguise." That really means you are moving forward on *"The Train of Life™"*.

When you are moving forward in truth (rather than story), Source Energy will assist you in that movement. However, if you are moving backward through stories, the assistance will still come, but it may not take on the form you want. You may feel out of sorts or uncomfortable while you are going through the process of realigning yourself with truth. However, once the intended lesson of the story is experienced, you will again move forward in truth and you energy vibration will increase.

When we are thinking consciously rather than subconsciously, we allow our Higher Self to take control of each life situation. By doing so, we allow ourselves to live in present moment awareness and bring Spiritual Body awareness to the forefront of our life situations. When we consciously do this, it brings us to a state of Grace where we accept what IS and simply go with the flow of life while staying peaceful during the process.

There will always be challenges that come and go in our life situations. Simply be the observer of what comes and offer no resistance to what IS. Every moment is planned out in the exact way you agreed to long before you showed up in this vessel called the human body. Therefore, enjoy each moment, even those that your ego may perceive as being bad. They are all here to assist you in healing the splintered part of your Soul that is holding your back and will take you into the next level of awareness.

Life is meant to be a beautiful sacred dance spent in daily joy/happiness and reverence for life itself. Bring that beauty to the forefront of your life situations and you will always experience the peace and grace of the Divine Universe.

Do We All Feel the Same Emotions

We each have the capability of feeling every emotion available to us. However, it is our vibration level that leads us to the progression of loving emotions. An excellent way to monitor this is to simply look deeply into what feelings are being experienced in each present moment. And then, check in with the internal Chakra Energy System to determine whether or not energy is blocked or free flowing. If your energy is blocked, you will feel a heaviness in the area or chakra that is blocked. It may even feel painful if you are holding on to some negativity or hurt that is very low in vibration. If this negativity is continuously held in the forefront of your life situation, it can even cause illness or dis-ease (disease) in the part of the body that is experiencing the blockage.

The more you discover how to check in with the Chakra Energy System, the easier it will be for you instantaneously feel any blockage that occurs in the body before it elevates to an illness or very low level vibration. There are many excellent books available which explain the Chakra Energy System in detail, including where each chakra is located, what organs are related to it, what colors are associated with them and what fragrance is linked to each. For my purpose in this book, I will explain the system, but will only take it to a level of understanding that is in alignment with the particular level of the *Conscious Clarity Energy Process*™ I am currently discussing. (The Chakra Energy System is very complex and the greater understanding your have of this system, the more you will be able to attune to each sector.)

As your energy vibration increases, you will actually begin to feel the flow through the body. You will understand how powerful the energy flow is to your Well Being. The flow of this energy is called Kundalini. Although, words like up and down are used to describe energy flow, in actuality, the Kundalini Energy is more of a vortex than an actual up or down flow in static direction. This vortex will be explained later, but for now all you need to understand is that the energy flows through the body and the chakras. Therefore, it stands to reason if one of the areas is blocked, due to some low-level emotion that is vibrating very low, it will eventually have its associated organ damaged by the continuous low-level vibration.

Knowing that you understand the importance of keeping the Spiritual Body in the forefront of everything you experience in this life situation, it starts to make sense that monitoring the energy flowing through you is very important. This may sound like it is very complex, which it is when first learning about it, but as you progress in the *Conscious Clarity Energy Process™* discovery, it will begin to be second nature to you. Like all intelligence that is revealed, when we first start out in the education process, it can feel very complex. This is especially true with spiritual education as for the most part you have been hypnotized by the old ego and false beliefs for a long time. However, as you progress and have a firm understanding deeply rooted in your consciousness, it will become easier to monitor the flow of energy.

Each feeling available to us has its own unique energy vibration level. This is why it is so very important to bring awareness to the surface of each emotion and how it affects the Spirit, mind and body.

Can Emotions Hold Us Back

Monitoring our emotions during the life situation process is the key to the choices we make in each moment. When we actually discover the importance of living life by being fully conscious of our feelings, we begin to understand how each thought can either limit us or expand us.

Negative emotions hold us back from realizing our true potential in this life situation. When we engage in limiting low-energy level vibrations, it becomes a negative ride down the trail of uncertainty, judgment and unhappiness. When we are conscious of what we are feeling through our emotions, we can stop the downward spiral of negativity before it drags us down in vibration.

Through Conscious Clarity of the emotions we are feeling in any given moment, we can learn to make better choices which are based upon a higher level of vibration energy. If you feel a tightness or closed energy path anyplace in your chakra system, simply identify the area of the blockage and then attempt to remember what you were thinking just prior to feeling that blockage. Most likely, you will find you were thinking of something you did not want in your life or were focusing on some negative false belief.

Therefore, if you were thinking of something you do not want in your life, you have just begun the process of manifesting that which you do not want into your reality. Yes, as is always the case, we manifest exactly what we think about mostly. So be very conscious of your thoughts, because your thoughts are a spring board into the visualization process and manifestation of form.

We are far more powerful than the mind could ever comprehend completely. And, the emotions we feel are the key identifiers of how each life situation unfolds for the physical body. Therefore, if you are *not* experiencing all the joys of a spiritual life, you are holding yourself back based upon being out of alignment. This means the Spiritual Body is not in the forefront of your life situation. And therefore, the choices made during negative emotion manifestation bring about that which is not wanted.

This is a challenging vocation when old ego is involved with its constant bombardment of negativity but can always be identified by monitoring the flow of energy in the body. By allowing your Higher Self to quickly identify the emotions in the body, you can release the negativity as it bubbles up in each life situation and remove uncertainty in a heartbeat.

Why Do Some People Seem Emotionless

There are two sides to this question. First, are we talking about what seems to be a lack of emotion based on inner fear coupled with hardness on the surface? Or are we talking about what seems to be a neutral external appearance rooting in Love and acceptance to what is?

Fear is a catalyst for many people which on the surface may cause them to seem emotionless. They have a wall up so that their fears can be hidden. In many cases, they have experienced deep pain in their life situations and will put on a false front in order to hide. This could be hiding behind a rigid exterior while inside they are feeling insecure and vulnerable. Many times these people will have positions in society that place them in a false position of power, which is driven by ego. This could be someone that is typically living an

252

existence of "what's the worst that could happen" and takes action based upon those fears.

If you have someone in your life that appears "hard as nails", be careful not to judge them. Now that you are living your life with the Spiritual Body in the forefront of awareness, it will be easier for you to understand them as simply a lost Soul. Many of these individuals are unaware of their own emotions and the energy they produce; therefore, they cling to the ones they know best. For example, someone that has experienced perceived unbearable pain may feel more comfortable reliving that pain through mind-altering substances because the pain is anchored into their belief system. This can lead to extreme depression and a dark outlook on life situations as the mind continues to make up stories of worst case scenarios of unworthiness.

On the other hand, Love and acceptance of what IS can be misinterpreted to be a weakness by ego-rooted individuals. When you have an outward appearance of simply going with the flow of life, you may be judged by egoistic individuals as being too neutral or passive emotionally or emotionless. For example, if you believe that you will go on spiritually long after the body dies, you may have an outward appearance of being emotionless or too happy when someone dies. While everyone handles this type of grief differently, it can be misinterpreted as non-caring or emotionless. If a person truly believes when the body dies and that's all there is, it could be very difficult for them to see your point of view.

Living in awareness of emotions is the stepping stone to energy flow. They allow us to feel energy levels within ourselves, which would be otherwise clouded by the mind. When we allow ourselves to experience feelings without judgment, we can gauge where we stand from a vibration viewpoint. Lower vibrating emotions bring out the worst in us as humans and are controlled by the ego's stories of whom we may think we are.

If someone is living life on the surface with the Physical Body in the forefront of their existence, it may bring about negative emotions rooted in fear. Conversely, higher energy vibration and living life deeply embedded in Love with the Spiritual Body in the forefront of our daily existence brings about inner peace. During this state of *Being* rather than *doing*, the mind becomes engaged in acceptance to what is. This flows with emotions that are realized at higher levels of energy vibration.

In each case, we have a choice to bring our emotions to the surface for everyone to see or we can hold them deeply within us in fear of being discovered. What is your current pattern?

Does It Hurt to Hide Emotions

Spiritual Beings never have anything to hide including emotions. When the Spiritual Body is in the forefront of each moment, the emotions that bubble up after mind is brought into a life situation are always peaceful and content with

Knowing action will follow from an open heart philosophy of Love. The way we bring our purpose to the surface of life situations is simply a natural state of being and we flow with life, rather than offering resistance to what is. Through awareness of who we really are we live life through a state of Conscious Clarity. Therefore, because we are always alert to what is brought in the present moment; solutions come to challenges as if by magic.

Once we are living the life we are meant to lead and are in alignment with our purpose (by understanding our Original Source Agreement with Source Energy/God), we flow through life with lightness of Spirit; we know we are safe with nothing (no thing) to be fearful of in our life situation. When we understand that everything is in the exact correct order for us in each moment, we simply accept that which IS and let the life situation manifest in harmony with the current energy vibration we are transmitting to the Universe.

If someone in your life seems to be troubled, but is not openly discussing what they are experiencing, it is a good bet they are living with the Physical Body in the forefront in that current moment. This is a common occurrence in someone that has not mastered the Soul Merge process. They find themselves shifting back and forth and have not yet accepted they are responsible for every moment of their life situation. They still have not accepted the reality of being the one that designed their own Original Source Agreement. However, the moment they realize they are shifting back into old ego patterns and control dramas they then return to the present moment awareness and renew Spiritual Body alignment.

Remember, when the Physical Body is in the forefront of life situations, the next "unnatural phase" is the Emotional Body misalignment. This misalignment is not your natural state of being and it is certain to block your Kundalini energy flow. Therefore, pay close attention to your chakras and feel the blockage, so that you can clear the obstruction quickly. In truth, the present moment is never anything more or less than it actually is. It's the old ego mind belief system that creates a false story. It's really that simple so don't make it anything more than what it is

Therefore, if you momentarily slip back to the control drama of old ego and then catch yourself doing so, you will quickly overcome any negative emotions which have been hidden based upon Physical Body misalignment. Your Chakra Energy System will always provide you with a distress signal if you are out of natural alignment with Higher Self. Always trust this Truth!

How Do Emotions Affect Health

If for some reason you have slipped back to the old ego-based Physical Body misalignment condition, the Physical Body will be affected immediately. You will feel out of balance and the natural harmony of Spiritual Body alignment will be disrupted. You will feel heavy and the chakra that is blocked will feel the lower vibration which, in turn, could eventually cause disease (dis-ease) in the body.

You will feel a ripple effect to every negative emotion you manifest into your body. The more you consistently understand the negative affect of these emotions, the better off you will be. Once you learn to always side step that which causes disease in the Physical Body, you will be living life at the Universal Level of Consciousness. This is a beautiful place to live, for the Universal level is the stepping stone for all abundance found at the Monadic level of Conscious Clarity.

The ripple effects of negative emotions are not just singular in life situations. They have a ripple affect on groups, communities, nations and the world as perceived by the mind. We must always remember, thoughts and actions driven by fearful emotions have an affect on the mass consciousness of the world. That which is brought into the life situation through the lower vibration of fear-based thought, manifest into disease and ripple through all of humanity. It's like a cancer that spreads fear-based seeds and causes a conflict in the mind. This is how all wars are created at a much amplified state of unconsciousness.

If a nation is at war (fear-based disagreement), it cannot manifest that which is naturally peaceful. Through Love and higher vibration states of Being, all unrest in the world is diminished. Therefore, when people follow a country leader that is fear-based, the whole country suffers as a result.

When we closely examine the actual emotions we manifest, we begin to realize why it is so very important to consciously monitor our emotions. By bringing awareness of self-limiting emotion and thought to the surface of our existence, we have a much better chance of manifesting that which will serve us well.

Monitoring our emotional state is a stepping stone to all that is possible to manifest balance and ultimately harmony in the world. If you think this is naïve or far too easy to comprehend, then perhaps it would serve you better to stop thinking and instead bring into awareness that which you feel mostly in your heart. Love will always override any fear-based patterns brought on by old ego misalignment.

Remember, each emotion brings with it a certain vibration frequency which either empowers us or diminishes us. Therefore, negative emotion drops our energy vibration and positive emotion increases our energy vibration. It's really very simple to understand once you begin to open your heart further so that you live in harmony with your Higher Self perception.

What Are Some of the Different Emotions

Remember, all emotion is based upon the two root emotions of Love or fear. The two cannot be experienced at precisely the same moment. All other emotions are derived from the two core emotions of Love or fear. Therefore, if you are feeling uneasy about something in your life, ask yourself what root emotions you are currently experiencing that lead you to what you are feeling. This discovery is extremely valuable for your overall Well Being.

We are each responsible for whatever emotion we are currently experiencing, because each is based upon our thoughts and the story we are telling ourselves in each moment. Our subconscious mind cannot distinguish between what is true and what is false! Therefore, it is extremely important to understand the power of thought and how emotions about those thoughts change our energy vibration in each present moment.

By monitoring our emotions and physical feelings in the body, we bring awareness to our current life situation and the perception of the mind to our circumstances. One of the most valuable tools you can use to better understand your feelings is using the two root method of comparison. You are either living a life based upon Love or fear in each present moment. Learning to balance the two until you can consciously live a life completely through Love with reverence for life itself will bring you into a State of Consciousness never experienced before.

Below is a list of emotions/feelings derived from the two root emotions of Love and fear. Ask yourself how often you experience each of these daily. And then, remember how you felt when focused on them. Happiness and sadness are choices we make each day and understanding our emotions leads us to emotional Well Being.

Emotion Chart - Love or Fear Comparison

Love	Vs.	Fear
Calm/Peaceful/Tranquil	-	Anxiety/Nervous/Worried
Humility/Humble/Modesty	-	Arrogance/Egotism/Superiority
Willing/Enthusiasm/Ready	-	Unwilling/Reluctance/Opposition
Appreciation/Gratitude/ Admiration	-	Criticism/Disparagement/Disapproval
Kind/Gentle/Thoughtful	-	Unkind/Cruel/Spiteful
Unity/Agreeable/Harmony	-	Separate/Disconnected/Divided
Confidence/Self-confidence/Composed	-	Doubt/Hesitation/Uncertain
Empathy/Understanding/ Compassion	-	Judgment/Opinionated/Dogmatic
Strength/Powerful/Assertive	-	Weak/Failing/Limited
Respect/Reverence/Valued	-	Disdain/Contempt/Despise
Compassion/Empathy/ Consideration	-	Self-Pity/Decadence/Victimization
Patient/Serenity/Tolerance	-	Impatient/Annoyance/Intolerance
Understanding/Considerate/ Thoughtful	-	Objecting/Inconsiderate/Selfish
Acceptance/Open-minded/Recognition	-	Rejection/Closed-minded/Denunciation
Hope/Trust/Optimism	-	Despair/Hopeless/Depression
Joy/Bliss/Ecstasy	-	Misery/Sadness/Gloom
Caring/Helpful/Considerate	-	Uncaring/Indifferent/Callous

Each emotion/feeling has a certain energy vibration which we feel in our bodies at the exact moment we are experiencing them. By paying close attention to what we are feeling in the body, we can determine whether we are balanced and at peace or blocked and fearful.

Remember, our natural state of being is always peaceful. If you are experiencing anything other than peace, you are actually in some manner living in fear and your Kundalini energy is blocked which causes disease (dis-ease) in the body.

Ever Been Called Emotional

We've all heard the phrase at one time or another "You're being so emotional." What this really means is that our beliefs have been triggered and we are creating new drama in our life based upon stories of the past, or worse, stories of the future that are simply not true. The emotions that are brought to the surface, based upon fear, never serve us well. Perhaps, the person making the statement "you're being so emotional" observes the life situation in front of us from a different perspective. They are not aware of the underlining story that is triggering the belief. And of course, in most cases, is probably a false belief based upon some fear based old ego drama.

This is not to say that some emotional outbursts are not based upon some perceived truth. However, in that particular moment, you should realize that which does not serve you well is in control of the alignment of the Four Body System. It is almost a certainty you have shifted back to a lower vibration level where the Physical Body is in the forefront of your life situation and you are experiencing emotions based upon fear. When this happens, it's easy to play the role of victim. When in victim (fear) mode, you shift to the story of something happening to you (which never serve's you well) rather than something happening around you. Never forget - nothing ever happens to you, it's your limited perspective that creates the victim!

In many cases, drama that starts to unfold in our mind is based upon some belief where we think we have been wronged. This creates false stories that come from when the label of "being so emotional" is placed on our perspective of the life situation. It's a good bet, in some way, the old ego perceives being attacked which always brings about false beliefs and lower-self induced drama.

A first-class example of this was previously mentioned in the story of how people are being victimized all over the world. I'm not saying people are not actually being abused by other people in some manner. This is truly the case; however, the reason for the abuse is due to the mass consciousness level (energy vibration) that is in alignment with the fears associated with the abuse itself. It's like a big snowball rolling downhill out of control where the longer it rolls, the more fear it picks up along the way.

In life situations where survival is the primary focus in life, it is very easy to be perceived as a victim. If we are living life worrying where our next meal is coming from and, perhaps, where we are going to sleep that night, we are vibrating at a very low level of energy. At this low level of life experience, it is very important to re-evaluate your beliefs and make some changes to improve the life situation.

No matter what your life situation, there is always some small opportunity for improvement waiting for you within your reach. It may not be easy to manifest a change if the life situation is very low energy, but it is always possible to make a minor change for the better. If you sit for a few moments to silently examine your beliefs and feelings, you will always discover inner solutions to outside challenges. In moments of silence, Higher Self guidance can be heard - so pay attention.

What Does "You Hurt My Feelings" Mean

We have all heard the statement "you hurt my feelings" and have probably even said those exact words to someone before. The truth is no person can hurt your feelings. You can only bring feelings of hurt or upset to yourself. Remember, when the Spiritual Body is in the forefront of your life situations there are never any victims. The only way you can feel victimized is if you experience life situations with the Physical Body in the forefront of your reality. It's the old ego that is always looking for someone to blame for what we have brought to ourselves.

The expectations created by the mind (ego) can be difficult or unreasonable when matched to the actual possibilities available to us in any current moment of our life situation. In many cases, we may have not communicated what our feelings are to someone in advance so that they understand how we feel.

<u>Here's an example:</u>

Perhaps, there is something you want to do with your spouse on a particular day as a team. However, you have not let them know in advance how important this is to you. Then when the day comes, they wake up and decide they are going off alone to do that very thing you wanted to do but with them. It could be something as simple as shopping for a birthday present for a loved one in the family. Because that family member is important to you, you wanted to make it a joint effort to pick out a present. You could judge them for your perceived disappointment and could feel offended, because they did not at least ask if you wanted to go. Of course, they had no way of knowing you wanted to go. However, that doesn't change your perception. So then you start acting out in a negative way. Is that fair to either of you? Of course not, but it doesn't change the fact that there was simply a mis-communication between you and nothing to be upset about.

How we treat others whether consciously or subconsciously can certainly influence a perspective of how they feel about us. However, in reality, we are never truly responsible for how anyone responds or feels when it comes to the outside influences of life situations. In most cases, when people believe you are responsible for their feelings, they are simply out of alignment with their own essence of being. Again, let me emphasize, we are never responsible for how someone else feels, especially if they are not communicating at a level of Oneness in the partnership.

We are all powerful Spiritual Beings. Therefore, having a human experience, which is form based, can never harm us in anyway. Once we bring that into our awareness that which happens or is said around us should have little or no influence on the way we respond to life situations. In the example above, all the spouse had to say was "so and so is very important to me too and I'd like to go with you." With the Spiritual Body in the forefront of daily life, it would be observed as nothing happening to anyone. Only shopping was about happen and that required some action which, in this case, was simply a statement that the spouse would like to go too.

Each person is responsible for their own feelings and actions. Although we are all One in truth, that which is perceived as harming us, is all a resultant factor of the ego. The more we discover how to live life with an open heart (open chakra system), the more we realize we have a choice of feeling victimized or simply allowing that which is to BE. By living life in acceptance to what is, we allow that which does not serve us well to simply flow around us. By doing so, it opens up a field of energy that is healing rather than plummeting into low energy emotions.

The more we practice living life in this state of grace and gratitude for all that comes to us, the more we embrace our authentic power. The old ego is always looking for ways to separate us from others and living with the Physical Body in the forefront of daily life situation is the perfect catalyst for hurt feelings.

265

Therefore, if someone makes a choice to say something to you that is unexpected, simply understand that it is not about you at all. People say what they believe to be true, based upon their own plans, beliefs, thoughts and emotions. Simply allow them to be who they are and understand that everyone, including yourself, is doing the best they can in each moment.

Through open spiritual communication (without conflict of old ego opinions), you allow yourself to open up to even higher states of awareness. In that advanced state of awareness, you will experience the loving grace of forgiveness if someone else is not acting in Spirit. Jesus said, "Forgive them for they know not what they do." He did not judge, he simply allowed the energy vibration to be what was and continued spiritual healing.

The next time someone says something to you that has an affect on your emotional stability; simply let them know how you feel, immediately.

Here's an example:

You could say, "Did you know when you say something to me like that, which seems to have a low energy vibration, I wonder what is going on with you internally that would cause you to say such a thing." By making a statement like this, it allows the other person to reconsider why they made the comment in the first place. And then, an open discussion may result, which could determine the root cause of what each person is feeling.

We never truly know what is going on in someone else's mind. Also, if you feel the message you are receiving from them is not in alignment with your energy flow, simply walk away and allow them to experience their own truth.

Many people go through most of their human experience with a chip on their shoulder based upon some past event which has anchored into their subconscious mind. They feel victimized and play it out on everyone around them, mainly because they have not discovered how to purge those low vibration emotions. Once they discover how to do so, it will make an enormous difference in how they perceive their life situations.

Can Exercise Help Negative Emotions

Negative emotions are typically brought on by memories of a past story that are anchored in the subconscious mind. Therefore, if you bring past negative memories into your present life situation, you are likely to re-experience the same negative emotions. And, while experiencing these negative emotions, you will most likely find yourself slipping back into old ego control characteristics. The past never equals the future, therefore as soon as you become aware that you are bringing the past into the present, just stop it!

Exercise is one of the best resources available to us to create an attraction to a higher energy vibration which, in turn, is a catalyst for the mind to feel energized.

One of the wonderful positive aspects of exercise is the way it brings awareness to your body. It excites the Physical Body to a point where you become very aware of the areas that are being exercised. And, it follows that if you bring awareness to the current moment, the past memories will float away as if by magic.

<u>Here's an example</u>:

If you are running outdoors, you become very aware of your surroundings. You pay attention to what is immediately in front of you and begin to focus on the present moment. You experience things happening around you that you would not see if you were driving a car. All the little things in life like hearing birds singing, feeling the wind in your face, feeling the beat of your feet on the ground and sun on your face. These subtle experiences are amplified in your awareness and it brings about the higher vibration of experiencing nature surrounding you.

Subconsciously, without any thought on your behalf, your breathing changes as your heart rate increases and you take in more oxygen to fuel the body which in turn produces the life-force chemicals that bring on a feeling increased energy. As you continue to run, you naturally hold your head up higher as you become a conscious observer of the wonders of life surrounding you. Without trying, you begin to experience a nature harmony with the higher energy vibrations available to you by being outdoors.

Whether you are exercising outdoors or indoors, most of the Physical Body affects are the same. You become more focused on what you are doing in the immediate moment and pay attention to your surroundings at a higher level of awareness. And, as long as you are being present, you stay in alignment with that which serves you best. In this state of Being, the past stories are no longer brought into the current moment.

Each time you exercise, you have the opportunity to bring more awareness to the present moment. And, you will find yourself living each moment in a state of gratitude. No matter what you current life situation is you can always find something to be grateful for. Exercise is one of them. Spiritual exercise is no different; in the meditative state of silence, the Soul is energized with the beauty of Highest Self awareness.

Do Emotions Lead to Depression

In each moment of life situation, we have a choice to live from the perspective of having the Spiritual Body or the Physical Body alignment system controlling our emotions. If the ego is merged with the Soul, the life perspective is in alignment with Love, Peace and Light. The emotions are in harmony with abundance and the Physical Body is merely the vessel to be used on our journey.

The Physical Body is never who we really are, but it is part of our overall being while we are here in this form-based reality. Now that you are living life with the understanding that you are a Spiritual Being having a human experience, the ego/mind will not have the control over you that it did when you were misaligned. The fog of limited understanding has been lifted and you are now walking the path of inspirational thought rather than the resultant aspects of Physical Body limited emotion control dynamics. Releasing yourself from merely a Physical Body alignment perspective allows you to grow in awareness of the Spiritual Body and its unlimited possibilities.

Depression is a state of mind and, therefore, only possible with a Physical Body mis-alignment where self-limiting emotions are in alignment with a misaligned Four Body System and guide the mind into misdirected stories. Therefore, depression is some "thing" you have to "do" by bringing past or future stories based upon wrong thinking belief structure into the present moment. Whereas, wrong thinking is merely a statement saying you are misaligned. Spiritual Body alignment never brings on depression; it is always in alignment with Love, Peace and Light and in harmony with abundance and truth.

If you learned nothing else from this guideline for realignment than to understand the importance of always walking the path of Spiritual Body alignment, you would be living a life of "heaven on earth" in each moment. We are always meant to be happy and experiencing life to its fullest.

That is what the Original Source Agreement has in store for each one of us. To live life out of alignment with our Original Source Agreement is to live with a fog placed over the abundant possibilities available to us.

As previously discussed, the easiest way to realign your Four Body System is through daily meditation. It's in this silent peaceful state of being that all the secrets of the Universe are revealed. The more your energy vibration is raised through daily meditation, the more you will experience the truth about the Original Source Agreement and the incredible abundance you have at your finger tips. It's all planned out with every possible journey you could ever imagine, but it's up to you to make the choices along the way. Your choices will lead you down a unique path that can only be experienced by you directly. You may allow your path to be influenced by others, but ultimately no one knows the best choice for you other than yourself.

You should now understand that you have to DO depression, which is only possible in a Physical Body misalignment where the Emotional Body fuels the Mental Body with false beliefs about your lower-self reality.

You can bring your true vision to light by simply understanding your limitless Higher Self. One of the most powerful ways to do so is to quiet the mind and listen to the guidance that comes through during the pure peacefulness of the meditative state.

What Is Depression

Mind games and ego control dynamics are the catalyst for "doing" depression. The medical industry defines depression through various hypotheses which are all based upon a Physical Body misalignment system. If your Four Body System was aligned properly, with the Spiritual Body in the forefront of your life situation, you would never be depressed. In fact, the Spiritual Body does not even understand the term depression. It accepts that sadness comes and goes based upon the life situations that are happening around us, but it never allows the ego to take control of us and bring false beliefs into the spiritually enlightened mind.

"Wikipedia defines Major depressive disorder (MDD) (also known as recurrent depressive disorder, clinical depression, major depression, unipolar depression, or unipolar disorder) as a mental disorder characterized by episodes of all-encompassing low mood accompanied by low self-esteem and loss of interest or pleasure in normally enjoyable activities. This cluster of symptoms (syndrome) was named, described and classified as one of the mood disorders in the 1980 edition of the American Psychiatric Association's diagnostic manual. The term "depression" is ambiguous. It is often used to denote this syndrome but may refer to other mood disorders or to lower mood states lacking clinical significance. Major depressive disorder is a disabling condition that adversely affects a person's family, work or school life, sleeping and eating habits, and general health. In the United States, around 3.4% of people with major depression commit suicide, and up to 60% of people who commit suicide had depression or another mood disorder.[1]

The diagnosis of major depressive disorder is based on the patient's self-reported experiences, behavior reported by relatives or friends, and a mental status examination. There is no laboratory test for major depression, although physicians generally request tests for physical conditions that may cause similar symptoms. The most common time of onset is between the ages of 20 and 30 years, with a later peak between 30 and 40 years.[2]

Typically, patients are treated with antidepressant medication and, in many cases, also receive psychotherapy or counseling, although the effectiveness of medication for mild or moderate cases is questionable.[3] Hospitalization may be necessary in cases with associated self-neglect or a significant risk of harm to self or others. A minority are treated with electroconvulsive therapy (ECT). The course of the disorder varies widely, from one episode lasting weeks to a lifelong disorder with recurrent major depressive episodes. Depressed individuals have shorter life expectancies than those without depression, in part because of greater susceptibility to medical illnesses and suicide. It is unclear whether or not medications affect the risk of suicide. Current and former patients may be stigmatized.

The understanding of the nature and causes of depression has evolved over the centuries, though this understanding is incomplete and has left many aspects of depression as the subject of discussion and research. Proposed causes include psychological, psycho-social, hereditary, evolutionary and biological factors. Certain types of long-term drug use can both cause and worsen depressive symptoms. Psychological treatments are based on theories of personality, interpersonal communication, and learning. Most biological theories focus on the monoamine chemicals serotonin, norepinephrine and dopamine, which are naturally present in the brain and assist communication between nerve cells."

When the Spiritual Body is guiding your life, the emotions that come from an acceptance of what is happening around you are always positive; therefore, a higher energy vibration. When there is no victim perceiving something happening to you, it is not possible to experience the negative feelings or low self-worth and negative labels which are in alignment with the term depression.

In view of the fact that depression is a state-of-mind, it would be an understatement to say staying In-Spirit or inspired by the higher energy found in keeping the Spiritual Body in the forefront of everything your experience would enhance your overall Well Being.

Which following statement is your truth "I am my body" or "I have a body"? The answer will bring awareness to your current alignment. If you are not your body, who or what are you?

Who Does the Labeling

Misguided society has a powerful approach to manipulating the old ego into focusing on the lower vibrations found in negative energy. One of the tools these controllers use is that of labeling. What we need to remember is that we are not the roles we play, we are Spiritual Beings observing that which is happening around us. The role we are playing can change in a heartbeat and is guaranteed to continue to change as we spend more earth years in the Physical Body. All that happens around us is a form-based reality which we are merely observing as we continue to heal ourselves and the collective Soul of the Universe.

As we explore deeper into the reality of which we *truly are,* we begin to relate more to our Spiritual Body association in the experiences of life, rather than the Physical Body form-based perception. Then we discover the occurrences surrounding us are merely a reality based upon the collective actions we have taken throughout our form-based experience thus far. As we continue to evolve in Spiritual Body awareness, Conscious Clarity of our actions becomes more important to our healing. We now spend more of our time participating in our Spiritual Body evolution and endeavor to surround ourselves with like minded people to enhance one another's awareness of Higher Self energy vibration. Who you spend your time with can have a major influence on how quickly your energy vibration increases to a higher level of understanding.

By now, you should be sitting in silence at least once or preferably twice per day. You have discovered the depth of knowledge available to you through the silence of meditation (quieting the mind) is an extremely important part of your Well Being. This aspect of an inspired life is provided for our peace of mind and Spiritual Body growth. This higher state of energy vibration is where all the solutions are to all challenges that arise from living unconsciously. Once you consistently tap into this higher state of energy vibration, you will discover the "controllers of society" have little or no influence on the outcome of your life situations.

When we turn off the outside negativity and constant bombardment of limited perspective thinking, we align ourselves with a powerful sacred guidance system. By simply listening to this inner guidance, we allow the world to evolve naturally as we continue to live in a state of Conscious Clarity and everything on our path becomes clearer.

It's important to remember, the vast majority of people you interact with each day are still living from a Physical Body perspective of life as their reality. They may continue to vibrate at the lower levels of awareness and may continue to doubt your new perspective on life. Simply accept this as a fact. It will become increasingly clearer to you that people choosing to live from this unconscious state of existence will need to be left behind as you grow in spiritual awareness. It can be a very difficult decision to let these people go, so be sure to give them the opportunity to grow with you before you make your final decision to move on.

We must always remember that although we are all connected in Oneness, we still have the free will choice to take action in life based upon our current belief system, conscious evolution and vibration level. While keeping this in mind, it becomes easier to simply allow people to evolve at their own rate of awareness, while you evolve at yours. Overall evolution is always in its proper order. The proof is simply that it is what it is - no other proof is necessary.

As you continue to develop your new spiritual relationships, you will feel a definite change in your level of peace within. Those that now come into your life (in harmony with your energy vibration) will also realize that the shift in vibration rises exponentially in Oneness. As you spend more time with these new friends who live life from this higher state of energy vibration, you will understand that you have an opportunity to change many of the roles you have planned until now.

Now that you have aligned yourself with people of equal or higher energy vibration, you will feel an understanding that it is not your business to even care how most of society role plays in their illusion of limited form-based reality. You simply accept fully that everyone evolves at their own rate of awareness and you make yourself available to those that choose to increase their energy vibration. Leaving old friends behind is not always an easy task, but it may be the best thing you can do to advance your own spiritual evolution.

As you revisit *The Train of Life™* analogy in Illustration E, you will see that the level of energy vibration you are now living is in alignment with a "Resultant Reality" stepped up to a life of Conscious Clarity and awareness. The unconscious mind no longer has the same influence on your reality, because you have stepped up into the energy vibration of a fifth dimension reality.

Now, you begin to cultivate this new fifth dimension reality into your Life Plan and take yet another quantum leap in awareness to sustain or continue to increase your level of energy vibration. This is accomplished through living life daily from a state of Grace, focused on Love, Peace and Light.

Therefore, the labels society may place upon you, no longer influences your personality which has grown to understand that no fear-based, false reality can hold you back from natural Spiritual growth.

Chapter 6 Suggestions - Getting in Touch With Feelings

You discovered in Part One of this program that all it takes to complete the Soul Merge Process is to keep the Spiritual Body in the forefront of everything you experience in life. And, one of the best ways to achieve this is through sitting in silence at least once each day communicating with the Highest Self (God-Self). By sitting in a state of meditative bliss, you have a direct connection with Source Energy (God-Self) where you actual hear the Divine guidance of the Universe. There is no greater power on Earth to assist you!

"Meditation is not some "thing" you do; it is the experience of Being that which you are." – Terry Swejkoski

- The most important action you can implement in your life to better understand your emotions/feelings is to sit in silence daily, preferably twice per day.

- Feel how the life-force energy in your body is flowing through your chakras by training your mind to be still. You will then experience a true conversation with Source Energy.

- The Divine wisdom of God-Self is always guiding us. Through this wisdom, we can choose to always experience a life filled with Love, Peace and Light. It's our choice and all we need do is listen to the inner guidance and all solutions to every challenge in life will be revealed.

- In order to hear the guidance from God-Self, you must raise your energy vibration to the level of stillness. By removing the cluttered thoughts of the mind, you will hear solutions for every challenge.

- The balance we can experience in life is equally proportionate to the way we monitor our feelings and how in touch we are with them. Our feelings are a mapping system for the body to alert us of where we stand in our energy vibration. If you did nothing else but pay close attention to the feelings you are experiencing and which part of the body you may feel an energy blockage, your life would always be in balance.

- All emotion is based upon the two root emotions of Love or fear. The two cannot be experienced at precisely the same moment. All other emotions are derived from the two core emotions of Love or fear. Therefore, if you are feeling uneasy about something in your life, ask yourself what root emotions you are currently experiencing that lead you to what you are feeling. This discovery is extremely valuable for your overall Well Being.

- Depression is a state of mind and, therefore, only possible with a Physical Body mis-alignment where self-limiting emotions are next in line and guide the mind into misdirected stories.

- When we turn off the outside negativity and constant bombardment of limited perspective thinking, we align ourselves with a powerful sacred guidance system. By simply listening to this inner guidance, we allow the world to evolve naturally as we continue to live in a state of Conscious Clarity and everything on our path becomes clearer.

Now that you have been living from a Spiritual Body (fourth dimension perspective), you are ready to take the next step in raising your energy vibration to that which is in harmony with unlimited possibility. If you have not yet reached this state of awareness, review all that you have rediscovered about your Higher Self to this point. Simply go back and re-read each chapter of this process and ask questions in silence pertaining to areas of confusion.

Chapter 7

12 Simple Steps for Staying On Track

How Many Steps Are There for Staying on Track

Staying on Track once you realize who you really are is really quite easy if you keep the Spirit Body alignment in place. By consciously moving your life forward with the certainty that you can succeed in any endeavor you are committed to, you will see beyond the ego's need to control you.

It is imperative that you understand the ego will still pop in from time to time. Its controlling patterns will diminish with time, but you must always be on the lookout for little tricks the ego will use to confuse you. Based upon this knowledge, it will be easier for you to continue your journey forward in new light. Simply understand that challenges in life will always come, but they are nothing more than a test to keep you on track. In fact, at times, the tests can be very challenging, because you have a never-ending movie called your life that keeps unfolding in surprising ways.

There will be many times when you feel as though you are experiencing challenges that you did not bring to yourself. At these times, it is important to remember you agreed to every situation that happens around you. You agreed to every single life situation you experience long ago and signed on the dotted line in your Original Source Agreement. In that agreement, you experience a bigger picture of life other than just yourself. This means, although you are here to focus on "your life primarily", you are also responsible for assisting others that are in harmony with your energy vibration in each current moment.

In the last chapter, you learned about emotions/feelings and how they are part of your inner guidance system for staying on track. This ultimately means to stay In-Spirit or inspired to continue to move forward. Just as with any journey, the journey of life comes through living it. You must learn to appreciate it fully and accept every life situation with open arms. Even when the outward appearance seems challenging, there is a purpose for that challenge. You may not understand the purpose at the time you are experiencing it; however, if you have faith and allow that which is meant to unfold around you blossom, the purpose will eventually be revealed in a beautiful manner.

You have the free will choice to either float through life unconsciously in a never-ending spiral of emotional disconnect (as most people do) or you can take complete charge of your journey by realigning with your Original Source

Agreement. Now that you have learned to blend your Mental Body (mind) with your Spiritual Body, you have the knowledge available to you to move forward in quantum leaps of Conscious Clarity. You must now focus on your Original Source Agreement as never before, with a burning desire on that which is truly the destiny for your greatest good and the greatest good for all of God's creation.

The logical mind is programmed to take steps to achieve that which is first only imagined and then manifested. It is programmed to set goals that can be achieved in alignment with your energy vibration; therefore, the higher the energy vibration, the greater the achievement. Please understand the first part of any creation is seeing that which you desire. This desire is something that comes to you in the form of a vision. When you learn to silence the mind from the daily misinformation that surrounds you, you see your vision with Conscious Clarity. Therefore, by now, you know you must sit in the silence of a meditative state daily to experience the complete guidance coming your way. Then when the mind is clear, you can set goals to manifest the vision into your current reality.

As you tunnel down deeply into the vision of your Original Source Agreement, you will begin to discover that you have the power to exponentially move your energy vibration up to a higher level of understanding, one that makes it easy to deal with the outside occurrences or challenges of life situations. As you continue to build your authentic power (God-Self realization) through the tools that have been previously outlined for you in the *Conscious Clarity Energy Process™*, you will see with growing clarity that life is meant to be a blessing each day. You are the one that has the power to bring your vision to light. You are the only one that is responsible for your life situations as they come to you. You must always remember that which comes is always in alignment with or directly proportional to your current energy vibration at the time you manifest it. This is a Universal Law of Attraction.

You will always receive that which you focus on the most. It will be brought to you through the power of Universal Intelligence once you ask for it. Therefore, you must be prepared to accept that which you manifest into your life experience and never doubt that you have a reason for being in the exact life situation you are experiencing in each moment. When feelings of disconnect arise (and they will), simply sit in silence and ask for guidance so that you can receive the Universal power available to you.

This is an amazing time to be here on this planet. We are here to rediscover the incredible power of working together as One for the betterment of all of humanity, not just for own personal perceived needs.

The number of authentic power steps available to you that will enhance your energy vibration is limitless. However, only you know how many steps are required to actually move forward at a pace that is comfortable for your own personal overall Well Being. And, those steps must be taken one step at a time.

In the next few sections, I will share with you a general strategy or steps for pursuing goals during your journey. At this juncture in your rediscovery of true Self (God-Self), you will begin to open up to your greatness in new exciting ways and your faith will grow exponentially.

Do I Need to Do These in Order

The path to enlightenment is a never-ending process which is experienced one step at a time through balancing the categories of life situation. These categories are detailed for you in Illustration D of the *Conscious Clarity Energy Process™*. Review the chart now so that you will re-familiarize yourself with the concept of sectioning your Life Plan into mini categories that are easily manageable. By sectioning your Life Plan into categories, the mind can quickly comprehend what it takes to balance all eight categories of life situation.

For those of you that have a hard time when it comes to planning, simply keep in mind you already made this plan before you entered the current body you are using. Therefore, the plan will be revealed to you or rediscovered easily in detail through the process of peaceful meditation.

There are two categories that should be focused on first to increase your energy vibration, especially if you feel that the challenges of life are becoming a major burden for you:

The first is the "Spiritual Life" where all Highest Self guidance comes from in your Spiritual Body alignment. If your goal is to live life from a joyous state of being, be certain to do so by aligning the Spiritual Body in the forefront of everything you do without exception.

The second most important category is the Soul Merge where you consistently reassure the ego that everything is under the control of the Highest Self energy vibrations, not the mind alone. Once the ego and Soul are merged together, they work in harmony to bring balance to the rest of the categories of life situation.

If you feel yourself slipping to a lower-energy vibration, simply focus on the first two categories to bring yourself back into harmony with your Highest Self hub of life balance. Now is the time to form new habits and to create a new level of understanding as to why you must balance your life situation in alignment with your highest vision for life rather than simply wandering through life unconsciously.

Each one of us has a vision of what our life is meant to be. That vision is found in the silence between the thoughts of the mind. Now that you are spending a minimum of twenty minutes each day in stillness through peaceful meditation, you will experience Source Energy guidance as never before. Even during times of challenge when your energy vibration may have slipped, all you need do is take a few deep breaths, sit still for a few moments in silence and you will regain your natural higher energy vibration. Source Energy will always be there to guide you, especially during moments of uncertainty. Always remember, *you are never alone!*

When you are sitting still or in a state of inner peace during meditation, the challenging outside influences of life situation simply fall away like ripples caused by a stone dropping into an otherwise calm body of water. Know that the ripples of challenging life situations are merely temporary. The key is to live in awareness of your feelings, so that you can quickly re-adjust your thoughts if you feel you are slipping away from the peaceful inner harmony that is your natural state of being.

You should always remember that life is meant to be experienced to its fullest in each moment. However, even though you are a beautiful Spiritual Being, you are housed in a body that is form-based and that body is not always in alignment with your highest purpose. The ego will attempt to trick the mind into believing you are less than you really are. So pay close attention to your thoughts and simply learn to accept all that is in your life situation, as it unfolds in each moment. And then, re-align your thoughts with the reality that everything happens *around you* for a specific purpose. That which you are experiencing in each present moment is leading you to your ultimate destiny. Although you may not be aware of it in the current moment, even the challenges are there for a purpose, because they allow you to make choices. And there is always one choice that is far better than the other which will move you forward to your ultimate destiny.

As the other six categories of life unfold for you, you will be given many opportunities to grow exponentially in faith. It is faith that will assist you in moving forward through life situations that seem overly challenging. And it is faith that will allow you to stay calm during the challenges that surround you. All of life is a lesson to be accepted as a stepping stone into the next moment of higher awareness. Stay alert and you will be amazed as your categories of life become more balanced. And the more balanced you are, the more your energy vibration will increase, taking you to higher levels of understanding and happiness where your life will have a synchronistic flow as if by magic.

Outward happiness is not measured by how enlightened you are in each moment. It's more about how many times you bring enlightenment into your life by staying in alignment with your Original Source Agreement. And, when you are in alignment, you will radiate with an inner joy that will always keep you smiling, even during challenging times that are not understood by others living life at lower-energy vibration levels.

Remember, with Spiritual Body alignment in the forefront of everything you experience, life will change for you. Life will unfold in a synchronistic, perfectly choreographed dance of joy, where your Highest Self will flow through life in alignment with your Original Source Agreement.

What Is Synchronicity

Typically, people believe synchronicity is the alignment of events from history that align with the current moments in Earth time. In a matter of speaking, this is true, but there is a higher level of awareness definition for synchronicity, too. This higher awareness definition is simply being in alignment with your Original Source Agreement, so that events unfold in your life situation based upon your pre-planned direction from a Highest Self perspective. You will always be the author of your own destiny when you are in Spiritual Body alignment. By staying balanced and in alignment with your Original Source Agreement, you will manifest you life situation in a manner that you would not experience if you were out of alignment.

Yes, synchronicity is a wonderful word to use to place meaning on events as they unfold in your form-based life. However, it can have an emotional association as to how you observe life situations. Simply learn to allow that which is in front of you to unfold in its own manner as it is manifesting based upon your current energy vibration. This means, don't take life situations too seriously as they are form-based and will eventually have an end. Never forget, the harmony of each event is all based upon your current energy vibration and can only be experienced to its fullest if you have Conscious Clarity of what is happening around you.

If you have learned to accept that you are the author of you own story, you will find yourself way ahead of the majority of the rest of the population. It's this acceptance or ownership of the responsibility of your own destiny that will guide you into the direction of your highest purpose in life. When you are in balance with your pre-planned life, your feelings about how you arrived in the current moment will feel in harmony and peaceful. However, when you are out of alignment, you will feel a lower-energy vibration and emotions will control you. Then you will experience a disharmony where chakras begin to block in some manner and your inner peace will diminish. By paying close attention to these feelings and how the energy is flowing through your body, you will know when change is necessary to get back on track.

Life is a balancing act based upon your perceptions of what reality is and whether or not you feel as though you are on the best path for your continued spiritual growth. Through Conscious Clarity of thought, you can allow yourself to grow in awareness because you will live life with an inner joy and that joy will radiate outward to everyone around you. All the right people will show up at exactly the right moment to assist you in moving forward in your life and you will feel the excitement of being in the flow of a balanced, high energy, blissful lifestyle. Everything around you will begin to unfold in a synchronistic manner that is totally in alignment with your highest purpose for being here. And, everyone around you will benefit in some way by sharing their time with you.

We can never be certain how life will unfold if we live it unconsciously, because by living unconsciously, we place ourselves at the beck and call of others that ultimately control our life. When we give away the control of our destiny to others, we are not thriving in life. We are simply surviving and losing out on all the wonders of a balanced life. This typically leads to feelings of inadequacy in some manner as we know in our hearts that there is something more to life than what we may be experiencing when others are controlling our destiny. And, we may even feel victimized by others. Then, our energy vibration diminishes and we fall short of our goals for our higher purpose in life.

If you would rather live your life in a state of balance and harmony with your Original Source Agreement, I recommend that review how each of the categories of your life are unfolding for you right now. Only you know if you are in balance and only you can make the choice to change your current life situation. You have the authentic power to bring Love, Peace and Light to each moment of your existence, never give that power away to someone else. Therefore, anchor in the fact that you have the authentic power to make a decision *right now* to get back on track and move out of whatever blockage you have brought to yourself by living unconsciously.

Now, you are ready to take the necessary steps to fulfill your ultimate destiny which is based upon being in harmony with your Original Source Agreement and Conscious Clarity of thought. Simply follow the steps and they will provide you with the necessary guidance to answer most questions that may arise.

12 Steps to Fulfill Your Ultimate Destiny:

Step 1 – *Spiritual Being Awareness*

Knowing that you are a Spiritual Being having a human experience is the first step to maintaining a life filled with joy. There's a difference between saying I am a Spiritual Being and actually having a Knowing you are a Spiritual Being. When you experience life from a state of consciousness that you *are* a Spiritual Being, all the life situation challenges that come your way are perceived as a simple form-based movie. And, we already know a movie can be re-scripted at anytime during its production.

As you look in the mirror each morning, see the Spirit that is beyond the body; through the eyes of the Soul life's experience is lived at a higher state of consciousness. You are not the body; you are merely using the body for a short period of measurable form-based time. The Spiritual Being that you truly are will use many different bodies during its journey through life. The Spiritual Being is eternal and, therefore, formless in cosmic time.

When we look at life as a never-ending journey through cosmic time, we begin to feel the Spiritual Being awareness of the Highest Self that is not experienced from the limited perspective of Physical Body belief. If you haven't had an "aha" moment by now with respect to this truth, perhaps this would be a good time to simply sit in silence with this understanding for a while. Just close your eyes take a few deep cleansing breaths and *feel* the unlimited energy pulsating through your body, Knowing you are far more than the Physical Body reflected back in the mirror.

Feel and understand that all the life situations you experience through the Physical Body are merely a drop of water in the ocean of cosmic life. The physical life you are currently experiencing is minuscule in comparison to your actual cosmic eternal life. This is why it is imperative that you change your limited perspective of yourself and rediscover your true Spiritual essence. When focused on the big picture or cosmic eternal life, the challenges of form-based life situations soften quickly and are perceived as opportunities for growth, rather than the lower-energy perspective of victimization.

Your Spiritual Life is the absolute, the omnipresent and is shared with all other Spiritual Beings through the level of Oneness. At this level of energy vibration, all of us have the opportunity to view life from an unlimited perspective and understand what it truly means to live in harmony with each other. At this level of energy vibration or perspective, we understand that we are all connected in the Universe and, therefore, our choices affect the entire Universe, not merely our limited form-based bodies.

At this level of understanding, we are all connected with Source Energy and it is that energy that provides the unlimited power of Universal Oneness. All of our life situations are orchestrated as a beautiful symphony that is meant to be experienced from a level of understanding beyond that of the limited mind. Therefore, because we are all part of Source Energy (God), we are capable of performing in this form-based movie called human life at the level of unlimited possibility. With that understanding, Knowing that you could not fail at anything you visualize, what would you change in your current life situation?

We all chose to be here in this physical world to continue to rediscover what we each agreed to in our own Original Source Agreements with Source Energy. Therefore, the sooner you start to live your life from the awareness of unlimited possibilities, the more you will become aware of your part in the big picture of life.

Once you truly *know* you are a Spiritual Being, your life will be miraculous every day, because you will be in alignment with your Original Source Agreement.

Step 2 – *Original Source Agreement Awareness*

Relax - Breathe and eliminate thought to hear the Highest Self guidance available to you every day. You will become more aware of your Original Source Agreement with Source Energy through the silence of deep meditation. The quieter you become, the more you will hear the direct messages coming from Source Energy guidance.

You do not know what you do not know until you eliminate thought and bring your energy vibration in harmony with Source Energy. This is the only way you will experience the truth about your own personal agreements that were made prior to entering you current form-based body. If you are still having difficulty eliminating thought, then it is very possible that you have not yet accepted the fact that you are a Spiritual Being having a human experience. If this is the case for you, simply accept where you are and focus on increasing your faith and peacefulness.

There will always be third dimension skeptics questioning everything that is provided to you by people living in fourth dimension spiritual awareness. This is mainly due to spiritual ignorance or lack of understanding only available at Higher Self levels of energy vibration. By learning to quiet the mind through easy breathing exercises where you simply relax breathing deeply and allow the mind's limiting beliefs to slowly drift away, you will begin to experience the direct conversation with Source Energy. Breathe in deeply (from the diaphragm) for a count of four (4), pause and then, exhale completely for a count of six (6); eventually, you can increase the exhale count to eight (8) as you progress. Everyone is capable of accomplishing this technique with practice without exception.

You have a wonderful plan already laid out for you. Call it your destiny or whatever other words you choose to assign to the Original Source Agreement and remember, you personally created the agreement. All that matters is that you consciously become more aware of your true essence each day; use whatever means that seems to resonate with you most. The ego will still continue to sneak in to disrupt your stillness from time to time, but only until you have completely surrendered to the higher powers within you. The moment you totally surrender and therefore reach the Soul Merge level of energy vibration, the harder it will be for ego to gain control of your choices in life. Stay focused on maintaining this higher level of awareness and you will feel the blissful joy radiating from within.

Remember, you are always responsible for your choices; however, you do not have to be prisoner to the ego and the manipulations of its lower vibration levels of fear-based reality. By allowing yourself to surrender fully to the presence of Source Energy in your life, you will begin to slowly eliminate the negative thoughts that may still be controlling some of your daily life situations. Each day you can make the choice to live in acceptance of what is, thereby increasing your energy vibration to offset the challenging life situations happening around you.

Only by opening up to Spirit level awareness, will you be able to flow through life peacefully and achieve your Highest Self destiny in your daily experiences. The Original Source Agreement will be heard loud and clear once you release the limited expectations that you have placed upon yourself by only believing in Physical Body intelligence. The mind will attempt to manipulate you into believing the physical intelligence of the mind is superior to Spiritual Self awareness during this human experience. However, you should always remember that that in itself if living from a state of limitation. The only limitations you have are those that are form-based and self-inflicted.

The cosmic intelligence of the Universe is what is available to you when you are living your life in a meditative state of reality. This means you are living at a level of energy vibration where the subtle messages or guidance received in each moment overpowers the limited beliefs and doubts of mind-based reality. This may still be very difficult for some of you to grasp consistently; however, if you are patient with yourself, you will slowly (but surely) increase your energy vibration through faith. When living life from this beautiful peaceful state of awareness where faith overpowers you limited beliefs, it changes your perception of what happens around you on a daily basis.

Bring your faith to light by meditating at least twice daily for a quiet mind hears what you think you do not know. As you grow in the awareness of which you truly are, you will find that each moment becomes more and more relaxed. When living life in this relaxed state of alignment with your attention focused on Original Source Agreement awareness, you will find your life quickly changing for the better.

Step 3 – *Daily Connection With Source Energy*

To hear the guidance that is in harmony with your Original Source Agreement, you must train your Physical Body to exist in a state of meditative peace. By placing your attention on the intention of quieting the mind, it will be a catalyst for understanding the depth of the messages being brought to you at the higher levels of awareness. This guidance is brought to you beyond the levels of neurological brainwaves of the Physical Body. There is a state of enlightenment or a level of energy vibration that is beyond that which the Physical Body can comprehend. This state of Being is Spiritual Body awareness and available to you at any given moment.

It is during the state of enlightenment or Spiritual Body awareness that you begin to experience the non-word conversations with Source Energy. Therefore, it is imperative that you begin to quiet the brainwave activity of the physical brain if you are to hear the guidance available to you. At first, it can be very challenging to accomplish "the quieting of the mind" because we are so pre-programmed (especially in Western civilization) to live from a state of action or agitated Physical Body alignment with society.

Through Brainwave Entrainment, science is just beginning to understand the correlation between the brainwave activity of the body and how it affects our state of consciousness. Although, the studies have been increasingly more in depth including comparisons between scientific thinkers and highly-realized meditative monks that sit in quiet-mind awareness for hours at a time, humanity is still at the beginning stages of understanding. The current mass consciousness level of understanding which pertains to living life in a meditative state of mind is at a very low level of energy vibration. Therefore, it is imperative that we "enlist the mind to serve the Soul" if we are to continue with our human evolution, whereas the majority of humanity begins to understand the significance of this new fourth dimension limitless lifestyle.

If you are planning on contributing to the fourth dimensional world which is becoming more attuned to the unlimited possibilities available to us by placing the Spiritual Body in the forefront of our daily activities, you must change your beliefs. You must begin to reach deeper within or outside the box of conventional lower-energy thinking and bring your Higher Self wisdom to light.

To start, you must begin to understand the workings of the brain and how you can focus your attention on the intention of raising your spiritual energy vibration by lowering your physical brainwave activity. This may seem like a lot to comprehend at first, but let me assure you it will serve you well. It is first important for you to have a general understanding of the physical brain so that your mind will begin to merge with the Soul with Conscious Clarity. As an example, you could compare the Soul Merge process to learning a new language.

Just as you do not understand what is being communicated to you with words in a language you are unfamiliar with, at first you will not understand the messages that are being transmitted to you from the higher levels of energy vibration if your do not train your physical body to quiet the mind or brainwave activity. It is at the zero level of brain activity where the non-word language of Source Energy is revealed and the spiritual Kundalini energy rises up to welcome it. During these moments of enlightenment, you will experience "aha" realization and clearly remember your Original Source Agreement in detail. And, once you experience a glimpse of this level of understanding, you will never go back to vibrating below your true potential.

Even though brainwave scientific study is just now beginning to break through the barriers of the ego, it is important to remember that most of society is still living in the dark ages of what it all truly means. There are many skeptics, you may be one of them; however, by learning to quiet your mind through the practice of daily meditation, you will bring yourself to a state of Conscious Clarity as never before. You will experience that which was unseen and unheard of before and you will change your beliefs from skeptic to true believer.

We all have the power to quiet the mind and bring our physical brainwave activity to zero within a few heartbeats, but you must be willing to accept that which you have denied up until this moment and open yourself to new levels of understanding.

The following chart details typical brainwave activity, as measured during Brainwave Entrainment research:

Brainwave	Cycles/Second	Mental States & Associated Processes
GAMMA	30Hz to 60Hz or 40Hz to 99Hz*** There continues to be some disagreement in regards to where GAMMA Starts (30 Hz or 40Hz) ***	Compassion, Empathy, Decision making under stress, higher brain functioning and processes, influences sensory organization processing and integration. Believed to strongly influence the organization and interpretation of sensory data. Believed to have a strong impact on social consciousness and right and wrong. Enhanced self awareness and insight. GAMMA frequencies are found naturally in higher amounts in long term practitioners of various forms of meditation. Believed to enhance the ability to achieve goals. Improves clarity of thought and believed to improve intuition.
BETA	13Hz to 30 or 12Hz to 39Hz	Wide awake – sensory motor awareness. Focused and alert, analytical thinking,

		learning new information quickly, complex mental processing. Usually associated with peak mental and physical performance. Also associated with stress and anxiety. Can be used to enhance the absorption and processing of new information.
ALPHA	8Hz to 12Hz	Associated with lighter meditative states. Associated with super learning. More relaxed. Relaxed yet alert but not necessarily engaged in active processing. Ready to respond, positive thinking, creative problem solving. Mood elevations, stress reduction, enhanced creativity, bridges the consciousness with the unconscious mind, better access to resources involved in creativity, can be a source of motivation and inspiration.
THETA	4Hz to 7.5Hz	Dream state, creative inspirations, hypnologic state, enhanced visualization, deep meditation, sleep spindles, deep relaxation, inner peace

		and sense of well being, long-term memory. Believed to increase inner wisdom, enhanced intuition, reduce stress and transformational help for limiting beliefs. May negatively affect attention disorders such ADD and ADHD.
DELTA	.6 Hz to 3.5 Hz	Deep sleep, no dreams, physical healing and recuperation, healing of the limbic system, may positively improve symptoms of PTSD, empathy. Believed to help with inner growth and wisdom, recovery from trauma
SUB-DELTA	.1 HZ to .5Hz	Positive effect on the limbic system, healing, believed to be the source of deep inner wisdom peace and Divine knowledge.

You will notice that the upper frequencies are more associated with "thinking" and how the mind processes the various brainwaves. Then, as the frequency drops, as in the Theta, Delta and Sub-Delta levels, the mind is released or quiet. As this occurs, it allows us to focus clearly on the guidance that is transmitted at the Sub-Delta levels. At these levels, we are capable of communicated directly with Source

Energy and begin to understand our true purpose based upon our Original Source Agreement or True Life Plan.

At the Sub-Delta level, brainwave activity is almost non-existent and we have the ability to transcend the mind's limited understanding of reality. At this level of "non-thought", you are capable of manifesting healing authentic power at the level of cosmic creation and are in direct contact with the Universal Oneness. This is the level of existence or enlightenment that most spiritual seekers attempt to obtain and brings about a quantum leap in energy vibration into the higher levels of fifth and sixth dimension awareness once it is achieved.

Special Note: The higher levels of dimensional awareness will be discussed at a later time. For now, all you need do is accept what is being presented to you in the current moment. You have just begun to touch upon the levels of awareness available to you. This would be a good time to review Illustration E, *Energy Vibration – Life Fuel Source* and see how the lowering of brainwaves brings about clarity and Higher Self awareness at higher vibration levels of consciousness.

By now, you should understand the rationale and importance of training your physical body to exist in a meditative state of peace. Therefore, train yourself to observe silence at least twice daily as you develop your Higher Self awareness. As you progress, you will actually discover that you can (and will) exist in a constant state of meditative peace throughout the day. At this level of understanding, the guidance received from Source Energy will be heard during your normal daily activities and you will be guided in each present moment through Conscious Clarity of your Spiritual Higher Self awareness.

Step 4 – *Become an Active Observer*

Believe in yourself and the gifts you have been given to accomplish your purpose for being here. Understand that you are here to assist in transforming the world to the next level of evolution and that it was actually a choice you made to come here to accomplish this purpose. By listening to your inner guidance and accepting assistance from others, you can achieve anything you actively plan during your journey. Yes, you can truly be an "Active Observer" of your destiny. Actively plan what is planable; and then, simply sit back and observer it unfolding in your life as the Universe manifests it into form-based reality.

The secret to being an "Active Observer" is to listen to the guidance you receive during meditative states and, then, take action on that vision observed by mapping out a detailed plan with realistic goals. Focus on your goals and your life will become the reality of your vision. Walk away from the naysayer mentality and keep your Higher Self aligned with your Spiritual Body in the forefront of every action. By doing so, you will stay in alignment with your Original Source Agreement which is what you actual see in your visions during meditative states of Being.

Always remember the most important truth about meditation:

"Meditation is not some "thing" you do; it is the experience of Being that which you are." – Terry Swejkoski

When you know you are a Spiritual Being having a human experience, you walk a path that is in alignment with Divine wisdom which can only come from Source Energy harmony. This wisdom or cosmic intelligence is the voice you witness during your periods of non-thought which produce the physical vision from the cosmic realm of reality. Pay attention! Your vision will never fail you and it can always be called upon in a heartbeat if and when you require additional guidance during challenging times.

The purpose of goals is to obtain that which is formless (Original Source Agreement Vision) and align it with a physical plan to manifest it into form-based reality. Once you observe the vision, it is absolutely mandatory that you write it down to anchor it into your subconscious mind. By doing so, you establish a plan that the mind can then understand from its limited intelligence capacity. Each conscious action you take will move you forward one small step at a time toward your ultimate vision. And, your subconscious mind will align with what you write down. Before you know it, your vision will manifest into form-based reality.

I recommend always carrying with you a small pocket-sized notebook (for quick access) to transcribe the visions that come to you. This can even be placed at your bedside, so that you can record the messages received while your Spirit travels home while the body is resting during physical sleep cycles. During these physical sleep cycles is when some of the most inspiring messages will be received. Therefore, it is imperative that you write them down as soon as you receive them. Your mind will tell you that you will remember them and that it's okay to wait until later to transcribe them; this is the ego stepping into your spiritual awareness, attempting to hold you back from your vision. I implore you not to be tricked by this inaction (mis-step) for it is simply a test to see if you are In-Spirit or wavering on the edge of inaction, better known as procrastination.

In truth, because the mind typically lives in duality, it is necessary to understand that for every action which moves you forward, there will always be an opposite action (within the mind) that will attempt to move you in the opposite direction. This is true even during goal setting opportunities. For every goal you write down, there will be a negative force attempting to hold you back which is nothing more than some limited reason or story that tells you to stop taking action. This is why most people procrastinate. They literally make it a goal when their visions come to light to not take action and, then, they wonder why their life is filled with what they do not want. They think about why their goals can't be achieved more than they focus on the action necessary to manifest their vision into form-based reality. This in turn brings their energy vibration level down to the reality of physical inaction.

To offset this inaction, deep within your body and at the level of spiritual understanding, there is a spiritual goal-seeking and goal-achieving system that always has the power to dissolve any negativity that may arise from limited thinking. This spiritual system is the Kundalini Energy System. It alerts you when you are out of alignment with your true purpose for being here or your vision for life. If you are not taking action, it will alert you by providing some form of blockage or dis-ease within the flow of energy circulating in the body. You will physically feel the blockage. And then, you will have the opportunity to sit in silence to receive the guidance necessary to remove the blockage. The choice is yours alone to either stay blocked or clear it. Pay close attention to your decisions at these times.

When you finally realize with certainty that inner guidance is a *spiritual constant* which is always providing you with feedback, you will begin to listen to these subtle messages when they are transmitted. However, you must be at the level of non-thought to hear the Divine guidance with Conscious Clarity so that you can anchor it into your subconscious mind. It may not seem possible for you right now, but you have the power to bring non-thought Conscious Clarity to your Higher Self in an instant. I assure you; *you have the authentic power to change limited beliefs at any moment* and can experience non-thought Conscious Clarity at any moment if you choose to do so.

Once you master eliminating unnecessary thoughts from your consciousness, you will understand what it means to live from a state of meditative peace and enlightenment. At this level of understanding, each step you take will feel as if you are gliding through life or walking on a cushion of light energy. This level of understanding allows you to fulfill your every desire in life and will let you know quickly if you are not in harmony with your true purpose.

If you choose inaction once you have observed visions coming to light, you will continue to ride someone else's Train of Life™. You will be pulled along unconsciously through life and will give up your own authentic power which would otherwise lead to abundance. Therefore, by settings realistic goals, you will experience a Purpose Driven Life and will feel your Kundalini Energy flowing through you unburdened by fear.

Each small step forward will take you to your vision in life and will provide you with opportunities which only you can choose to take action upon when Divine guidance is provided.

What's holding you back from moving forward right now in this moment?

Step 5 – *Understand Why You Procrastinate*

Procrastination is a debilitating sickness of the mind and is driven by the ego's fears of you escaping into a life filled with abundance. The ego wants you to stay locked in self-limiting beliefs, worries and fear. Conversely, your true Highest Self visualizes your Original Source Agreement Plan of action as an unlimited, multifaceted dance filled with Love. Again, as always, the choice is yours to either live your life as a prisoner of the ego or you can defy self-limiting beliefs, by propelling yourself forward in life through realizing your true unlimited potential. Yes, you can fly inspired and defy the gravity of self-limiting beliefs and soar through space as if you have rockets on your feet. You have the potential to overcome all challenges in current life situations by simply opening your mind to the unlimited possibilities of a Spirit Driven Life.

The best way to overcome the restrictions of the current limited mind/ego is to dive in head first into understanding why you procrastinate. Just be totally honest with yourself and you will begin to see a pattern emerging that has been holding you back all your life right up until this very moment. You have been held back by the greatest fear of all - the fear of self-limiting beliefs. And, until you make a choice to break free from this prison, you will continue to live a life of limitation based upon what the delusion of self-imposed fear brings to your life.

Now is the time to soar and allow your Universal truth to be told to the world. Now is the time to stop your self-limited beliefs from holding your back. Now is the time to align your life with the abundance it has been pre-programmed for based upon the visions available to you in your Original Source Agreement. Now is the time to bring your ego into harmony with you Higher Self and to realign yourself with your Original Source Agreement Divine Plan. Now is the time to take charge of a life filled with all that is "really important" in order to achieve your Highest Self vision and goals.

All that has manifested in your life up to this point has been in preparation for you to be launched into the universal power of Oneness. You have the ability to see beyond what the ego will ever allow you to see. You are a Spiritual Being having a human experience and it is time for you to fulfill your destiny and fly!

You are at a junction on *The Train of Life*™ where you have the opportunity to fully merge the personality with the Soul. Up until this point, I have only referenced the Soul Merge process as a possibility for the mind to contemplate as a possibility. From this point forward, you must always keep your life on track, whereas, you bring to the station all that is available to you by releasing the ego of its burdens. Once you release the ego completely, you will move into your greatness which can only be found in the spiritual awareness of Divine guidance.

Now is the time to realign the rest of your form-based illusion of life with a set of goals that will be laid out for you in detail during periods of living in a meditative state of being. Ask your personality this one very important question "What would I do if I knew I could not fail?" The answer to that question is the catalyst for setting your goals in place. Write down your answer and then post it someplace so that it can be seen daily. Then sit in silence and interact with the Divine guidance that comes which is the greatest vision for your life and in harmony with your Original Source Agreement.

Your new plan for achieving the greatest vision for yourself will not fail you. You are pre-programmed and it can be easily compiled by formatting your goals using the Categories of Life as a guideline to get you started. This is when it all starts to come together for you. This is the time in your life that you will begin to truly manifest in harmony with the Universal power of Oneness. This is the time when you truly take the next step forward in living a Spiritual Body alignment lifestyle. This is the time for you to welcome the personality into your game plan for achieving your true Highest Self goals. You can and will achieve Conscious Clarity of thought and consistent Soul Merge!

You can start by consciously opening your mind to this understanding; *your mind is only here to align your spiritual vision for life with your life situations.* You will now see the power of bringing your true vision to life situations and understand why you have yet to achieve everything you desire. The authentic power of the Higher Self will guide you along your new journey. Fear can be left at the train station and you can now bring about all abundance in your life that has been put on the back burner until now.

Remember, all doubt is only in the mind and it is a fear-based reality. That self-limited belief is an illusion of fear which is rooted in procrastination. Release those fears and allow yourself to be what you truly are - a magnificent Spiritual Being using a physical body to bring your vision to light.

There are two of my favorite quotes that come to mind which sum this up nicely:

"You must be the change you want to see in the world." – Mahatma Gandhi

"Our deepest fear is not that we are inadequate. Our deepest fear is that we are powerful beyond measure. It is our Light, not our Darkness, that most frightens us."– Marianne Williamson

If you are ready to move out of your ego-based shell and step into the light of your life's greatest achievements, take an oath to bring your Original Source Agreement to life. Pull out a piece of paper and actually write this down, *"I will no longer allow the ego's demand for control. I will step into my greatness and bring my vision to light by writing down my vision for all categories of my life situation."* Now, sign it and place it someplace where you can see it every day until you change. By doing this, you will anchor the mind into the unlimited potential you are about to commit to on paper in the form of realistic goals!

<u>Step 6</u> – *Document Your Desires and Vision for an Abundant Life*

When you pay attention to the limitless possibilities that are brought to you during the silence of meditation, you are actually listening to the harmony of the Universe. This is where all creative juices flow and are always in alignment with your Original Source Agreement. The visions you manifest are subtle flashes of your agreement coming into your awareness and are your guidance to follow if you truly want an abundant life.

Always remember, you are in this world, but you are not of this world. You are far greater than you mind will ever comprehend and you are part of the Source of all creativity. Knowing that you are a Spiritual Being having a human experience removes the limitations of the mind. When you actively focus on that which comes to you during meditation life becomes easy and relaxed. There is a deep Knowing that whatever you perceive and visualize during periods of silence can be brought into form-based reality.

Let's get started now by making a list of all of your desires for each category of your life situation. Simply write down every possible desire you would like to bring into your life based upon the eight categories of life situation as detailed in Illustration D. This includes your wildest dreams no matter how farfetched they may seem to you at this moment. Whether you want a new car, new career, new relationship or whatever the mind can perceive as something you desire, write it all down. Let the thoughts come randomly throughout the day, simply keep a record of what comes to mind. In fact, keep these lists in each category going for a few days to ensure you have documented ever possible desire that comes to mind. Let yourself be free of limitation, just write down all that you wish to achieve in your lifetime. This is the beginning step to manifesting that which you are truly here to accomplish on this leg of your journey. This is the beginning of your true "blueprint" for achieving your life's purpose.

You may find yourself observing what other people have, whether it is a beautiful home, a relationship that appears perfect or a career that allows them to have all the material things they could ever want. Write down everything that comes to mind and don't be afraid to let your mind drift off into your wildest fantasies. There are simply no restrictions to what you desire; this is just the substance of what is important to you. This will be the foundation for what you actually achieve in your lifetime, so don't hold yourself back from all that you desire.

Your current physical age will have an influence on your desires. You may have already achieved some of what you thought was truly important to you. Now is the time to step up to the next level of awareness to achieve a fulfilled life. As you contemplate what is most important to you, you may find yourself settling for less than what you really desire. This is not the time to settle, this is the time to finally put down on paper that which you truly desire. You may currently be stuck in a career that is not fulfilling of your true abundance path.

This is the time to write down your true career intention. Focus on that which you feel is best for you, not what you already achieved or what you have settled for in the past. This is the opportunity for you to bring your desires and vision to the forefront of awareness.

Each of us has a vision that we never brought to our conscious awareness, whether we thought it was out of our reach or we told ourselves that we did not deserve having it doesn't matter anymore. You must now be honest with yourself, allowing your desires to formulate in your mind. If you are driving a Chevy, but always wanted to drive a Cadillac, now is the time to write it down as a desire. Remember, you are the creator of your own destiny, so no matter what limits you have placed upon yourself in the past has no relevance to this exercise. You must learn to get out of the box, stop settling and start paying attention to all the desires that come to mind. If these desires are a byproduct of what you visualize during meditation, pay special or close attention to them.

This type of exercise is nothing new. The first time I conducted this exercise was at the age of 20 when I was first discharged from the Marine Corps after serving two tours of duty in Vietnam. I believed I was invincible and could accomplish anything my mind desired. I had hundreds of desires on my lists. Each time I thought I had every desire written down, more would formulate a few moments later. I found myself paying close attention to everything I observed throughout the day and added new items to my list of desires as they came to my attention. I never discussed this with anyone as it was my understanding that it was just the beginning of my journey. I set up various plans to achieve all my desires and modified them along the way as necessary. If something stood in my way to block achieving my desires, I found a way to work around it. I knew great things were in my future and I was determined to do everything humanly possible to achieve my goals and I did so with perseverance.

I found myself slowly but surely revealing my desires to others that were close to me. I was searching for feedback and was ready to bring others along with me on my journey. What I learned was that many of my family members and closest friends thought I was a dreamer. I found that the more desires I revealed to others the more they thought I was expecting too much out of life. At first, this bothered me and then I realized because others were limiting themselves to less than what they really desired I was not about to follow in their footsteps. I become more closed to what others thought and continued on my journey based upon my perception of what was important to me. I was determined to create my own destiny and I did so.

I achieved most of what I wanted in life at an early age. I was content with the reality that I had accomplished so much in the material world. I was competing with others that had the same desires and I was winning. I was proud of my achievements and was envied by many of the people that competed with me. I had a substantial house with acreage on the lake, drove new cars, had multiple boats, took vacations and had plenty of friends that we aligned with my desires. All of this was possible because I made it my Life Plan to achieve all the goals I had set out for myself. I could pretty much right my own ticket for all the best things in life in accordance with the goals I set for myself.

By setting "written goals" in harmony with your desires, you too can achieve the same results and assist many of the people you care for financially along the way. You can have every material thing you could ever want in life and can accomplish whatever your mind desires!

Until you take the time to write down all of your desires and visions you will not be ready for Step 7 in Staying on Track. You will miss the whole point of this exercise and you will regret not following through with this simple exercise. This exercise will bring your True Life Purpose or vision to light in the next step.

Now is the time to document your list of desires and visions so that you will be ready for the next step in this process. This exercise is absolutely essential if you are to discover your true purpose in life. If you are someone that tends to procrastinate when it comes to these types of exercises, "CHANGE NOW" or you will continue to be lead through life by others that think they know what is best for you.

Before you move on to Step 7, spend at least one week (7 full days) writing down all your desires and visions that come to you. To make it easier, simply use Illustration D as a guideline. Don't even think about moving on to the next step until you have generated a list based upon your wildest desires and dreams – this is extremely important!

Step 7 – *Learn to Distinguish Between Desires and Purpose of Life*

Welcome back! It should be seven days since your last time reading. Have you generated your full list of desires and dreams? I know some of you overachievers have not because you wanted to keep the reading momentum going - if this is you, STOP RIGHT NOW and go back to Step 6 to complete the exercise!

Each of us has an instinctive deep spiritual understanding of what we are actually here to do. This is your spiritual vision or purpose for life and it is always in alignment with your Original Source Agreement. When you listen to the guidance that comes to you during periods of stillness or meditation, your creative juices flow and you will be amazed by what you feel and how much clarity you experience. However, the mind has a tendency to cloud this spiritual reality with the desires of the mind which can confuse your understanding of your true purpose. It is important for you to discover the difference so that you can then re-focus your energy on that which is your true purpose in life.

During my explanation in the last section pertaining to what I had achieved in my earlier years of this life situation, there was one aspect of my life that I intentionally left out which I had not achieved. I was not truly happy and, worst, I was seldom joyful! I discovered I was temporarily happy when I achieved some form-based thing, but it was not everlasting. I was happy because I had some "thing" new to focus on; however, the enjoyment of playing with my new toy was clouding my True Life Purpose for being here. My heart was closed spiritually and my actual spiritual energy vibration was at an all-time low. I was so busy doing what I had planned on accomplishing based upon my desires that I was missing out on discovering my true purpose for being here.

I discovered the destiny I had written was all based upon what my mind thought was important to me or my Physical Body. I discovered my endless search for true Love and connection with my Higher Self awareness was put on the back burner while I set out to achieve all the form-based desires of my mind. I allowed my ego to take control of my life situations and I was actually on a run-away train based upon what society perceived as important in life. I was unhappy inside and found out quickly that all the material things in the world cannot replace the burning desire I had hidden deep within my true Higher Self. That burning desire was simply *to Love and be Loved at the level of Highest Self awareness*! Most of my time was spent on achieving form-based results that were pleasing to the mind, but not my Spiritual Self. I knew something was missing and that's when I truly started to become conscious of my true identity as a Spiritual Being.

It's important to understand your ego will always put itself in the forefront of your life situations until you discover the essence of your true Spiritual Being. By allowing the mind to document the desires it has perceived as important to you, which are typically based upon Physical Body alignment, you will automatically discover the areas that are not in alignment with your Higher Self and Original Source Agreement. Outside you may appear content, but inside you will "feel" the disharmony of being in a state of ego-based dominance or Physical Body alignment. This is a perfect time for you to discover this misalignment. Even if you have been on a spiritual path for some time, the ego will play tricks on you and take you back to its lower vibrations of life. Life is truly a dance back and forth from Physical Body alignment to Spiritual Body alignment. Only you make this choice in each moment, no one else does it for you.

Now that you have a better understanding of why it is important for you to document your desires, this may be a good time to simply sit back, take a few deep cleansing breaths and relax before you complete your category lists. Just take five minutes to sit in silence without thinking about whether or not you have discovered anything about yourself before continuing. Enjoy your special five minutes ...

... OKAY, five minutes of peace have passed, now revisit what you wrote and finish writing your lists of desires and dreams and then prepare yourself to discover whether or not they are in alignment with your true purpose for being here.

What you think about most you always get in life. It may not come at the moment you expect it to, but it will always arrive eventually. It may take moments or it may take years for you to discover your true purpose for being here. One thing I will promise you, when you are in alignment with your true purpose and Original Source Agreement, you will feel easy and relaxed. Life will flow through you and you will "feel" the essence of your true Highest Self revealing your destiny as never before. You will "feel" the sense of spiritual guidance that emanates from the higher vibration levels of pure Knowing. You will live each moment as the miracle it truly is and you will escape from the lower level of ego-based domination. You will always feel inner Love and peace while experiencing a truly joyous life.

Until you align yourself with the Spiritual Body in the forefront of everything you do during this life situation you will be lost in the ever-changing desires of the mind.

However, when you live with Spiritual Body alignment in the forefront, your true purpose for being here will be revealed to you from a higher level of understanding. From this level, you will learn to distinguish between desires and purpose of life. And, you will be ready to set realistic goals that are in harmony with the gifts you were given to use while you are on your journey in this incarnation.

In the next section, you will discover how to weed out the desires of the mind that do not serve the Spirit. When we "enlist the mind to serve the Soul", life becomes a unified dance of pure Love, Peace and Light!

Step 8 – *Align with Spiritual Body to Embrace Joy*

Vibration is the key to all growth. The lessons you discover along the way can be experienced the hard way through mind-based desires or the easy way through loving spiritually-based alignment with your true purpose. It's really that simple and you are the only one that can feel whether or not you are in alignment with Spiritual Body energy vibration. The higher you are vibrating, the easier life will be for you. Therefore, doesn't it seem obvious that you would like to vibrate at the highest frequency possible? Can you believe it's as simple as living from a state of Love rather than fear? Do you believe you have the spiritual authentic power within you to live each moment in a state of joy where miracles are commonplace?

Now is the time for you to become the illuminated Being that you are by ending the false illusions you have of yourself. You cannot expect the Universe to align with your Highest Self possibilities if you are still living a life based upon Physical Body alignment with ego and its confusing control dogma. You must now break free once and for all of the prison you have allowed yourself to be housed in. All you need do is stay aligned with the Spiritual Body in the forefront of every feeling, thought and action. It's your natural state of Being!

The main purpose of documenting your desires was to discover whether or not you are in alignment with the Physical Body or Spiritual Body. The physical will always be predisposed with mainly material based manifestation which will bring temporary happiness. Conversely, the Spirit will always be predisposed with an everlasting joyful state of being and guidance in harmony with your true purpose for being here. By paying close attention to how your feel or the level of your energy vibration in each moment, you will be able to distinguish from what you desire and what is in alignment with your Original Source Agreement plan or your vision for life.

Spiritual Body alignment allows you to make an accurate assessment of each category of your life and the vision you have for manifesting the spiritually important aspects of your life's purpose. All physical form-based illusion of reality is secondary to spiritual purpose. Yes, you can still have all the material by-products associated with desires, but there's a difference in how you receive them when you put your Spiritual Body first. When you are aligned spiritually, all the material pleasures of life come in abundance as a relaxed resultant of joy rather than a forced demanding resultant of ego-based doing.

When you choose to "enlist the mind to serve the Soul" you become aligned with Soul Merge mentality. When the mind follows what the Spiritual Body (Soul) is providing through deep inner guidance, life becomes easy and relaxed with unlimited possibilities for manifesting that which is in alignment with your Original Source Agreement. When you are aligned in this manner, you become the creator of your true spiritual destiny rather than the false illusionary reality of ego-based material possessions as your driving force.

Now that you understand the difference, it's important for you to revisit your desire and vision lists to determine which path you have chosen for yourself. If your desires are not in some way in harmony with your vision, you have been tricked by ego to believe that your desires have more importance than your spiritual purpose for being here. You must now re-examine your lists with an open heart and feel the energy as it flows through your chakra system. Focus your attention on the intention of being in alignment with your Original Source Agreement and you will easily feel whether or not you have energy blockages within your body. If the energy is blocked, you will feel it at the energy point or chakra where the blockage is present. This will quickly be your guiding light in the face of lower-energy illusions brought about by ego-based mind manipulation.

Although in the beginning, it may require a focused effort on your part to determine your level of energy vibration in each moment, it will be worthwhile for you to learn to "feel" these energies in the long run. This will become natural and easy for you in no time at all. You have the spiritual authentic power within you to determine your alignment at any given moment in time. Do not allow your mind to cloud your vision in the beginning as it will only bring you that which you do not want. Focus only on what you do want in life which is in alignment with the Highest Self guidance that comes during the periods of silence or meditative Conscious Clarity. Your desires will align naturally with your vision as you become more and more adept at Soul Merge.

Learn to BE the vision you have in harmony with God and, then, you will experience a joyful life every moment!

Step 9 – *Write Goals Based Upon Spiritual Body Alignment*

Forget about your past or any regrets you may be carrying with you and put depressing thoughts behind you once and for all. The only thing you need to remember about your past is that it has made you the person you are today. That person is a wonderful Spiritual Being housed within a physical body that is now ready to transform into Divine greatness. It is truly time to position yourself into the next phase of your spiritual growth.

Now that you have had the experience of documenting your desires and assessing whether or not they are in harmony with your purpose for being here, it is time to establish goals to take you to the next phase of your Life Plan. If you have not taken the time to weed out desires that do not serve your Highest Self purpose, now would be the time to do so. Simply review you list one more time and eliminate the desires that are only driven by ego dominance. By doing so, you will find it easier to focus on "blue printing" a set of realistic spiritual goals that are guaranteed to increase your energy vibration.

Go back to the Categories of Life (Illustration D) and determine which one stands out for you that you feel will require the most immediate attention to balance your life. Obviously, the Spiritual Life and Soul Merge categories are the most important areas that everyone should focus on first. Once you are living your daily life with the Spiritual Body in the forefront of everything you do, it will serve you best if you concentrate on the Soul Merge area to ensure you have "enlisted the mind to serve the Soul". Then, move on to the next category which you feel needs your immediate attention.

Once you begin evaluating your current life situation pertaining to each category, it will be very obvious to you which ones are out of harmony with your True Life Purpose. If you are still unclear of your true purpose, do not allow your mind to influence your assessment. Simply sit in silence and feel the energy as it flows through your body as your review each category. The one that stands out as blocking your energy the most is the one that you need to focus on now. Then rank the categories with a number between 1-10 (one meaning needs the most attention) and focus on realistic spiritual goals that will increase the energy vibration of each category.

Once you have conducted a thorough assessment of each category and have written down realistic spiritual goals for each one, it will be necessary for you to revisit your goals on a daily basis to ensure you have not set yourself up for failure. You ego will continue to pop in from time to time in an attempt to sabotage your spiritual Conscious Clarity. One of its favorite manipulations is writing goals that are unrealistic, meaning your egoist mind influenced your goal writing process. This is typical of how the ego works until you have fully integrated the Spiritual Body alignment system into your daily life.

Example:

If one of your goals is to create Financial Freedom in one month and you currently have six credit cards at their maximum charge limit, this is an unrealistic goal. First, you must develop a strategy to eliminate the debt one credit card at a time. You can set a goal to pay down the highest interest rate card first by paying say $100.00 more than the minimum payment each month, while simply paying minimums on the rest. Of course, if your current career is not paying you enough to follow this strategy, then you may need to change careers. Therefore, the category Career may require immediate attention rather than Financial Freedom, because the new career will realistically assist you in obtaining financial freedom.

In truth, if you are not a good shepherd with your current money the Universe will hold back your abundance until you create a mindset that allows you to better control your desires pertaining to spending money you do not have. Money is nothing more than "green energy" and, if you are not yet vibrating at the level of Financial Freedom, you must first increase your personal energy to bring the higher energy of Financial Freedom to you.

Obliviously, the areas that are farthest out of harmony with abundance will require more immediate attention. You will notice quickly that the areas which require the most attention are the ones that ego had controlled the most in the past. This is why it is so very important for you to realign your Spiritual Body in the forefront of your daily life situations. Your old ego has not served you well. It is time to change and bring ego or the false personality into alignment with the Spiritual Body alignment and your *True Personality*.

If you are having difficulty in bring Spiritual Body alignment to the forefront of your daily life situations, it could be possible that you have relationships that are out of harmony with your Highest Self purpose for being here. It could possibly be that you are being negatively influenced by the energy of the relationships you currently embrace. If you truly intend to experience spiritual growth, you must immediately place yourself in life situations that are vibrating at a higher energy frequencies.

Example:

If you currently associate mostly with people that are vibrating a very low level and do not intend to join with you in spiritual growth, it may be time to say goodbye to those relationships and develop new ones that are more in alignment with your purpose for being here. It's a choice to move forward in life and it's also a choice to stay stagnant and in alignment with others that do not want to consciously change. (Review Illustration E, paying close attention to "Life Fuel Source" as this will help you to understand how others can influence your growth.)

Once you begin engaging with others that have the same intention to focus their attention on spiritual growth or raising their energy vibration, you will begin to transform to a higher level of balance in every other category of your life situation. You will start to notice how each category appears to perpetuate the others to bring true abundance to your life. You may even find yourself in a position to be offered a bright new career path more in harmony with your spiritual goals just because your developed new relationships with like-minded individuals.

The Universe or Source Energy is always available to assist you with developing your true purpose for being here. When you begin to demonstrate that you are spiritually in alignment with your True Purpose, your life will become more easy and relaxed along the way. Abundance will come naturally and you will feel more connected with God than ever before because you will be vibrating at a frequency where you actually hear the guidance being offered to you.

Step 10 – *Focus on Spiritual Transformative Education*

In the third dimension secular reality, the main focus is on egoist-self or personality and what can I (Physical Body) do to increase my worth for myself first as a physical being living from a Physical Body alignment perspective. Values are formulated based upon the experience of others in this limited society and the academic secular education system is typically in the forefront of understanding based upon third dimension achievements, rather than fourth dimension spiritual guidance and Knowing at a higher level of understanding or vibration. Every*thing* is based upon what can be achieved from the limited perspective of form-based thinking for the benefit of the Physical Body illusion and a secular academic education limited perspective.

The vast majority of the mass consciousness of the world is still living life in survival mode which is based upon the self-imposed limitations of third dimension perspective thinking. Success is measured and judged by others, typically based on society's limited third dimension thinking. Most people are brought up in an academic secular education environment leading to limited success. They go to secular academic school, get a degree and then work (labor) for someone else. Most of these people work for large "old world" corporations that are based upon maximizing profits for the benefit of the corporation, its leaders and lastly the share holders. This scenario limits the typical individual from achieving their spiritual greatness and only focuses upon achieving a limited amount of success. This limited success is measured by how much money they make and what their status or ranking level is within the corporation based upon pay-grade. This scenario locks them into third dimensional thinking because they "think" they are doing very well. However, bonuses are given only to the leaders in the corporation that have learned to achieve success over their perceived competition within the corporation, rather than spreading the wealth to the actual team members that accomplished the goals of the corporation. Even with corporations that provide profit sharing to its employees, it is only a small percentage in comparison to the amount the leaders of the corporation receive. The executive staff typically receives large salaries, bonuses and stock options.

Following this form of secular education system limits, the abundance one can personally achieve as a non-executive is limited to personal judgments of others. The major goal is usually outdoing the competition for the benefit of oneself, the corporation, stock holders and its executive leaders. This third dimension thinking perspective brings about a hierarchy of success from a have or have not point of view. There are laborers that provide all the technical work processes and, then, there are the leaders or executives within the corporation that provide the guidance as if they are superior to instead of equal to the rest of the staff. And, regard to equality is further measured or judged based upon how many diplomas, certificates of certification and rewards for accomplishment one has achieved from the third dimension secular education system perspective. In other words, it's all based upon the judgment of those perceived as being superior rather than equal.

In effect, most of the population is brainwashed into believing this limited secular education system is superior to any spiritual level of understanding for their careers to move forward. The corporations ensure that they control every aspect of staff members' growth that can be achieved throughout their career, usually based upon keeping those close to them that agree with their philosophies for business. Then, to add to this control, these corporations lobby the government to ensure laws are written to enhance their chances of bringing about this limited perspective illusion. Therefore, most people in the corporation that plan to emerge to the executive level align themselves with leaders above their pay grade and do whatever they can to follow those leaders up the ladder of perceived success.

The good news is that this "old school" mentality of third dimension illusion is now changing due to the new age fourth dimension level of understanding. We are witnessing a rise in overall mass consciousness energy vibration which is questioning the "old school" standards. We now live in a fourth dimension world where the times are changing for the benefit of all of humanity rather than the select few that have been considered privileged. Although on the surface this shift is still in its infant level of growth, there are more and more spiritual organizations being formed each day that are teaching the new fourth dimension spiritual transformative realities to the general population of the world. We still have a long way to go to transform the illusion that has been in place for so long but rest assured we are now seeing quantum leaps pertaining to this spiritual direction.

When we clearly understand and embrace the fact that we are Spiritual Beings having a human experience, it becomes possible to see beyond the smokescreen of the egoist lifestyle of someone perceiving that they are superior. By bringing the Spiritual Body into the forefront of your daily life situations you will become part of the new age evolution which is on the path to changing how the world thinks about the future. The evolution of the world depends on us moving forward into this new lifestyle where we actively begin to use our gifts for the betterment of all of humanity. This shift is necessary if we are to accomplish our true purpose for being here.

By working in harmony with the Universal Law of Oneness, we shift our perspective to consciously bring awareness to our thoughts and actions, always based upon what is best for everyone. We are destined to be of service to all by using our gifts to fulfill our purpose for being here at the spiritual level. Therefore, living from a Spiritual Body perspective, it is important to seek out new relationships that are in alignment with shifting the old paradigm of "what's in it for me" to "how can I serve to bring about change and enlightenment to the mass consciousness of all humanity."

The fourth dimension or spiritual realm is now coming to light as never before. You now have the opportunity to move forward into your true purpose and actually utilize your gifts for everyone's benefit. With this alignment, abundance comes to you naturally rather than by always doing more and more to achieve the limited illusion of self-centered success.

If you are ready to make this shift, it is time for you to let go of those that are holding you back. By releasing those that are stuck in third dimensional intelligence, you will find yourself in a position that brings just the right new relationships to you (at exactly the right moment) to assist. This synchronistic flow of energy will continue to grow around you and you will be amazed at how much happier your outside world becomes.

With Spiritual Body alignment in the forefront of your daily life, it's easy to focus on your desires and visions that are in harmony with others feeling the same attraction to change. Then you will be able to set goals that are based upon using your gifts to their fullest potential from a spiritual perspective. When you position spiritual awareness and spiritual growth in the forefront of your connections with others, you manifest that which is in alignment with your Original Source Agreement.

You should always remember change is not something the typical third dimension thinking person is ready to endorse. So understand or accept that on the surface, you will not be taken seriously by those fearful of change. However, once you align yourself with others with the same level of understanding, the path will become very clear for you and most of those that have doubted you will fall along the wayside. They will both join you and increase their energy vibration to move forward or they will be left behind in the third dimension as you continue to grow spiritually. The shift has been going on for a number of years, but only now are we seeing the magnitude of its momentum building to a level that it is being taken seriously.

Take a few moments now to review *The Train of Life™* analogy illustrations to see if they are becoming clearer to you, especially Illustration A which clearly demonstrates the significance of releasing the boxcars (people) that are attached to you that want you to stay connected at the lower levels of egoistic understanding. The more people you continue to drag along on your Train of Life™ that are influenced by low levels of vibration desire only, the more it will encumber your journey. The train is coming into the station and it is time for you to step up your momentum and leave beyond that old third dimension reality of control or you will be one of the many left behind. Immerse yourself in Spiritual Transformative Education and you will quickly experience joy in your life every day.

In the next step, you will begin to examine one of the most important aspects you can experience everyday from a loving perspective!

Step 11 – *Cultivate Spiritual Partnerships*

Cultivating Spiritual Partnerships is the most important catalyst for moving forward in spiritual development. Listen to the guidance that comes during periods of silence and then follow your instincts as spiritually aligned people begin to show up daily to assist you with your spiritual growth. When you are aware of the unlimited possibilities available to you from forming Spiritual Partnerships from a Spiritual Body alignment perspective, just the right people will show up when you need them. When focused on developing relationships with those around you with spirituality in the forefront of their daily existence you will find the lower vibration relationships will begin to slip away naturally. You will develop new Spiritual Partnerships just by being at the same energy vibration or in harmony with those you seek. It all becomes very synergistic the more you believe or have faith that lifelong Spiritual Partnerships are not only possible by the natural flow of your enhanced lifestyle.

As you continue to increase your energy vibration, you will be amazed at how many past dreams become a reality for you. You will certainly have many opportunities to share your spiritual beliefs with others around you and they will then make a decision to either move forward with you by living life from a fourth dimension reality or they will simply be left behind in old school, limited, third dimension reality. You are not here to convince anyone that spiritual awareness is the best path for them. Your purpose is simply to present your plan for your future and how you intend to live your daily life. The choice of whether or not they want to be part of your intention is always up to them. Your increase in energy vibration will be very difficult for some people to accept, mainly because they are so locked into living from ego or third dimension, fear-based dogma.

It takes only a moment to see the light or benefits of living life from a Spiritual Body alignment perspective, but most of humanity is still so locked into fear they simply do not allow themselves to step into the light. Each of us has the choice to live freely in Love awareness or continue to stay prisoner to the ego's fear-based demands.

It's important for you to realize that not everyone is ready to move forward into fourth dimension Spiritual Body alignment. This can be a real challenge when it comes to your current intimate relationship with your spouse or partner. If one person is increasing their energy vibration and moving forward while the other is not, it creates even more fear in the mind of the person vibrating at a lower level. It's imperative that you discuss this in detail with your spouse or partner so that the two of you can choose a path that works best for both of you.

In some intimate relationships which were born out of ego-based levels of understanding, a shift into spiritual awareness can mean the end of the intimate relationship. This does not mean you do not allow the other person the opportunity to grow spiritually with you. However, it also does not mean that you should stay in a relationship indefinitely that is not serving both of you to the ultimate spiritual growth possibilities of the relationship. At times, it is best for the relationship to shift from an intimate relationship to a friendship for the benefit of both people. This can be a very difficult choice if there is a large gap between the energy vibrations of the two. There are no guarantees that it will be a congenial shift, especially if one person feels victimized based upon a fear-based limited reality.

Many times we hear statements by couples such as, "we have grown apart" and are splitting up. Depending on the spiritual maturity of the relationship, this could mean different things. In one scenario where ego and third dimensional reality is in play, it could mean one person no longer believes in the relationship from a materialistic view point. They want different things or live life from a fear-based perspective while the other person lives by faith.

However, from a spiritual viewpoint, it could simply mean they are vibrating at different frequencies and are no longer in harmony with one another spiritually and need to move on for additional spiritual growth to manifest. It can actually simply depend on how the relationship started at the beginning. In truth, if two people are experiencing life with opposite Four Body System alignment, it can be very challenging for both from each other's different point of view. If this is the case, the best possible scenario is to release the intimate relationship and allow each person to continue to grow, but separately from one another.

The truth is there are no limitations to the number of spiritual relationships you will have in your cosmic spiritual lifetime. You may return to different bodies many times and during these bodily life situations you may have multiple intimate spiritual relationships, as well as, many friendship spiritual relationships. There are no hard set Universal rules of physical bodily relationship in each incarnation you experience. If you are aligned with Spiritual Body awareness in the forefront of your life situation, you will quickly realize that each spiritual relationship will only last as long as each person is alignment with the other person's spiritual growth. If the relationship does not continue to grow equally, one person will request a shift to bring about the next possible spiritual growth relationship; whether it is intimate or friendship is irrelevant.

There is one exception: Right now, you are not aware that you only have one true Spiritual Partner or Cosmic Soulmate, but you will discover this in the Monadic level of the *Conscious Clarity Energy Process*™. This level teaches cosmic planetary alignment and how we are each destined to bring our energy level up to that of Source Energy (God) awareness by aligning with our Cosmic Soulmate. Each of us has a Cosmic Spiritual Partner that is our mirror and destined to be with us throughout our cosmic (never-ending) lifetime. This Spirit will arrive at the exact moment you are ready to experience the highest levels of spiritual awareness. This may take many incarnations in which you may spend multiple human lifetimes together or apart preparing for the ultimate awareness that you are Cosmic Soulmates. This Spirit will be in harmony with you at every level of understanding and you will be the same for them. This is where the physical need for separation no longer exists as the two of you will reunite at the level of Oneness as you have always meant to be.

Until you reunite with your Cosmic Soulmate, listen to your current intimate partner to understand what they believe about Spiritual Body alignment; be aware of their energy vibration and their level of spiritual understanding. Discuss your beliefs with them and ask them to be honest with you pertaining to their beliefs. Are they in alignment with your purpose for being here or are they stuck in third dimension reality? Do they have the same balanced mindset about merging the Soul with the mind and do they support your journey with regard to spiritual development? Spiritual development discussions should be part of your daily communication with your current partner; if not, then a shift in awareness needs consideration. Holding back is not healthy for either person's Well Being.

However, it is possible that you are now living your current life situation with your true Cosmic Soulmate and do not know it, only because you both need to increase your energy vibration to bring awareness to this possibility. If your household and outside relationships are filled with the power of authentic Love, Peace and Light, you are heading in the right direction. However, if your household and outside relationships are centered in fear-based Physical Body misalignment, it is surely time for a change so that you can enhance your spiritual growth.

Listen to the guidance you are receiving from Source Energy and be aware of those that are being sent to you. You will have many spiritual relationships in your cosmic lifetime, but you will only have one spiritual partnership with someone that is ready to be there for you every step of the journey. When they appear is determined by your level of spiritual understanding and connection with Source Energy (God).

Step 12 – *Know Source Energy (God) Is Always With You*

Desperate people do dysfunctional things which are always triggered by fear-based stories they tell themselves and lack of faith in Source Energy (God). They believe their life situation is hopeless, so instead of going deeper within to find a solution to whatever challenge they are experiencing, they go outside themselves to find a solution. They typically perceive themselves are being a victim of whatever life lesson is being presented to them in the moment.

No matter how challenging a life situation may seem, God is always available to provide guidance, but will not interfere with our free will choices in life. We must take "proper action" if we are to grow into our true greatness. We must understand that God is not here to step in and change what we have decided to experience based upon our free will choices. What many people do in times of perceived crisis is create a Physical Body alignment story that is anchored in past and future reality rather than the present moment reality and Spiritual Body alignment. God watches this and allows us to experience the moment in a way that is meant for us to learn and spiritually grow from the experience. And, until we learn to keep our Spiritual Body alignment in the forefront of our daily life situations, we will continue to have Physical Body alignment results.

Whether we choose to step into the greatness of our Original Source Agreement or not is totally our own decision, not God's. God is always providing guidance in the background, but we must be living in a state of awareness to hear the guidance being provided. If we sit in silence, the guidance will be heard which really means quieting the mind and eliminating the self-imposed negativity of the stories that we manifest out of a feeling of hopelessness or separation from God. God always sends us messages throughout the day, but they may come in a form that we do not recognize, especially if we are living a fear-based existence. When challenges come, there is always an opportunity that comes along with the challenge to change our perception so that we can step up our energy vibration to Spiritual Body alignment.

God will never stand in the way of our choices and will always provide lessons that allow us to clearly experience the results of the choices we have already made. Therefore, if we keep making the same choices, we will naturally continue to experience the same results time and time again. It's a realistic Divine cycle, God allows, then sends a lesson and, then, we rinse and repeat the same level of energy vibration choice, typically expecting a difference result if we are living Physical Body alignment reality. The truth is, no matter how much we "do" to change our life situations, until we align ourselves with the Spiritual Body in the forefront of our daily experiences, we will continue to see low energy vibration results. Until we surrender spiritually to what is and live in acceptance of what we are experiencing, we will not move forward or increase our energy vibration.

The easier path would be to live with the belief that God is always within us to provide lessons which bring us in alignment with our Original Source Agreement. If you are experiencing a challenge in your life situation, simply shift your belief from victim to the spiritual awareness that you are having a human experience which is meant to provide a lesson. Once you begin to view each occurrence in your life situation as an opportunity for spiritual growth or increasing your energy vibration, you will begin to understand that a shift in your perception will enhance the possibility of achieving that which you had already planned out for yourself before arriving here in this current life situation. And never forget, we are all here to assist one another with our spiritual growth, therefore, something that you are experiencing may be for the benefit of someone else, too. We never experience anything that we did not agree to in our Original Source Agreement. This *truth* is far beyond the understanding of most ego-driven personalities.

When difficult challenges arise, the mind may believe that God has forsaken you. However, it is during these times of difficulty or challenge that you are being called upon to take action of a positive nature to bring about change and realignment with your spiritual greatness. Whenever there is pain associated with an experience in life, it is typically anchored into the subconscious mind. This is embedded to allow you to feel the emotion of the experience so that if a similar challenge presents itself in the future you will be prepared. Yes, you will be triggered to the past pain and then you will have an opportunity to change your outcome and heal. This is spiritual growth in its infinite state of awareness. You will always be provided opportunities to learn from the lesson provided and then make a different choice, rather than repeating the same action over again. If you continue to experience that which you do not want over and over again, there is always a reason beyond your current level of understanding or energy vibration.

God is within you and surrounding you at all times, ready to provide the life you truly deserve. However, you must surrender to faith in order to hear the Highest Self guidance that comes to assist you in making better choices so that your life situation can improve. Learn to sit in silence and you will be amazed at how your life situations increase in energy vibration. And always remember, what you resist, will always persist.

Chapter 7 Suggestions – 12 Simple Steps for Staying on Track

If you have truly surrendered to the *fact* that you are the author of you own story, you will find yourself way ahead of the majority of the rest of the population that is looking for answers outside themselves. It's this acceptance or ownership of the responsibility of your own destiny that will guide you into the direction of your highest purpose in life. When you are in balance with your pre-planned life (Original Source Agreement), your feelings about how you arrived in the current moment will feel in harmony with the Universe and an inner peaceful state of being will be your natural experience every day. However, when you are out of alignment, you will feel a lower-energy vibration and negative emotions will control you. Then, you will experience a disharmony where chakras begin to block in some manner and your inner peace will diminish. By paying close attention to these feelings and how the energy is flowing through your body, you will know when change is necessary to get back on track.

Staying on Track once you realize who you really are is really quite easy if you keep the Spirit Body alignment in place. By consciously moving your life forward with the certainty that you can succeed in any endeavor you are committed to, you will see beyond the ego's need to control you.

Consider the 12 Simple Steps for Staying on Track a recommendation to assist you in rediscovering your Original Source Agreement; only you can find the way, through inner Self awareness and Conscious Clarity of the present moment.

- Step 1 – Spiritual Being Awareness

- Step 2 – Original Source Agreement Awareness

- Step 3 – Daily Connection With Source Energy

- Step 4 – Become An Active Observer

- Step 5 – Understand Why You Procrastinate

- Step 6 – Document Your Desires and Vision for an Abundant Life

- Step 7 – Learn to Distinguish Between Desires and Purpose of Life

- Step 8 – Align with Spiritual Body to Embrace Joy

- Step 9 – Write Goals Based Upon Spiritual Body Alignment

- Step 10 – Focus on Spiritual Transformative Education

- Step 11 – Cultivate Spiritual Partnerships

- Step 12 – Know Source Energy (God) Is Always With You

You have the free will choice to either float through life unconsciously in a never-ending spiral of emotional disconnect (as most people do) or you can take complete charge of your journey by realigning with your Original Source Agreement.

Now that you have learned to merge (blend) the Mental Body (mind) with your Spiritual Body, you have the knowledge available to you to move forward in quantum leaps of Conscious Clarity. You must now focus on your Original Source Agreement as never before, with a burning desire on that which is truly the destiny for your greatest good and the greatest good for all of God's creation.

Chapter 8

Take the Path of Least Resistance

What Will Resistance Do for Me

By now, you should be experiencing glimpses of Spiritual Body alignment in your life, even if you are allowing your mind (ego) to continue to dominate your life. The seeds have been planted for a better way of life and your subconscious mind is questioning the current Physical Body alignment dynamic you have survived in thus far. The only thing holding you back from experiencing a limitless, Divine life where you thrive rather than survive is resistance to change.

Resistance (reluctance) to shift from Physical Body alignment to Spiritual Body alignment is typically based upon the low vibration emotion of fear and the ego's continued control over your life. Living in fear is not in your best interest, it will only keep you imprisoned in an illusion of limitation because what you resist will persist. Now is the time to change and take the path of least resistance so that you can experience the never-ending Joy that comes from living in Spiritual Body alignment.

For many of you, the effort of changing to a new way of looking at life is more challenging than the current pain and limitations you are experiencing with a Physical Body alignment perspective. In reality, holding yourself back from Spiritual Body alignment is a setback in moving your life forward. You block experiencing the limitless possibilities available to you each time you allow the ego to control your life. You don't realize that living life with Spiritual Body alignment in the forefront of your existence is your "natural state of Being". The ego is strong willed and will trick you into false beliefs about your Higher Self and your ability to change your current life situation.

Resistance to change spiritually is guaranteed to keep you locked into a life of lower vibration emotion, pain and setbacks. If you still do not believe this, perhaps you should consider taking an inventory of how well you rank yourself in all the eight categories on *The Train of Life*™. How has the old paradigm of living life through Physical Body alignment served you up until this very moment? Can you identify with a pattern of stagnation due to the limits of the mind? Have you been telling yourself a story based upon half truths about what you deserve in life? If so, maybe it's time to stop this lower energy conversation with yourself and blossom into the light of Higher Self awareness.

There are many reasons people are infected with the resistance-to-change disease, especially when it comes to making a change in core beliefs that have been programmed into the mind (ego) since infancy. When it comes to spiritual

Well Being, if you are still locked into your limited sensory perspective of life or Physical Body alignment, you will not achieve the full potential of what you planned for yourself in your Original Source Agreement. Always keep in mind, the major plan for your life is already available to you to review and can be found easily in the silent moments of awareness through living a life in a meditative state of Being.

Resistance can be overcome in a heartbeat once you discover the subconscious reasons the mind has for holding you back. To live life to its fullest potential you must, "recruit the mind to serve the Soul". Only then, will you be guaranteed to have a Purpose Driven Life, one that is in complete harmony with your Original Source Agreement.

Every day, each of us receive opportunities to listen to the inner guidance that moves through us from Source Energy (God). However, if you are still locked into Physical Body alignment and resistance to change, your state of consciousness misses most of the opportunities or the guidance that is available to you; this lower energy vibration is blind to the Divine wisdom of the higher energy messages being transmitted to you throughout the day. By staying locked in Physical Body alignment, you are making a free will choice to ignore guidance that is found in the higher energy vibrations of Spiritual Body alignment.

The mind (ego) is a powerful, intelligent tool that was created to guide the brain to accomplish worldly or form-based manifestation of things. However, you must always remember, the ego will trick you into staying locked into living a limited spiritually misaligned life that is typically controlled by others or false beliefs about yourself which are based upon a fearful Physical Body alignment mentality.

Until you give up your fascination with Physical Body alignment, you will not be free of the self-imposed prison you willingly locked yourself in which limits you from experiencing your True Life Purpose to its fullest. Resistance to change is guaranteed to provide you with a life of survival rather than one where you thrive through the limitless possibilities of a fully inspired lifestyle.

What Will Non-Resistance Do for Me

The whole balance of the *Conscious Clarity Energy Process*™ is based upon Spiritual Body alignment being brought to you in an easy, natural progression. The understanding that you are a Spiritual Being having a human experience is the catalyst for your spiritual enlightenment and discovering how to always live in the present moment. This allows you to increase your energy vibration slowly and feel the miraculous benefits from living in non-resistance of what is. Therefore, when you live life in the present moment and non-resistance with complete acceptance of what is, you have no need to judge or care whether or not someone judges you. Each day in life's journey becomes a beautiful dance with Source Energy (God) as your partner. And during peaceful meditation with your partner, you are provided guidance for whatever challenge is present. You live each new day with a higher reverence for life than the day before.

"Meditation is not some "thing" you do; it is the experience of Being that which you are." – Terry Swejkoski

When you look at the big picture of your life in this manner, you understand that through non-resistance you will experience your Original Source Agreement to its fullest potential. You will have a feeling of understanding beyond that of mind because you will be experiencing the form-based world from a non-form-based perspective of unlimited opportunity and manifestation. You live your life as the Spiritual Being you are rather than simply "being human" which is based upon a beginning and end. You discover how to use the gifts you were given to fulfill your true purpose for taking on human form in this world and your life becomes miraculous every day.

Unfortunately, most people believe they are simply the human body and live from a Physical Body alignment perspective which is not only self-limiting (beginning and end), but a detriment to personal overall Well Being. This is a low vibration existence and will only take you as far as limited beliefs allow which is based upon experiences of the past and hopes or dreams of the future. With this alignment perspective, the present moment is lost in the delusional belief that the past equals the future; when in fact, "the past *never* equals the future". Yes, we remember the lessons of the past, but only the present moment exists in true reality. Remember each future moment can only be experienced in the present moment. Therefore, if you are living in the past or future, the present moment cannot be experienced to its fullest potential. When you live life this way, your energy vibration becomes locked at its current level or frequency until you stop resisting what is available to you in the present moment.

For a visual representation of the above explanation, take a few moments to review Illustration C, *Energy Transformation*. Just sit with the image of the illustration in your mind's eye for a few moments to anchor in the message embedded in it. Allow the experience to open your perspective to a higher level of vibration and prepare for a new level of understanding. Bring yourself back to the meditative state of being which you are and simply feel the guidance that is coming to you from Source Energy through the higher vibration frequencies. And always remember, you can only hear the guidance coming through if you are in alignment with its frequency. It is extremely important that you understand this Universal fact.

Through the spiritual education thus far, you have been experiencing glimpses of spiritual enlightenment which in truth means you are becoming more aware of who you really are. As your energy vibration increases each day, you will experience the true power of transitioning to Spiritual Body alignment. You will feel the gentle harmonic balance of Kundalini Energy (life-force) flowing through the body and you will experience the balancing aspects being brought to each of the Categories of Life as referenced in Illustration D, *Life Plan Balance*.

When you live life through non-resistance or acceptance of what is, your perception or Conscious Clarity awareness will begin to shift. You will no longer set unrealistic goals for a straight, steep and tiresome path to seeking Spiritual Enlightenment. You will traverse a slow easy and relaxed steady pace as if traveling up a mountain using a switchback trail rather than attempting to climb straight up. This enhanced steady climb in energy vibration will come to you in a peaceful, easy and relaxed manor. You will feel at home with your true Higher Self identity and you will blossom more each day to the beautiful reverence for life that Source Energy always planned for you. You will learn to appreciate each moment for the miracle it actually is and discover how peaceful life can be no matter what challenges are occurring around you. Feeling this way will become your new norm.

The choice is yours. Will you continue to resist and merely survive or will you accept what is and live a life of non-resistance as the Spiritual Being you truly are?

How Do I Learn to Live Life Without Resistance

The key to living life without resistance to what is becomes very clear once you release the old ego and replace it with the new ego. The new ego or evolved ego serves the Soul or Spiritual Body alignment reality by merging the spirit with the mind (Soul Merge) for the benefit of all. Once you make this shift to the new awareness of what is, your feelings change and you take on the new role of observer rather than victim; being the observer ultimately leads to an easy, relaxed, joyful spiritual existence and a happy physical lifestyle.

Important Note: When speaking of living without resistance, it is important to understand this does not mean to live a passive life of submittal to all that is of the Physical Body. It is all related to the resistance of affirming Spiritual Body alignment existence of your true Highest Self reality. Therefore, it is natural to defend your Physical Body and its surrounding environment if attacked by some other Physical Body force. Taking the "Path of Least Resistance" is spiritually defined here as living life through a Spiritual reality rather than simply a Physical reality of ego dominance. The alignment of the Four Body System is the focus of enlightenment. Always remember, you are an eternal Spiritual Being having a temporary human experience.

This can be very challenging for someone that is deeply rooted in old ego dogma and victimization control tactics. Once we transcend the perceived need to control and manipulate others to get what we want, we discover how much easier it is to live life with an open heart philosophy of acceptance to what is. One of the best ways to demonstrate or bring light to this limitless awareness is the example provided earlier in this writing:

We all consist of a Four Body System and how deeply we are integrated into the various parts of that system determines how we approach our life situation on a daily basis. If you could discover how to simply acknowledge that you do indeed have these multiple aspects of the body without allowing them to control you, your physical lifetime would be a lot happier. Through meditation, you can consciously stay connected with the highest power of this system, the Spiritual Body.

As mentioned throughout this book the actual sequence of the Four Body System is of the utmost importance with respect to our perceived level of happiness. Therefore, it is naturally aligned when in the sequence below.

The natural Four Body System alignment consists of the:

1. Spiritual Body
2. Mental Body
3. Emotional Body
4. Physical Body

Example – Typically Out of Alignment:

The vast majority of humankind lives their life based upon having the Four Body System reversed, where control is perceived at the Physical Body first.

- Physical Body - When the Physical Body is first, it identifies as situations happening to me (identity) or a physical reality.

- Emotional Body - This in turn excites the Emotional Body, whereas, now a feeling is generated due to what is perceived as having been done to my physical identity.

- Mental Body - These emotions then excite the Mental Body into thinking about what has happened to me (my story) usually based upon thoughts of the past and false beliefs that then lead to some type of reaction to the life situation experienced.

- Spiritual Body - Then finally, after much self-inflicted torment, the Spiritual Body sends a message that perhaps you may be over-reacting to the situation at hand. At that point, an inner dialog or discussion within lower self begins and a decision is consciously made to either build on the story (which the Mental Body created) or to drop the issue in acceptance of what is.

The difficulty with this type of pattern is it usually leads to fear-based action unless you have learned to catch yourself when you see this destructive pattern emerging.

Example – Naturally in Alignment:

If we analyze the same situation and reverse the control mechanisms of our Four Body System, there is a completely different result.

- Spiritual Body - When the Spiritual Body is in control and a life situation occurs, it is first acknowledged as what is and acceptance is immediately allowed. The perception is merely "this happened", it did not happen to me, it simply happened.

- Mental Body – Then, the Mental Body activates to confirm; yes, this happened and some type of action may be required.

- Emotional Body - Next, the Emotional Body ignites with a feeling of empowerment to the challenge; it creates positive solution-based emotions and provides action to resolve the issue, rather than focusing on the perceived problem.

- Physical Body - The result is the Physical Body feels peaceful and excited that there is a challenge to resolve. The Physical Body remains stress-free and the solutions appear from a higher knowledge base. The beauty of this type of pattern is the Four Body System then works in harmony without fear and feels peaceful Knowing that Love through Divine power and wisdom can bring light to any life situation.

In each of the above examples, the resultant actions will vary dramatically depending on whether you are living your life in a state of Love or fear. This may sound rather idealistic to some of you; however, if you make a focused effort to realign yourself with the Spiritual Body (through meditation), your life will be more balanced and in alignment with the higher level of understanding which is experienced through Love, Peace and Light.

The best way to stay connected with your Spiritual Body in the forefront of life situation is through the practice of daily meditation. When you discover how to keep the Spiritual Body in the forefront of your life, your level of awareness in any given situation will have a higher energy level and ultimately Conscious Clarity. When the mind is quiet and Kundalini energy is flowing unrestricted the highest level of spiritual communication is possible. It is in that clarity of mind that your true purpose is revealed.

When living a life of Spiritual Body alignment and non-resistance, the victimization role is transcended into the higher vibration level of observer and the end result is a balanced physical lifestyle in harmony with the Divine power of the Universe.

Are Non-Resistant People Happier

There are varying levels (vibrations) of happiness, meaning you are only going to be as happy as the level of harmony you are allowing yourself to experience which is limited by the beliefs of the mind. Conversely, our natural Spiritual way of Being is focused on the absolute abundance the Universe has in store for us. Therefore, as you dig deeper within, you will discover the more balanced you are in each category of your life, the happier you will be externally or on the physical level. That's because happiness is an external thing measured by the form-based perception of the circumstances surrounding you in your life situation.

In most cases, the ego controls happiness based upon your limited beliefs about yourself externally. However, your true Higher Self is always there attempting to break through the barriers or smokescreen of the ego. Therefore, if you are feeling unrest with your life, it is because you are resisting life itself. When living at a level of vibration where resistance falls away, every*thing* (external) changes and you begin to live a life filled with the Joy that flows from within you or from a Higher Self perspective of life. However, the challenge with only living a life focused on external happiness (as your main objective) is that happiness for the most part is limited to the external elements surrounding you. Those external elements are limited by the ego's interpretation of what life should be. This is known as living a superficial lifetime without any depth or spiritual guidance.

If you truly believe you are only the Physical Body and constantly resist life experiences, then you are limiting yourself to the control dynamics surrounding you rather than the true Highest Self guidance which comes from within you. Non-resistance to what is is the catalyst to the Spiritual *Joy* that is housed within the body. This is very confusing for those living a life of Physical Body alignment, because they have not yet stepped up their energy level which allows them to even hear, let alone understand the incredible opportunities that are possible for them if they could hear the Divine guidance.

The Divine guidance from God comes to us in a whisper, not in some outlandish display of power or excessive words. Therefore, when the Physical Body (mind/ego) is quiet or sitting in silence, the guidance can be heard with Conscious Clarity and personal spiritual abundance flourishes as it was meant to. When the mind is quiet, the Divine guidance we all have available to us is heard loud and clear and, more often than not, it is simply felt through conscious awareness of the Kundalini energy flowing through us. We learn to feel the energy and can therefore tell when our energy is blocked by some external life situation occurrence that limits the natural flow of Kundalini energy.

Abundance is not measured by any "thing" external to yourself; this is simply one of the many big misinterpretations of the mind.

Abundance is the realization that you are not regulated by some outside factor on a chart that society choose for you; it is the natural level of awareness you consciously attain and focus on that creates the "perceived level" of abundance you experience or the flow of energy.

Please, take a few minutes to sit in silence for that spiritual reality to sink in to your mind. Most people measure abundance as having more, rather than less of some *thing* external to themselves. It may be materialist in nature or a delusion of the mind, either way it is not an accurate representation of true abundance. Abundance is measured by the level of Kundalini energy flowing through the body and the gratitude you bring to each life experience.

Therefore, true abundance is the Joy experienced by living life fully present in each and every moment without dwelling on the past or worrying about the future. True abundance is sharing your deepest heartfelt gratitude with those surrounding you; bringing out the Joy in others by allowing your Self to surrender to the harmony that comes in a relationship of faith and trust. By allowing your innermost expression of Love to shine as a beacon of light to assist others in the challenges they may be experiencing. Whereby, your Kundalini energy is flowing in its natural state rather than limited or blocked by the minds misinterpretation of life situations.

When you begin flowing with life through the gift of acceptance to what is and experiencing it as it grows more and more powerful in Divine light, you finally discover the true secrets to happiness. Therefore, yes, it is true, a person that lives life without resistance is typically happier. They are least likely to judge others and are accountable only to themselves for their own chosen action which is based upon their current energy or vibration level. Their outside life situations for the most part are a direct reflection of their inner emotional stability.

In summary, wherever you are vibrating in life today is all based upon your collective personal decisions to date. Yes, you may be influenced by others surrounding you but when it comes right down to it, you have the final say before you decide to take action. You choose to resist life or go with the flow of the experience. The final choice is always yours and yours alone. It is your responsibility to manage your own life situations and stop giving power to others that may be attempting to control your flow of Kundalini energy. Therefore, if you want to be happier, simply take charge of your own flow of Kundalini energy by consciously living a life of non-resistance to what is.

So Just Go With the Flow

Life is a process and like any other process it evolves over time. Many of you expect to have all the answers all at one time, especially some of you that are younger. My best advice to you is to allow life to be the enlightening journey it is meant to be. You are growing with every breath and your experiences in life are all related in some way to your purpose for being here. Enjoy the progression of increasing your energy vibration a little bit at a time until it is in harmony with your true purpose.

Each new "aha" moment or moment of insight is designed to help us grow the Spiritual Self to its fullest potential so that you inspire yourself and others around you. You are far more important in the big picture of the evolution of this planet than you may realize. The proof is that you are here, *Now*. This is a period in our evolution where we all rediscovering the essence of our true being like never before. At times, this may mean going through some tough challenges that will bring you closer to your purpose; especially if you are having difficulties bringing your true purpose to light on your own.

The progression of life is truly an amazing experience once you realize you are the only one responsible for where you are right now. Although we can be influenced by others in many ways, the truth is we all make our own choices and experience the results of those choices. Therefore, if you aren't happy with your life in this moment, make better choices!

We all have a God-given right to be joyful and in harmony with the peaceful abundance life has to offer us. If you have a true reverence for life, you will feel the cosmic flow of energy surging through you each time you are faced with a challenge. You won't look at the experience as problematic; you will grow to understand that each challenge is a stepping stone to lift you up to your Highest Self purpose. By flowing with life instead of resisting it, you become better at dealing with the challenges that come your way.

Your true life, meaning your spiritual life, is never-ending. It is a compilation or series of small journeys that continually increases your energy vibration to align with the Universe. Each smaller journey in your true spiritual life cycle is increased or decreased in energy vibration based upon the choices you make during each journey. Yes, that means you are incarnated into many form-based lifetimes, perhaps more than your limited mind can comprehend. And each smaller form-based lifetime is one of the many smaller journeys you will make in the unlimited life of Spirituality. Each return journey brings you back at the level of energy vibration you were at when you left the last form-based reality.

There's no escaping the cycle or progression of increasing energy vibration from one incarnation to the next. You will continually grow at your own pace and only you can change that rate of growth. When you finally decide to believe in the Divine power that daily assists you to fulfill your spiritual life Original Source Agreement, your smaller journeys will be experienced with joy and complete harmony with the Universe. That is what is meant by a true non-resistant lifestyle. When you grow beyond the limited barriers of the mind (ego), you will begin to experience a journey of unlimited possibility. You will stop asking yourself why this or that is happening to me and understand that all that happens in a form-based lifetime is happening around you, not to you, and that which is happening around you is happening to assist you with your spiritual life growth or evolution.

Therefore, each experience in life is meant to be a stepping stone to prepare you for the next lifetime experience. You can choose to be engaged in life fully as a positive influence on others in each incarnation or you can resist it and hold yourself back from your greatness. Be assured that by playing out the role of victim when challenges arise to teach the lessons of life, you will continue to live a lifetime of limited reality or survival. Or you can simply make the choice to allow that which is meant to teach you to unfold around you with the wonderment of where each non-resistance step may take you next.

Only you can choose to experience the benefits of living a non-resistance lifestyle. When you make the shift to non-resistance, you will understand the joyful experience manifested based upon living through Love, Peace and Light which ultimately means going with the flow!

What Are the Physical Benefits Of Non-Resistance

The biggest physical benefit from living a life of non-resistance is a constant unrestricted flow of Kundalini energy through the body. This, in turn, provides contentment beyond the limited beliefs of the mind and brings about a deeper understanding of how Love channels happiness in the

Physical Body reality. When the Kundalini energy is flowing without blockages, the chakras of the body are relaxed, stress free and wide open. When experiencing this unrestricted flow of energy in the body, it brings about harmony with life at its deepest level of being; *living life at the level of Conscious Clarity of Spiritual Body awareness.*

Most people think about, rather than feel, the Physical Body. They trap themselves in a never-ending delusion of mind control and imprisonment over their life situations. By today's standards of fourth dimension or Spiritual level understanding this is like living in the dark ages. It causes a conflict within the mind and shuts down the Kundalini energy that is attempting to align with the Higher Self consciousness. To better understand what this means to the Physical Body, review Illustration E, *Life Fuel Source.* The type of fuel (thought) that is feed to the brain by the mind has a significant impact on how the Physical Body responds to life situations. Therefore, if you are still living Physical Body alignment, this can be detrimental to Well Being because the perceived conflict between the Physical and Spiritual realm of consciousness is resistant to life itself. This creates a false sense of reality because negative emotions then drive *The Train of Life™* awareness through unrealistic ego dominance.

Learning to step out of the Physical Body alignment paradigm is not an easy task for most people. The ego is strong and will use whatever tricks it can manifest to convince you that all there is to life is the physical realm of being. Therefore, again, until you believe you are a Spiritual Being having a human experience, you will trapped in the low energy vibrations found by fueling the brain with "Dark Fossil Fuel" thoughts. Until you break this self-destructive pattern, you will not understand the joy of the eternal life journey as it was meant to be experienced. You will stay stuck in the low vibrations of self-doubt, false beliefs, anxiety, resistance and possible self-imposed depression. And, you will likely continue to associate most of the time with people that are vibrating at the same lower energy vibration because the ego has convinced you that you are not a Spiritual Being.

At all levels or vibrations of life, the resultant factor of the chosen "Fuel Source" is directly proportional to the life reality you have decided to live. You are the only one in control of your thoughts and until you change your thinking by asking better questions about life and living in acceptance of what is, your Physical Body reality will remain blocked of the Divine life-force energy available at the level of Joy which is found deep within yourself. Therefore, you must go deeper within to release your mind of the unnecessary burdens found by living a life controlled by ego and the manipulating egos of others surrounding you with their low energy influence.

When you stop resisting the natural flow of your Higher Self attempting to guide you, you will begin to climb out of the state of self-imposed depression that you have created for yourself. You will look at life from a different higher energy flow perspective and you will begin to align your Physical Body in the proper order for a happier life. Then, your Kundalini energy will flow in its natural state of being and you will experience happiness like never before. The human body has an amazing ability to heal itself from the inside out. This is true for emotional as well as physical cellular dis-ease.

Today's society has grown in scientific knowledge like never before and we are on the verge of finally understanding how the Spiritual healing capabilities from within influence the Physical Body healing process. There are miracles just waiting to unfold around you, but you must be conscious and living life from a higher level of vibration to experience them as they come to you.

You and you alone are holding yourself back from the greatness that is in store for you and just waiting to be released into the world. Your Physical Body will begin to respond the moment you decide to live your life fully present instead of being trapped in the past or hoping for a better future. Simply pay attention to what is unfolding around you in the present moment and have faith that all is in Divine order. You have the spiritual power to change the world, starting with yourself!

Does Path of Least Resistance Mean Be Passive

When speaking of living a path of least resistance, it is important to understand this does not mean to live a passive life of submittal to all that is of the Physical Body. It is all related to the resistance of affirming Spiritual Body alignment existence of your true Highest Self reality. Therefore, it is natural to defend your Physical Body and its surrounding environment if attacked by some other Physical Body force. Taking the "Path of Least Resistance" is defined as living life through a Spiritual reality, rather than simply a Physical reality of ego dominance. The alignment of the Four Body System is the focus of enlightenment. Always remember, you are a Spiritual Being.

Life is all about energy and the movement or dance of that energy as it flows through you. You can choose to let the outside circumstances of life situations flow through you or you can choose to let them embed in your Physical Body. From a spiritual perspective, this is typically known as blocking the flow of energy within the body, which in turn causes anxiety and eventually dis-ease. It's important to understand that what you believe, whether it is true or not, can have a crippling affect on your overall Well Being. If you are constantly resisting the experience of your lifetime, you will eventually create an abnormal blockage of the energy that is meant to naturally flow through you; this natural flow is the Kundalini energy.

Life situations can be very challenging at times. There will always be influences that are not in harmony with your natural state of being which is designed to be peaceful and relaxed. It's the stories made up in the mind that cause most of the unrest you may be feeling when challenged. However, if you simply learn to allow that which is meant to naturally flow through or around you, you can then take a path of least resistance and the resultant feelings change. At times, it takes a conscious effort to see what is actually happening around you clearly. It's not an easy task if you allow the mind to burden you with over analysis of any given life situation.

If you can learn to become the observer of life challenges, it allows you to step outside the life situation. Many times challenges may seem unbearable and it may feel like you are never going to get past whatever it is that is causing the uncertainly in the moment. If you feel as though you don't know how to respond to a challenge in life, sometimes it just simply best to allow it to unfold as it may. One of my favorite sayings is "this too shall pass". Whenever a challenge feels like it's beyond your control, allow time to heal the wound.

I can remember periods when I had absolutely no idea how to resolve challenges that presented themselves in my lifetime. In these cases, I simply stated aloud, "this is beyond my control, please bring a solution as quickly as possible." Then, I simply released it to the Universe and went to bed for the evening. The end result was always the same; a solution presented itself either in the middle of the night or first thing in the morning.

It's important to remember how powerful the mind is and how it can bring you right down to your knees at times. In today's unstable world, it can be a real challenge to keep your energy up to a level where the outside occurrences of life do not in some way stick to you. However, it's still a choice that you make, whether something outside of you bothers you or not. It's typically the analysis of a life situation that causes the discomfort you may be feeling. We are a society of overachievers, the mind wants to figure everything out in as short a time period as possible. The mind wants immediate answers to some really complex challenges which can in turn cause the buildup of embellished stories.

If you ever feel as though you don't know which way to turn next, sometimes it's just best to observe without making any judgments one way or another. If a challenge seems overwhelming, it's always best to simply sit with it for a while to ensure you are observing it for what it "really" is. Don't make it anything more or less, just sit in silence and ask for guidance or a solution. Then, let the Universe take over while you go on with your day without putting any more thought into the analysis of the challenge.

Allow yourself the luxury of living life in its natural state of Being where the body is relaxed and flowing with the path of least resistance. Remember, it's always the mind that causes unrest. Therefore, one of the best ways to deal with a perceived major challenge is to allow some time to pass before making any decision or taking action to resolve a challenge. Don't get caught up in the dogma of needing to take action immediately, unless, of course, it is an emergency life threatening situation.

How Has This Worked for Others

We each have specific teachers or gurus that come to us either by actively seeking them out or by them being sent to us through circumstances in life that are beyond our control.

Each of us has had the experience of someone showing up at exactly the right time to assist us in some way with a challenge in life. It may be someone you have known for a long time that you look up to or someone that is introduced to you when times seem tough. It doesn't really matter what the challenge may be, someone will eventually show up to assist you. Usually, this comes at a time when you surrender in some way. This could simply mean saying to yourself "I don't know what to do with this situation."

When you surrender to a greater power than your physical self, the Universe automatically goes into action to assist you with any challenge from a spiritual perspective. The reason this happens is because you have changed your energy vibration to align with the assistance that is always available to you from within.

The path of least resistance does not mean there will not be challenges in your lifetime. It simply means go with the flow of life and don't get all hung up on the drama of the mind when challenges arise. We all have unexpected experiences in life, it's part of what makes life interesting. It's the uncertainty of life situations that brings balance to the certainty of the things you do have under your personal control. All challenges are an opportunity to learn more about your True Self - your Spiritual Self!

One of the people I love to use as an example is one of the top known spiritual teachers in personal development today, Eckhart Tolle. One of his famous quotes is, "The realm of consciousness is much vaster than thought can grasp.

When you no longer believe everything you think, you step out of thought and see clearly that the thinker is not who you are." This is a very power statement as it gets right down to the core of our belief structure and alignment with the Spiritual Body. When we release the mind from the challenges before us, we open up to a higher vibration or realm of understanding that cannot be heard from a Physical Body perspective.

If you are not familiar with Eckhart Tolle, you probably don't understand the message being conveyed. He is internationally known as the master of living in the present moment. One of his most famous books is "The Power of Now" which has sold millions of copies worldwide. Eckhart Tolle has one of the most amazing stories of transformative realization into the understanding of Higher Self that has ever been told. At a time when he was faced with seemingly unrecoverable challenges in life and on the verge of suicide he told himself, "I can't take this anymore." It was at that exact moment that he became aware of his ego, the ego that had been controlling him and causing him to feel the way he did. He simply asked the question, "Who is this 'I' that can't take it anymore?" It was at that precise moment he became aware of the ego and discovered that the Physical Body or thinker is not who he really is. From that moment forward, he was determined to understand more about this false self and discover the power of living life from a Spiritual Body alignment perspective.

When we begin to understand the full extent of our spiritual power over the challenges of life situations, we begin to realize our full potential as Spiritual Beings having a human experience. By stepping outside the box of the thinker, we offer the world a fourth dimension spiritual perspective to achieving miracles in daily life.

Another one of my favorite quotes is from internationally renowned spiritual author Marianne Williamson. She states, "Our deepest fear is not that we are inadequate. Our deepest fear is that we are powerful beyond measure." The fear always lies with the ego mind or thinker, not with the loving Spiritual Self that thrives within our physical body. When we align with the power of the Higher Self perspective of being Spiritual having a human experience, we make a conscious choice to stop playing small and we step into our greatness. It is through Conscious Clarity of who we really are, aligning with the energy vibration of our Higher Self, that we create the everyday miracles available to us.

Many people that have been down and out, feeling as though they have nothing to live for are the ones that stand out the most in the spiritual transformative spotlight because their stories of overcoming unhappiness in life seem miraculous to us. When in reality, all they have actually done is stepped up their energy vibration to the greatness of their true Higher Self awareness. And, the truth a handful of people with this awareness can change the world as we know it today!

Can the World Change

Evolution of the World is always in motion. We have the power to move forward in the Universe by rising up to a higher level of energy vibration. Unless, of course, the inhabitants of the world choose to destroy what has already been increased by focusing on ego-dominated control dynamics. There is always a possibility that the world could be reduced to its natural raw state of creation or its common material based elements. The choice is truly made by the inhabitants of the world, not the core structure of the world itself as it was originally created. This is the beauty and, at the same time, the downfall of free will. The balance is actually based upon the current mass consciousness of the world.

Our planet was created and originally provided with all the natural ingredients to sustain life indefinitely. Only human beings are capable of destroying its natural balance and ultimately its existence. I believe we are now at a tipping point where we will awaken to the natural Spiritual Body alignment perspective of life which sustains life at its Highest Self level of energy vibration or we will start over again. We are now seeing more and more organizations stepping up to voice opinions that are congruent with sustaining life from a Higher Self perspective. But on the flip side, we are experiencing an unprecedented amount of dis-ease, too. Humanity is split between the high vibration of Higher Self and the extremely low vibration of ego dominated perspective. Manipulation by most governments is still an underlying control dynamic which is holding people at the prisoner level of their own egoistic beliefs.

Each day is truly a precious opportunity to assist others in bringing about change. One of the best ways to do this is to always align with Spiritual Self-improvement. This was clearly defined by one of the most enlightened beings to ever walk our planet.

You must be the change you wish to see in the world. - Mahatma Gandhi

Whenever you hear about some crisis going on in the world that simply does not resonate with your core beliefs and is within your area of control, get involved. Remember, you always have the opportunity to participate in righting some perceived wrong. Don't just take someone else's words for fact; get involved to confirm for yourself that some injustice has occurred. And then, if you *feel* you have the power to make a change, set in motion the necessary actions to make a difference that moves you higher in energy vibration. Listen to the guidance coming from Higher Self and if it resonates with you – *get involved.*

We all have incredible gifts to share with the world. When you align your gifts with a worthy cause, it manifests a higher level of energy vibration that is capable of creating change. Deep down inside of us, we can feel when our Kundalini energy is flowing at its highest state of vibration. By tapping into that flow of energy, we can "feel" what is in alignment with our highest purpose for being here. By utilizing this Divine life-force to its fullest, we can bring about a new loving dynamic which resonates with God's intent for not only our Well Being, but for the world, too.

The vast majority of the world is rooted in fear-based dogma that is just the opposite of what God intended for us. If you don't believe this, turn on late night television news and listen closely to how the stories are presented. We have been manipulated for centuries by the same fear-based control tactics. The presentation or media has changed, but the negative message is still the same. It's time to break out of this realm of life situation and move forward to the higher vibration of Love and trust in one another as a conscious humanity. What can you do today to assist in raising the mass consciousness of the world? Are you stepping up to the challenge of getting involved? If so, do just one good thing each day that matters for someone else and experience the awesome feeling of Love that comes from giving of your True Self personality!

Is Humanity Resistant

As stated previously, the vast majority of the world's humanity is rooted in fear-based dogma which is just the opposite of what God intended for us. This is due to most of humanity still living with Physical Body alignment in the forefront of daily reality and being locked in a third dimension mindset. This results in untrue stories or influences that affect life in a negative way because the old ego is controlling life situations from a much lower level of energy vibration perspective.

Until we raise above old egos' control dramas, life situations that are manifested from past and future ideology or stories seem very real. In truth, the mind perceives false truths as real and then action is taken by the body to align with this lower level of energy vibration to justify the false truth. This is especially true when it comes to adult influences on children. Until the age of twenty five, the mind is still in a state of chemical development and is highly susceptible to influences from outside influences both chemically and mentally.

Example:

If a child is constantly taught by observation in a household that drinking alcohol is a way to ease the pain of self-imposed stressful life situations, they can easily become a substance abuser or addict. Then, the alcohol or substance of choice holds them prisoner to false beliefs that are perpetuated by this altered state or false reality. This is truly living life from a resistant point of view, rather than accepting what is in the present moment without influencing life with a mind-altering poisons. Anything that alters the chemical structure of the body negatively is considered poison or toxic and should be avoided.

Furthermore, at this extremely low level of energy vibration, the mind falls so far below the true reality of life situations that the mind takes this altered (resisted) state of reality to a false state of action. This causes the natural chemical balance of the body to erode to a still lower energy level of delusional reality. This type of behavior can be detrimental to anyone in the immediate proximity of the person under the influence of their chemical poison of choice. This is where the label "mean drunk" comes from. The "mean drunk" is living life so far below the true reality of life that they believe what the mind observes as true when the chemical imbalance is further deteriorated by alcohol consumption on a daily basis. Consequently, those in the household are traumatized by the person under the influence of the poisonous mind-altering substance. This affect on the household can be traumatizing for life or until each person can seek mental medical assistance to eliminate the result of the long-term, emotional abuse.

In truth, all of life is a blessing and is meant to be experienced to its fullest potential in a non-altered state of reality. When we resist the experiences of life by attempted to alter the truth with chemical substances, we end up living a false life which is based upon the untrue beliefs brought on by fear or anything other than present moment reality. Conversely, when we fuel the body with nutrients that keep its chemical structure balanced and operating at its optimum performance both mentally and physically, we see life through a non-resistant reality or Conscious Clarity.

The sad truth is most of humanity or our western society has been influenced by the production of products that are detrimental to our health and natural Well Being. Even worse, we have become addicted to these mind-altering chemical substances and have unknowingly taken our energy vibration down to the level of the substance itself. Many of us are so addicted, we have the false belief that we cannot survive without the substance or chemical of choice. This, in reality, is truly going against the non-resistance current of life that God had naturally intended for us and the resultant reality can be very harmful to all of humanity.

How Is Going Against the Current Harmful

The intention for our existence has always been to flow through life in an easy and relaxed manner based upon Spiritual Body alignment. However, for some reason, we seem to have lost touch with Spiritual Body alignment reality. This is especially true in Western society where we have become a culture that exists very much like fish swimming against the current of water. We struggle in a frantic survival mode in Physical Body alignment and separation from Source Energy's (God's) intention and then expect our life situation to be in harmony with the Universe … how arrogant!

How many times have you found yourself going against the flow or current of a spiritual life? Do you truly understand what it means to be in harmony with life or are you still living in third dimension reality and just another one of the people that are struggling to survive a lifetime, rather than thrive with joy and spiritual abundance?

If your life is not everything you would like it to be, somewhere along the tracks of this lifetime you have taken a few misdirected detours that have not served you well. If you don't believe this, ask yourself if you are living your true purpose for being here. If you find it hard to ask that question or you really don't know what your purpose is, that is proof enough to come to the realization that you are not in touch with Spiritual Body alignment and your Original Source Agreement for being here.

Our Western culture is typically only concerned with a "what's in it for me" mentality of life. Most westerners swim with the little fish on the surface of life without ever diving deeply enough within themselves to understand who they really are. Many have lost track of the vision we designed for ourselves before taking residence in the Physical Body. In fact, most people still believe all there is to life is the Physical Body and, therefore, when the body dies, they die as well. This spiritual ignorance is so far from the truth, it's no wonder so many people are confused and are making poor choices. They are stuck between the spiritual guidance they suppress and the minds (ego's) non-stop conversation that seems to drive them to the brink of insanity.

When you are out of harmony with your true purpose, you become a prisoner to a false sense of being and simply exist rather than living life to its fullest potential. You become stuck in the "rat race" of society dictating what's best for you and move away from the happiness you deserve. You make up stories to justify your dysfunctional level of awareness and never really make an effort to realign with God's intention.

Physical Body alignment drains your life Source Energy through manipulating life situations to align with old ego-based false beliefs. Living with this limited level of belief or perspective quickly becomes very tiresome and many people choose to use mind altering substances to mask the pain which this Physical Body alignment manifests. By doing this, they fall still further below the level of spiritual awareness available to them and some eventually give up on life and feel hopeless. This is being stuck in a life that does not provide the happiness most are seeking outside themselves or the joy that comes from within the spiritual dynamics of our Highest Self reality.

When vibrating at this lower level of energy, the higher energy Divine life-force is masked by old ego-based dogma and the messages being sent from the higher levels of energy vibration are impossible to hear. This lower level of energy vibration manifests as a spiraling effect downward into a world of self-imposed doubts and half-truths. Then this negative story is amplified by more self-limiting beliefs from others surrounding them and the person becomes depressed with life itself. This life situation dogma continues to waste energy on low vibration stories that fuel the old ego and, in many cases, it becomes necessary to take mind-altering medications to even exist in society.

However, the astounding truth is that we, as Spiritual Beings, have the Divine power to intervene against old ego dynamics and awaken to a higher level of reality by simply realigning our Four Body System. This can be done in a heartbeat by just saying NO to old ego's demands and bringing Spiritual Body alignment to the forefront of our daily existence. One of the most effective ways to accomplish this realignment is to practice living in a meditative state of Being on a daily basis. Through silencing the mind and focusing on what is available to us in the present moment at the higher levels of awareness, we can completely change our perception of life and eventually the outcome of our actions.

Then, our life becomes the miracle it was intended to be and we begin to manifest non-resistant outcomes that are in alignment with our Original Source Agreement. Furthermore, we begin to feel the joy the bubbles up from within us and our vibration naturally increases to the level of Conscious Clarity (See Illustration E). Obviously, with this newfound clarity, we begin to see life in a new and exciting manner while bringing that awareness to everyone we meet in the form of Love, Peace and Light!

The truth is when we live life with the Physical Body aligned with other physical body dogma, we only experience half of the life we are here to ultimately enjoy. We only experience the lower vibration level or aspect of life because our vibration is too low to even begin to understand the purpose of the Spiritual Body leading our life situations. This resistance to Spiritual Body alignment being in the forefront of your daily life situations brings about limited results and you consequently never live a lifetime of true abundance because you are stalled or stuck in the third dimension of reality.

In true reality, everyone has the opportunity to realign with the Spiritual Body leading the daily phase of life. You too can achieve Divine greatness in your lifetime, but only if you are aligned with the limitless possibilities of experiencing both sides of the equation. By utilizing the Divine power of merging the Soul and ego together, you too can change your life to become a miraculous transformation that benefits all of humanity. Are you ready to become one of the examples of people that have gone through this exact transition? It's never too late!

What Are Some Examples of Non-Resistant Outcomes

Spiritual knowledge is the underlying secret to a successful existence on this planet. By utilizing the past experiences of your own life and the past experiences of others that are spiritually successful, you have the ability to completely change your life circumstances. You too can be in harmony with those that have come before you to make the dynamic shift from an old ego-based, third dimension lifestyle to the new age, fourth dimension lifestyle which is filled with limitless possibilities. It all starts when you choose Spiritual Transformative Education as the main learning tool for your life.

We have all been brain washed into believing that we are limited by the outside circumstances of our life and the amount of academic education achieved. Most people believe they have nothing more to live for than what the Physical Body alignment dynamic can offer. They have been convinced by well-meaning people (society) that they are only allowed to move forward at the rate of academic achievement they have manifested thus far. However, when you genuinely analyze some of the most successful people in the world, you quickly discover that many of them became successful without having a formal ego-based academic education that separated them from the rest of the human population.

Yes, an academic education is important based upon how our current society is structured. However, there is a far greater need today for a Spiritual Education than there is for any socially accepted, academic training. Our world is in the process of a major shift in reality and each one of us has the opportunity to make that shift for the betterment of humanity as a whole. As in the past, the societal dictators of the world are blinded by their own egos' and live in fear of any change that would benefit the mass consciousness of the world. They are locked in their ego-based dogma and are unwilling to step into the "light" of the unlimited possibilities of Spiritual Transformative Education.

There are many well-known people that have made the choice to move out of Physical Body alignment to experience the limitless possibilities of Spiritual Body alignment reality. They have been called to "discontinue" a lifestyle based entirely on society demands and have stepped into the light of Spiritual Transformative Education.

Dr. Wayne Dyer and Eckhart Tolle will always be remembered as two of the most well-known spiritually transformed people of our lifetime. Their stories of transition into Spiritual Body alignment are very well-known and are summarized for you below:

Example 1 – Dr Wayne Dyer

*Wayne was firmly planted in the Academic Education System and was held in high regard as an academic professor. Wayne worked as a high school guidance counselor in Detroit and as a professor of counselor education at St. John's University in New York City. He pursued an academic career, published in journals and established a private therapy practice. His lectures at St. John's, which focused on positive thinking and motivational speaking techniques attracted many students. A literary agent persuaded Dyer to document his theories in his first book called *Your Erroneous Zones*.

Wayne knew deep inside that he was not fulfilling his true purpose for being here. Therefore, Wayne quit his teaching job and began a publicity tour of the United States of America, doggedly pursuing bookstore appearances and media interviews ("out of the back of his station wagon", according to Michael Korda, making the best-seller lists "before book publishers even noticed what was happening"), which eventually led to national television talk show appearances including Merv Griffin, The Tonight Show and Phil Donahue.

Wayne proceeded to build on his success with lecture tours, a series of audiotapes and regular publication of new books. Wayne's message resonated with many in the New Thought Movement and beyond. He often recounted anecdotes from his family life and repeatedly used his own life experience as an example. His self-made man, success story was a part of his appeal. Wayne told readers to pursue self-actualization, calling reliance on the self as a guide to "religious" experience and suggested that readers emulate Jesus Christ, whom he termed both an example of a self-actualized person and a "preacher of self-reliance".

Wayne criticized societal focus on guilt which he saw as an unhealthy immobilization in the present due to actions taken in the past. He advocated readers to see how parents, institutions and even they, themselves, have imposed guilt trips upon themselves. Although Wayne initially resisted the spiritual tag, by the 1990s, he had altered his message to include more components of spirituality when he wrote the book *Real Magic* and discussed higher consciousness in the book *Your Sacred Self*.

Since then, Wayne has appeared on numerous PBS specials and has even been featured on a spiritual movie release called *The Shift*. Wayne's transformation into Spiritual Body alignment continued to grow daily and his life was based upon one of service to mankind through Spiritual

Transformative Education at the fourth dimension level of awareness.

(*Partial reference material from Wikipedia)

Dr. Wayne Dyer peacefully transitioned from his Physical Body during his sleep on August 29, 2015 in his home on Maui, Hawaii at the age of 75.

Example 2 - Eckhart Tolle

*Eckhart is a German-born resident of Canada, best known as the author of *The Power of Now* and *A New Earth*. In 2011, he was listed by the Watkins Review as the most spiritually influential person in the world. In 2008, a *New York Times* writer called Tolle "the most popular spiritual author in the United States".

Eckhart has said that he was depressed for much of his life until he underwent, at age 29, an "inner transformation". He then spent several years wandering and unemployed "in a state of deep bliss" before becoming a spiritual teacher. Later, he moved to North America where he began writing his first book, *The Power of Now*, which was published in 1997 and reached the *New York Times* Best Seller lists in 2000. Eckhart settled in Vancouver, Canada, where he has lived for more than a decade.

The Power of Now and *A New Earth* sold an estimated three million and five million copies respectively in North America by 2009. In 2008, approximately 35 million people participated in a series of 10 live webinars with Tolle and television talk show host Oprah Winfrey. Eckhart is not identified with any particular religion, but he has been influenced by a wide range of spiritual works.

<u>Eckhart's Inner Transformation</u>

One night in 1977, at the age of 29, after having suffered from long periods of suicidal depression, Eckhart says he experienced an "inner transformation". That night, he awakened from his sleep, suffering from feelings of depression that were "almost unbearable", but then experienced a life-changing epiphany. Recounting the experience, Eckhart says,

"I couldn't live with myself any longer. And in this a question arose without an answer: who is the 'I' that cannot live with the self? What is the self? I felt drawn into a void! I didn't know at the time that what really happened was the mind-made self, with its heaviness, its problems, that lives between the unsatisfying past and the fearful future, collapsed. It dissolved. The next morning I woke up and everything was so peaceful. The peace was there because there was no self, just a sense of presence or "beingness," just observing and watching."

Eckhart recalls going out for a walk in London the next morning and finding that "everything was miraculous, deeply peaceful, even the traffic." The feeling continued and he began to feel a strong, underlying sense of peace in any situation. Eckhart stopped studying for his doctorate and, for a period of about two years after this, he spent much of his time sitting "in a state of deep bliss" on park benches in Russell Square, Central London, "watching the world go by". He stayed with friends, in a Buddhist monastery or otherwise slept rough on Hampstead Heath. His family thought him "irresponsible, even insane".

(*Partial reference material from Wikipedia)

As with many other people that awaken to the understanding of their true Spiritual Beingness, our society in third dimension perspective views them as being out of touch with reality. In truth, they are out of touch with old ego dynamics and have transcended into the higher state of consciousness that has always been available through Spiritual Body alignment and now Spiritual Transformative Education in the fourth dimension level of awareness.

Is Our World Going to Learn

Our world, as we know it in the old third dimension, is always learning and evolving to the next level of understanding. However, the methods for discovering our actually abilities has shifted to a fourth dimension which opens up limitless possibilities to those aligned with the current fourth or Spiritual dimension.

Therefore, the evolution process is shifting from a beginning and end mentality to an eternal reality or Spiritual understanding of our true life which is endless. The choices we now make (to bring about change) in this lifetime is a learning process that will be the catalyst for how far we evolve and how quickly we can bring into alignment the wonders of universal growth or cosmic understanding.

We have gone as far as we can with a limited third dimension perspective of life. It has served us only to the point of realizing that something is lost in our daily life situations. The ability for us to transcend into a higher realm of reality is now in front of us and is knocking at the door of opportunity like never before. We have truly shifted into the Spiritual fourth dimension of reality. However, there are those that would rather stay stuck with old third dimension thinking and not move forward to the new reality before us. To those stuck in this limited perspective on life, I can only say, "I wish you well and hope that you will soon awaken to the new unlimited Divine power within you. You are far greater than your fear-based old ego will ever allow you to perceive yourself."

Humanity has evolved as far as it can from the limited fear-based reality of old ego, third dimension thinking. To believe we could evolve further at that level of understanding without consciously realigning with our true Spiritual Self is more continued arrogance of an old ego and fear-based control system that is on the verge of extinction. The old ego is so rooted in fear, it can't even begin to accept the change that is coming to merge the body and Soul together for the benefit of all.

It is the Divine power of Love that is moving us into the next level of awareness. Many light-workers are dedicated to assisting you with rediscovering who you really are, even if the level of third dimension reality does not understand the evolution that has already started to shift. Although, the choice to stay stuck where you are in the third dimension is always available to you, it is my hope that you will soon awaken and see what you are missing by staying aligned with the old paradigm.

Each one of us evolves at precisely the right moment for our own person growth. As a species, the Physical Body is lasting longer than it did in the past, but not nearly as long as it is designed to exist. We are capable of sustaining a healthy life for well over one hundred earth years, but many choose to destroy the Physical Body with chemicals that are highly toxic to the body's existence.

When we pollute the body with unhealthy foods, alcohol substances and mind-altering drugs, the chemical balance is destroyed which literally shortens the Physical Body existence. This is especially true in Western civilization where the "obesity factor" has reached the epidemic level of destruction. It's a sad reality. However, I believe we are finally experiencing a better understanding of the growing number of toxins causing brain altering levels of damage to the Physical Body.

Science has proven over and over again what we already know as Spiritual Beings, either we change or we will eventually cause our own physical destruction. We each make a conscious choice daily to ingest either healthy products that sustain life or chemically-altered products that drive up corporate profits at the cost of our human existence and overall Well Being.

As an example, take time to step outside your comfort zone and re-think what you put into your body each day. Write down the actual consumption of each product and then analyze whether these products are manufactured for your ultimate health or for bringing temporary pleasure to some form of pain you are experiencing through emotional instability.

Simply ask yourself, do these products serve my overall Well Being? Are they filled with all the nutrients my body needs to sustain a healthy active lifestyle? Be sure to analyze everything on your list, especially all the sugar-based additives that enhance taste at the cost of stimulating additional fat generated cells while addicting you to their additives. Don't forget to include the amount of sugar found in mind-altering liquors and wine products.

You will be amazed at the number of empty calories you consume each day simply for a false sense of comfort which you believe is enhancing you emotionally. These are typically called "comfort foods".

What Happens If We Don't Change

If we don't change our perspective of life from Physical Body to Spiritual Body alignment, we simply remain stuck in a world filled with life situations that are form-based, third dimension evolved and controlled by others. We remain in the illusion of form-based reality or third dimension thinking and we continue to allow those that have used the form-based power of fear to convince us that we are victims and have no power over what we perceive as happening "to us" in daily life situations. These illusions are typically reinforced by the insanity of believing we are nothing more than the Physical Body; a body that has a beginning and an end. Life as we know it will continue on in the same low-level vibration as it has in the past and we will remain a prisoner of the mind wondering why life situations are so hard and unforgiving. At the same time, we will continue to see those that have transformed to the Spiritual Body fourth dimension reality as a greater threat to us and we will build on that fear until it cripples us into feeling even more victimized.

Or we can choose to step up to our natural state of being a Spiritual Being which we truly are and awaken to the fourth dimension of Spiritual Transformative Education where the old ego is dissolved and gone for good. Once we acknowledge who we really are the life situations, we experience in everyday earth-life or life situations will begin to change completely. Why? Because our perception will shift from old ego to new ego (True Personality) thinking, this is the catalyst for the Soul Merge process.

By merging the mind together with the Soul and allowing our Soul to guide our everyday experiences and decisions, we regain the Divine power of an energy vibration that is in constant contact and in harmony with Source Energy (God).

To assist with understanding the Divine power of vibrating at a higher level of energy or Higher Self perspective, all we need do is look in the mirror each morning and state, "I am a Spiritual Being sent here to assist in healing the Earth." Then sit in silence for a minimum of twenty minutes each morning and listen for the guidance that comes to you between your thoughts. By beginning your day in this manner, you will jump start the natural process of spiritual guidance which actually comes to you each moment throughout the day. This guidance is always available to you, but you must be vibrating at a Higher Self energy level in order to hear the messages being sent to you in each moment.

Then, at the end of each day, allow yourself the Divine gift of sitting in silence again for a minimum of twenty minutes to anchor in what you have discovered during the day and to ready yourself for the return home while your body rests overnight. Yes, the body will rest or sleep while your true Spiritual Self travels back to Source Energy to refresh the energy vibration to an even higher level of awareness. This nightly out of body experience will become second nature to you once you have merged the mind and Soul together permanently into the "True Personality" reality.

Once the Soul Merge process is complete, you will no longer feel as though you are a victim of life situations or circumstances. You will be released from the insanity of believing you are only the Physical Body and you will begin to see with a third-eye perspective or spiritual outlook on life.

Furthermore, you will begin to significantly change your perspective about what's really important to you and your life will change as never before. You will experience a state of everlasting peace within you that will guide you through even the most difficult challenges. Life will be what it has always been meant to be and you will emerge to a state of Being rather than doing.

What's Really Important to You

Beliefs either balance your current energy vibration with the limitless Divine power of the Universe or with the typical third dimension survival instinct of our current society. Whether you realize it or not, your spiritual growth is the key to an abundant and peaceful human life experience. Your life up to this point has been based upon "what's really important to you" or what you think about most. If the lessons of life have not produced the results you have been seeking, then your evolution has been stuck in the limited beliefs of the third dimension and unconscious mind which produces outcomes based upon your current mindset and inner energy vibration.

It doesn't really matter how many self-improvement books you read or courses you take if your energy vibration is not in harmony with the Divine power of the Universe you will continue to struggle in life. Abundance is not about having more, it is about appreciating what you do have now. It is about using your gifts to fulfill your Original Source Agreement and thriving to better your relationship with others by assisting them in balancing their energy vibration. It's never truly about you and what you can get out of the human experience; it's about sharing yourself fully with everyone that surrounds you daily. Your daily connections are all part of you and together you can create an experience on Earth that aligns with the agreements you all made in the Spirit of Oneness.

When you step out of the dogma of current societies controlling "what's in it for me mentality" and start to serve others for the benefit of all, you will begin to balance your own personal energy vibration without even trying. You will experience a calm and peaceful life filled with a different set of agendas and you will begin to feel the actual Divine power of the Universe that is currently stuck inside you waiting to blossom into conscious awareness. You have nothing to fear on your journey because you are being guided each step of the way. All you need do is quiet your mind and listen to the guidance that comes your way in each moment.

Start asking yourself on a daily basis, "What's really important to me?" And then, be really honest with answering why? Are your answers are all based upon your own personal gains in some manner? Or are you serving the people that surround you each day? Are you ready to release the controlling dynamics you force upon others or are you actually satisfied with your life as it is today? What do you believe about yourself? What do others believe about you? Are the two in harmony or are you living in a false sense of security brought on by old egoist thinking? If your body died today, what would your legacy look like? How have you enriched others lives while you were here? What are the greatest lessons of your life to this point? What would you change if you had the power to do so? And yes, you do have the power to change in a heartbeat!

Why do you think many people that have *near body death experiences* completely change what's important to them after the experience? As someone that has had more than one near body death experience, I can assure you it's because they have been given the gift of having direct contact with Source Energy (God) at the level of truly being conscious of the experience! No human/earthly experience even comes close to the experience of listening to the message delivered by the Highest Self during a near death experience. The people that have these transitions are meant to accomplish some far greater task while in the body then their egos allow them to realize. Therefore, if they are off track, God steps in and does a miraculous job of reminding them what they are here to accomplish. In my case, I needed more than one reminder, because I was so deeply embedded in ego's control dynamics over the false self sense of reality.

Never underestimate the Divine power that is within you; it is just waiting for the right moment to blossom! Be patient and, also, be gentle with yourself for you are a Divine Spiritual Being just waiting for the Kundalini energy to align with your true purpose to co-create for the benefit of all. If you have not as yet stepped into your true greatness, there is no need for concern; you will soon experience another opportunity to do so soon. God is patient and will allow you to take as much time as necessary to awaken to the Divine power he shares within you.

In the meantime, God will continue to send you clues if you are out of alignment with your Original Source Agreement. These clues will continue to strengthen in intensity until you finally snap out of the old ego paradigm, mind manipulation of resistance and awaken to the beauty of your Soul or Higher Self guidance.

Chapter 8 Suggestions – 9 Critical Points - Take the Path of Least Resistance

By now you should realize the most important action you can take is to place the Spiritual Body alignment in the forefront of everyday life. If you are still struggling with this, be patient with yourself and realize the old ego is still controlling you. There will be a point in your life situation that you take a long hard look at your life as you see it now and you will awaken and say, "no-more". At that time, you will truly be ready to allow the Kundalini Energy to flow through you as it was always meant to.

It may be a challenging path for you, but until you are truly ready, you will continue to doubt the Divine power of Spiritual Body alignment and you will continue to be provided with lower vibration experiences to show you the insanity of Physical Body alignment and arrogance of egoistic beliefs.

Go back now and review the 9 Critical Points or Key Ideas to assist in making the transition from Physical Body to Spiritual Body alignment:

Resistance

Resistance (reluctance) to shift from Physical Body alignment to Spiritual Body alignment is typically based upon the low vibration emotion of fear and the ego's continued control over your life. Living in fear is not in your best interest, it will only keep you imprisoned in an illusion of limitation, because what you resist will persist. Now is the time to change and take the path of least resistance so that you can experience the never-ending Joy that comes from living in Spiritual Body alignment.

Non-Resistance

The understanding that you are a Spiritual Being having a human experience is the catalyst for your spiritual enlightenment and discovering how to always live in the present moment. This allows you to increase your energy vibration slowly and feel the miraculous benefits from living in non-resistance of what is.

When you look at the big picture of your life in this manner, you understand that through non-resistance you will experience your Original Source Agreement to its fullest potential. You will have a feeling of understanding beyond that of mind; because you will be experiencing the form-based world from a non-form-based perspective of unlimited opportunity and manifestation. You live your life as the Spiritual Being you are rather than simply "being human" based upon a beginning and end. You discover how to use the gifts you were given to fulfill your true purpose for taking on human form in this world.

Live Life Without Resistance

The key to living life without resistance to what is becomes very clear once you release the old ego and replace it with the new ego (*True Personality*). The new ego or evolved ego serves the Soul or Spiritual Body alignment reality by merging the Spirit with the mind (Soul Merge) for the benefit of all. Once you make this shift to the new awareness of what is, your feelings change and you take on the new role of observer rather than victim; being the observer ultimately leads to a happy, easy and relaxed physical lifestyle.

Non-Resistance and Happiness

In most cases, the ego controls happiness based upon your limited beliefs about yourself externally. However, your true Highest Self is always there attempting to break through the barriers or smokescreen of the old ego. Therefore, if you are feeling unrest with your life, it is because you are resisting life itself. When living at a level of vibration where resistance falls away, every *thing* (external) changes and you begin to live a life filled with the Joy that flows from within you or a Higher Self perspective of life. However, the challenge with only living a life focused on external happiness as your main objective is that happiness for the most part is limited to the external elements surrounding you. Those external elements are limited by the mind's (ego's) interpretation of what life should be. This is known as living a superficial life without any depth or spiritual guidance.

Physical Benefits

The main physical benefit from living a life of non-resistance is a constant unrestricted flow of Kundalini energy through the body. This, in turn, provides contentment beyond the limited beliefs of the mind and brings about a deeper understanding of how Love channels happiness in the Physical Body reality. When Kundalini energy is flowing without blockages, the chakras of the body are relaxed, stress free and wide open. When experiencing this unrestricted flow of energy in the body, it brings about harmony with life at its deepest level of being; living life at the level of Conscious Clarity of Spiritual Body awareness.

Success Story

One of the people I Love to use as an example is one of the top known spiritual teachers in personal development today, Eckhart Tolle. One of his famous quotes is, "The realm of consciousness is much vaster than thought can grasp. When you no longer believe everything you think, you step out of thought and see clearly that the thinker is not who you are." This is a very power statement as it gets right down to the core of our belief structure and alignment with the Spiritual Body. When we release the mind from the challenges before us, we open up to a higher vibration or realm of understanding that cannot be heard from a Physical Body perspective.

A New Dimension

We have gone as far as we can with a limited, third dimension perspective of life. It has served us only to the point of realizing that something is lost in our daily life situations. The ability for us to transcend into a higher realm of reality is now in front of us and is knocking at our door of opportunity like never before. We have truly shifted into the Spiritual fourth dimension of reality. However, there are those that would rather stay stuck with old third dimension thinking and not move forward to the new reality before us. To those stuck in this limited perspective on life I can only say, "I wish you well and hope that you will soon awaken to the new unlimited Divine power within you. You are far greater than your fear-based, old ego will ever allow you to perceive yourself."

Main Benefit of Realigning

We can choose to step up to our natural state of being a Spiritual Being (which we truly are) and awaken to the fourth dimension of Spiritual Transformative Education where the old ego is dissolved and gone for good. Once we acknowledge who we really are the life situations we experience in everyday earth-life or life situations will begin to change completely. Why? Because our perception will shift from old ego to new ego thinking, this is the catalyst for the Soul Merge process. By merging the mind together with the Soul and allowing our Soul to guide our everyday experiences and decisions, we regain the Divine power of an energy vibration that is in constant contact and in harmony with Source Energy (God).

Really Important

It doesn't really matter how many self-improvement books you read or courses you take if your energy vibration is not in harmony with the Divine power of the Universe, you will continue to struggle in life. Abundance is not about having more, it is about appreciating what you do have now. It is about using your gifts to fulfill your Original Source Agreement and thriving to better your relationship with others by assisting them in balancing their energy vibration. It's never truly about you and what you can get out of the human experience; it's about sharing yourself fully with everyone that surrounds you daily. Your daily connections are all part of you and together you can create an experience on Earth that aligns with the agreements you all made in the Spirit of Oneness.

When it really comes down to it, you are far greater than your old ego will allow you to comprehend. Until you make the shift to Spiritual Body alignment, you will stay locked in a dynamic that is limited. Each day is truly a precious opportunity to assist others in bringing about change. One of the best ways to do this is to always align with self-improvement. This was clearly defined by one of the most enlightened beings to ever walk our planet. *"You must be the change you wish to see in the world."* - Mahatma Gandhi

Chapter 9

Secrets for Discovering Your Life Purpose

How Do We Define Life Purpose

Until this moment, I have been focusing on bringing awareness to the fact that you are a Spiritual Being having a human experience. I have provided examples of people that have transformed their lives completely by discovering their own truth. Furthermore, you have been provided with the analogy, *The Train of Life*™, to assist you in bringing light to your greatness.

By now you have either decided to change your Four Body System alignment to move yourself into the next phase of spiritual growth by living each day with the Spiritual Body in the forefront of everything you do or you have decided to stay stuck in the illusion that you are only the Physical Body which has a beginning and end. These are your choices and only you have the power to be the change you want to see in yourself and in the world.

If you have not advanced to Spiritual Body alignment yet, it is probably best for you to review what you have already read until you change your perspective of who you really are. If you are not aligned with the Spirit in the forefront of your daily life, the next phase of this course in Spiritual Transformative Education will be completely meaningless to you.

Now is the time to *create a quantum leap* in awareness for those of you that understand the spiritual essence of your life existence which is eternal. If you are ready to bring balance to your life and fulfill your "true destiny" or "Life Purpose", hold on to your hat, because you are about to discover the secrets to understanding why you do what you do.

In the remaining two chapters of this course (Soul Merge), you will discover how everything comes together or aligns with your True Life Purpose. You may feel overwhelmed at times, as you may be discovering aspects of yourself that are hard for the mind to believe. Simply practice patience and gentleness as the awareness unfolds from within you.

Remember, this is book or course about Spiritual Transformative Education and some aspects may be new to you. Like any other education program it is a step-by-step process where each part builds in energy as you progress.

Life Purpose is all about Spiritual Growth and the release of Kundalini Energy to fulfill your own special purpose, not about how much success you have in the limited illusion of the Physical Body or false realm of reality. *Life Purpose* is about aligning completely with your Original Source Agreement and using your gifts to assist others in achieving their *Life Purpose*. You are about to discover how the

Kundalini Energy in your body flows to provide you with the balancing essential Divine power to accomplish that which the limited Physical Body is incapable of doing on its own.

The life-force energy known as Kundalini Energy is and has always been within you. It is the essence of which you truly are and will empower you to manifest that which is necessary to achieve your *Life Purpose* far beyond that of the typical Physical Body limited perspective. The Kundalini Energy has been coiled up at the base of the spine waiting until just the right moment to begin releasing its Divine life-force power to bring you to a state of spiritual enlightenment.

If you have not yet accepted the realization that you are a Spiritual Being having a human experience, you most likely have been experiencing a great deal of emotional and possible physical pain as the powerful Kundalini Energy has been excited during the previous content of this course. This is natural as the energy excitement begins its release to remove any blockages you may have in your chakra system. The Kundalini Energy is meant to flow "unrestricted" from the base of the spine through the top of the head, thereby interconnecting with the cosmic energy of the Universe. If you are not prepared when this begins, it can be very uncomfortable as the energy begins to surge through your physical body and identify blockages. Many view this as an agitation which they cannot explain and walk away from further spiritual discovery because of their fear-based thinking reality that has been so deeply anchored in their mind.

However, if you are ready to experience the truth about your purpose for life, by all means read on. Conversely, if you are still not ready to release the fear that has held you prisoner to the demands of the old ego, then simply stop now and review that which you have already read because until it brings you to a state of awareness that will allow you to move forward in Spiritual Body alignment (to experience the Divine Joy from within), you are not ready to achieve spiritual enlightenment or understand your True Life Purpose.

Does Kundalini Release Determine Life Purpose Realization Timing

The timing for discovering your true spiritual Life Purpose is dependent on the release of the Kundalini energy in the physical body. It is important to understand that everyone has a Divine inner drive or guidance within them to be special or unique at some-thing or career path. This is driven by the release of Kundalini energy which is in direct alignment with your Original Source Agreement, not your limited, ego-driven illusion of what life should be. This release of Kundalini energy typically happens multiple times or in layers as we are being brought into alignment with our Original Source Agreement.

Kundalini, a Sanskrit word meaning "circular power", is your true evolutionary Divine life-force. This energy is stored at the base of the spine and begins its release when it is ready. Your ego has no control over when the release begins and Kundalini has its own sense of direction as well. Although the natural flow is up the spine and out the top of the head, it may change direction at any given moment to clear blockages in the physical body that are hampering its natural pathway. Because we are all currently incarnated in human form with our own free will, the Kundalini acts differently in each of us. However, there is one thing we all have in common; the Kundalini energy pushes each of us toward the evolution of spiritual enlightenment or Knowing the God-Self (Highest Self) within. When this knowledge is unlocked from the personality, a blending of the old ego and Higher Self (Soul) makes its way to the surface of reality and we change how we perceive life. I call this the Soul Merge process. When this process is complete, the new ego or evolved ego known as the *True Personality* is born out of the Kundalini energy flow.

We are each called to fulfill our Original Source Agreement, some at an early earth age and some much later on. Some of us have known since childhood that our purpose for life is greater that which we are taught in the academic-focused, earth school. There is a feeling within us that is trying to provide us with guidance, but we do not necessarily listen to this inner guidance due to all the outside influences clouding our clarity. This typically results in a life filled with many challenges and setbacks until we realize our true purpose for being here.

If you feel as though you have been experiencing life as a limited being, perhaps it is time for you to accept that there is a better way. Instead of resisting the release of Kundalini energy, perhaps it would serve you well to learn more about how your "energy vibration" influences every outcome in life. The old ego will challenge your spiritual evolution and this may even result in you doing things you are not very proud of, but don't let this deter you from stepping up to aligning with your Original Source Agreement. Change can and will come in a heartbeat when you are fully aligned spiritually!

All matter has its own energy vibration or frequency, this includes our thoughts which are form-based and manifested by the perception of our own personal story or past experiences. When the story becomes unbearable, the simple solution is to change your thoughts and manifest a different story that is in alignment with the Higher Self Kundalini energy. By making this change, you will begin to experience a higher vibration, and thus, "matter" that is vibrating at a higher energy as well. Whether you choose to believe it or not, every "thing" you experience in life is brought to you based upon being in harmony with its "matter vibration frequency". Therefore, if you consistently focus on thoughts of what you do not want, you will continue to receive that which you do not want and you will block your spiritual evolution.

If you are feeling physical blockages at any of your chakras (Chakra, a Sanskrit word meaning "wheel"), the Kundalini energy will attempt to clear these blockages so that the various chakra energy vortices can activate unrestricted. You can choose to help or hinder this process of clearing blockages. I will discuss some exercises to assist you with clearing blockages soon, but first I believe you must discover how powerful you really are.

Kundalini is sometime called Shakti which is a focused, Divine spark of life-force. We each have the power to release a given amount of Shakti to assist in clearing blockages in the chakras. This can be done on our own chakra system or performed on others requiring assistance in clearing blockages. Unfortunately, there are those that would not like you to know about this Divine natural power, mainly because they fear the possible perceived advantage this could provide you over them. Many religions are fearful of Kundalini energy or Divine authentic power being discussed openly.

One important factor you should know is that Kundalini energy releases in layers and is unlimited. Therefore, as you flow through life, you will always have another layer of this Higher Self energy available to you whenever you need a boost to overcome a challenge in life. Furthermore, each additional layer is vibrating at a higher energy vibration than the previous layer released which means you will continue to increase your overall energy vibration each time more Kundalini energy is released. Once this process begins, there is no turning back and you will see life from a totally different perspective.

How quickly the Kundalini energy releases in your system will be determined by how quickly you stop living in the past third dimension reality and become more rooted in the present moment, fourth dimension reality of your spiritual enlightenment or spiritual evolution.

How Do I Assist Others in Realizing Life Purpose

The most effective way to assist other people in realizing their Life Purpose is to follow the guidance that comes to you from within. You will naturally manifest a serendipitous plan that will all fall into place by aligning yourself with your true spiritual purpose or Original Source Agreement. As a reminder, Source Energy will send you exactly the right people at the right moment to align with your Original Source Agreement and position you in harmony with the best outcome for you and those around you.

Source Energy is always in alignment with your Original Source Agreement. All you need do is focus your attention on the Spiritual Body alignment and the rest will come to you as if by magic. Through taking action on the guidance that comes to you in silence or the higher realms of consciousness, you will be guided step by step through the process of merging the old ego with the Soul. This will bring about that which is best for you and, ultimately also, best for assisting other people with achieving their own Life Purpose.

Once you begin to focus completely on Spiritual Body harmony with Source Energy, you will discover the outcome of your actions will automatically help others with realizing their true purpose. This is one of the most difficult lessons to learn for someone that is living life within Physical Body alignment constraints. Because they do not believe in anything that is not form-based or proven by science, they are judgmental of anything other than third dimension perceived beliefs. To take a leap of faith that Source Energy is watching over them is too far of a reach for these skeptics. The amazing reality is, as your energy vibration increases, these skeptics will fall away from your circle of friends and associates while new friends and associates will miraculously appear that are in alignment with your increased vibration.

Anyone that doubts your understanding of Spiritual Body alignment is not ready to move forward in their spiritual evolution. You cannot and should not attempt to convert anyone that is not ready to move forward. Everyone moves forward at their own rate of spiritual evolution. If their current energy vibration does not allow them to see that which is naturally in front of them, it's only a matter of time until they do. Until they learn to assist in releasing their own Kundalini energy rather than resisting it, they will remain spiritually unaware of their own capabilities to co-manifest with God. Simply allow these people to fall away from your life and focus on those that are newly coming into your life.

Remember, all people that come into your life are not meant to be there for a lifetime. That does not mean you should not stay friends with them at some level of understanding. However, you will discover that the more you grow spiritually, the more you will associate with others that understand your level of consciousness. Those that do not believe in your way of life will eventually fall away by their own choice. These skeptics will simply be left behind to experience their spiritual growth at their own pace and will continue to live a life based upon what they can perceive by the five senses only.

As of the year 2012, our planet shifted "fully" into the fourth dimension of reality and those that decided to stay in the third dimension of ego-driven dogma and the limited beliefs of Physical Body alignment were left behind to find their own way. These skeptics laughed at the possibility of a spiritual shift, because they are simply not vibrating at a high enough frequency to understand the importance of spiritual evolution. Earth is now fully in alignment with the Universal Divine power of Source Energy guidance. Each of us has a choice to stay connected with this Divine energy or to slip back into the lower energy vibration of the old ego dynamics perceived by the five senses. Furthermore, if you ask yourself, why would anyone choose to slip backward? I can assure you, all your answers will be ego-driven, because Spirit would simply state – they wouldn't even have the thought.

By placing your attention on the intention of Spiritual Growth or increasing your energy vibration, such that it is in harmony with Source Energy (God) and your Original Source Agreement, you will naturally align yourself with the Divine power of Universe. By using your multi-sensory awareness as a catalyst, you will continue to grow spiritually and your life will change forever.

You will experience a deep Knowing when you are in harmony with your inner guidance; this is also a natural tool readily available to you to assist others in moving forward in realizing their true Spiritual Life Purpose.

What Comes Naturally to You

Our society is driven by others (mainly immediate family) trying to plan our purpose for us. This is not (in most cases) intentional, but they do influence our mental decision or ego when it comes to the career path we choose in life, all based upon what they believe is best for us. Then, at least from the ego's perspective, there is the all important financial gain aspect of the decision. The vast majority of western society moves into a career based upon how much money or status the career will bring. When the career choice is made only based upon these perceived important factors, they are rooted in Physical Body alignment.

In reality, we are already destined for greatness and a perfect career that is completely in alignment with our God given gifts and Original Source Agreement. However, there is only a small percentage (at least in western society) that move into a career that is based upon Spiritual Body alignment; this small percentage listen to the guidance coming from within and discover how to "feel" what is best for them. They have a true burning desire to bring their Divine gifts to full realization. By following the guidance from within, they naturally align themselves with what they Love to do and, therefore, pursue their career with determination or purpose. This is what is known as a Purpose Driven Life.

When we Love what we are doing, we bring forth Universal assistance in accomplishing what we are destined to do in life. When we are peaceful and aligned with our Highest Self guidance, everything that is meant to flow into our life arrives easy and relaxed. We feel at peace with the choices we make and all the pieces fall into place naturally. When we are truly living a Purpose Driven Life based upon what we "feel" instead of what we "think", we co-create the results of our efforts in harmony with the Universal Laws of Abundance.

The outstanding news is that it is never too late to switch paths from an ego-based career to your true destined career path. Many of you will question the ability to change careers and say, I am too old, too deeply embedded in my current career, have too many obligations rooted in my current career, will disappoint others if I change now and on and on. The list of ego-driven excuses is never-ending. Yes, it is true; it may be challenging to change careers, but not as impossible as the ego would have you believe.

If you are currently "working" in a career that is not what you Love to do or you extremely dislike the idea of going to work each day, it's definitely time to change. This does not mean simply stop what you have falsely planned for yourself, but it does mean start today to plan an escape from your current "work" and move forward with changing the outcome of your life into your true life's work.

Based upon the laws of karma, there are certain seeds you have planted that will require your attention as you shift into your true destiny. However, the shift will be managed easily if you are living a Spiritual Body alignment lifestyle. Be relaxed and energetic about fulfilling your current responsibilities; slowly phasing into your new career with Conscious Clarity of where you are headed. If you are not certain of where you are headed, there are many tools available to assist you with a career transformation.

I have found one of the best tools to use as a catalyst to assist you in discovering your true destiny is the study of numerology.

In her groundbreaking book, *"I See Your Dream Job"*, career intuitive Sue Frederick discusses the details of Greek philosopher Pythagoras's numbering system. Pythagoras is the founder of our modern numbering system. In 580 B.C., he designed a theory of numbers based upon the digits 1 through 9. Pythagoras saw that everything in the universe operated in predictable cycles and his basic units of measuring each cycle were these digits.

According to Pythagoras, each number has a meaning or vibration and by adding the numbers within your birth date and reducing them to single digits, you reveal the nature of the work you came here to do. Furthermore, when analyzing the numbers of your name, it reveals additional clarity.

Your original plan was to be an inspired participant in the great human evolutionary adventure. You encoded this road map into the vibrations of the numbers of your birth and name so that you could tap into that code whenever you needed to remember your destiny. Your greatest potential for this lifetime, your highest, most meaningful work is all clearly outlined in your name and birth date.

Today, we still use the number system Pythagoras created, but we've disregarded the core meaning that was central to his system – that each number carries a meaning or vibration that goes beyond mere quantity. In her book, "I See Your Dream Job," Sue Frederick provides a complete blueprint to reinstate the core meaning of Pythagoras's numbering system.

The code implanted in your true Spiritual or Highest Self is your roadmap to leading a Purpose Driven Life. When you begin to analyze the true nature of your own person code, you start to see how your life has been pre-destined (in alignment with your Original Source Agreement) and encoded in what comes naturally to you.

Furthermore, the more you sit in silence or live in a meditative state, the more you will reveal (feel) the vibrations of your code by releasing additional Kundalini energy with Conscious Clarity and discovering how to follow the guidance that is deeply embedded in the vibration of this unique code.

Do Positive People Keep Showing Up

When you are living in the natural flow of your Life Purpose, you find that just the right teachers show up at exactly the moment you need them the most. There's no need to figure out how it happens, just accept the idea that they will always be there waiting for you. When living with the reassurance that you will always have spiritual guidance in some manner, you begin to live a life of acceptance of what is and the belief that you are always moving closer to your ultimate purpose for being here.

Teachers come in many forms, it may be someone in person or it may be just the right book or video that seems to catch your attention at the exact moment you need to discover something to enhance spiritual awareness. This awareness comes from the multi-sensory level of consciousness, not from only the form-based beliefs of the mind.

Source Energy is always sending teachers to assist you with increasing your energy vibration. If you are not yet vibrating at a high enough frequency to hear the messages being delivered to you in silence, Source Energy will guide you toward the spoken words that are necessary for spiritual growth. I've discovered the perfect book or other material appears at preciously the right moment to enhance spiritual awareness.

Remember, Source Energy always has your back and guides you toward alignment with your Original Source Agreement. If you don't yet believe this, I again recommend that you purchase a copy of *I See Your Dream Job* by Sue Frederick because it does an excellent job of explaining how numerology is a complete road map of your life. It's an excellent addition to anyone's library that is seeking the truth about who they really are and how they arrived at their current life situation circumstances.

I remember a time when I was not living in acceptance of what is and questioned everything. In truth, I was searching for the spiritual meaning or purpose of my life. I would look at life around me and say "is this all there is?" I felt as though there was something simple I was missing. And, believe it when I tell you, it was a hard road to travel, not being in alignment spiritually. My Kundalini energy was releasing in layers to bring attention to what I was doing wrong, but I could not see what was right in front of me. I was not listening to the teachers being sent to me and I was full of ego-based thoughts that were not serving me well at all.

When I first started to align with my spiritual truth or Life Purpose, I constantly bounced back and forth from Physical Body to Spiritual Body alignment. However, each time I aligned myself with Spiritual Body in the forefront of my life, I discovered new benefits of staying connected at that level of awareness. I was growing more each year, but I was still fighting the ego's control over me. I knew deep down inside that the life I always wanted to live was somehow coded within me, but couldn't find the right teacher to explain it to me physically. I was not vibrating at a high enough frequency to hear (feel) the guidance that comes directly from Source Energy in the silence of a meditative state of mind.

As my Kundalini energy released more and more, I soon became aware of the right teachers showing up in many different forms. I began to realize that I have complete control over my spiritual awareness and have the Divine gifts to fulfill my true spiritual Life Purpose. I began to live what I felt was a spiritual Purpose Driven Life rooted in spiritual awareness and I released all that was holding me back from growing spiritually. To guide me deeper into Self, all the right people and seminars started showing up directly; indirectly, all the best books, videos and articles started showing up again as if by magic. I became a true spiritual seeker and let the guidance from within continue to move me in the direction I "thought" I should go. What I didn't realize is how tricky old ego can be and how much control I was still allowing old ego to have over me.

What I learned thus far was incredibly valuable information, but I was still not completely converted into a Purpose Driven Life in alignment with my Original Source Agreement and Spiritual Body alignment. Although, the bouncing back and forth from Physical Body alignment to Spiritual Body alignment was considerably less frequent, I still did not fully understand or spiritually accept that I had total control over my life. I was living a half-truth that was not completely in alignment with a True Purpose Driven Life.

Then again, as if by magic, the perfect teacher showed up with just the right words to pull all the pieces together for me. That teacher was the before mentioned Sue Frederick and her book, *I See Your Dream Job.* I discovered through numerology and by analyzing my birth date and name with Sue Frederick's guidance that all the life lessons I had experienced thus far were directly in alignment with the valuable information provided in this small book. It was the

Numbering system that Pythagoras created way back in 580 B.C. that helped me to dissolve "old ego" once and for all.

The mind received the confirmation it needed to transcend to new ego or *True Personality*. A higher level of awareness anchored into my subconscious and all my dreams began to manifest in spiritual abundance. *This was truly my turning point and I've never looked back since.*

How Do Dreams Assist in Defining Life Purpose

Once you discover the secret to the Soul Merge process, your thinking changes from an "I can't do it mentality" to a "nothing's impossible mentality". What this actually means is that you have transcended the realm of limited possibilities or the old third dimension into the new world of limitless possibility of the fourth dimension. Your beliefs evolve to the state of spiritual awareness where you begin to co-create with the universe. You allow your mind to bring new creative energy to life situations which you had thought impossible in the past. You begin to tap into the creative force of the Universe and expand your dreams into reality.

Once the Spiritual Body is vibrating at an adequate frequency to hear the messages being delivered at the level of limitless thinking, we become aware of how our dreams influence us from a spiritual level of understanding. It's in the period of *theta dream state* sleep that you hear (feel) that which you are naturally in alignment with and your Original Source Agreement will be visualized.

Most people don't place much attention on dreams and what they represent. People typically make false statements like, "It was only a dream and doesn't mean anything." We've been programmed to think this way since childhood. Most of us have had the experience of "vivid dreaming" or dreams as real as life, as children or even as adults. When this happens, our parents or partners come to our rescue and tell us, "It was only a dream; don't pay any attention to it." Well, that may be true to a certain extent, but if you dig deeper into the level of *theta dream state*, you may be surprised at what you learn.

In truth, our dreams are part of an elaborate cosmic reality, one that guides us into the current life situation reality at a higher level of understanding. Every*thing* that you see with the eyes once came from a dream state. It is through the creative power of dreams and imagination that we create the material things that were once only a thought in the middle of the night. Whether it's a formula for mapping DNA by a chemist to the engineer creating new products to be used in everyday life, they all come from a state of awareness that transcends the old ego's limited imagination. The greatest thinkers of all time discovered how to transcend the old ego and have also been the greatest dreamers. They had the ability to tap into the higher vibrations of creativity found at the levels of lower brain wave activity and escalated spiritual energy vibration. In short, the gap between the thoughts!

Ask any Engineer when they feel the most inspired to create new products. It's typically when the mind is at peace and able to check in to the creative juices that naturally flow through us during theta brain activity. The level of awareness that is necessary to tap into the creative forces of the universe comes in the moments of silence or the gap between the thoughts. It's at this level, we are In-Spirit and can use the spiritual guidance found during the spiritually enhanced theta dream state to manifest new form-based evolutionary products.

Have you ever gone to bed at night with a challenge on your mind that required a quick solution? And then, suddenly the solution arrives in the middle of the night when all is still or silent. These solutions typically arrive during theta brain activity or when the mind is quieted from the excessive thoughts of the day. You experience the solution with Conscious Clarity and awaken with a perfect solution. However, most people simply drift back to sleep while thinking, "I'll write this down in the morning." Then, in the morning, they can't remember the exact details of their middle of the night revelation.

I recommend you begin the habit of placing a notebook next to your bed at night, so that you can record your theta dream state experiences immediately. This is especially useful for those of you that are required to consciously create solutions to complex challenges experienced in work-related endeavors. It's truly amazing the way the brain is capable of slowing down to tap into the creative juices of the Universe. What's even more incredible, you can train yourself to reach this level of creativity while in a meditative state anytime during the day as well.

As an evolving human race, we are just beginning to understand how the brain functions. We know from a scientific standpoint that we only actively use a small portion of our brain power. However, with the onset of new awareness from a spiritual level, we are now making breakthroughs at every level of academic education. What we once thought as impossible is now possible and our imagination (dream state) is opening up to a level of conscious awareness as never before. We are moving from only limited academic education to Spiritual Transformative Education and learning how to blend the two together for the betterment of humanity.

What if you were now working in a career that is completely in alignment with your Original Source Agreement? Do you believe it would hard for you to co-create with God during theta brain activity or when the body is in a meditative state? Do you believe you would be in a position to bring about change to the world in some manner? Do you believe it would be possible for you to standout from the crowd as an expert in your field of work? Do you believe the gifts you came here with would evolve into something special that would be beyond the thinking of typical third dimension man? Do you believe at the level of fourth dimension spiritual reality you are capable of tapping into the higher levels of understanding?

It is your choice to stay locked in the old paradigm of experiencing life only from a five-sensory perception which is found in the third dimension of reality. Or you can jump on board the fast train with new unlimited possibilities of transcending into awareness of the Spiritual Being you truly are. The dream state of awareness is more than just a passing experience found only when the body is at rest. The dream state can be experienced when the body is fully awake, as well. However, it takes an open mind, an open heart and a willingness to at least consider that there is another way to bring about the changes that are so blatantly necessary for humanity to evolve to the next level of understanding.

Be a dreamer and experience life as you were always meant to - by co-creating with God and living your True Life Purpose. Pay attention to your dreams and the small stuff; it will always serve your best interest and ground you deeply within your True Life Purpose.

Is Purpose Always Easy

Once you become aligned with your purpose, the simple truth about life is that it becomes easy and relaxed. This is mainly due to the fact that you no longer follow anyone else's idea of what is best for you. Once you discover your true purpose, you learn to follow your intuition without question and the path becomes a sacred blessing filled with gratitude and joy. It's not that you no longer experience challenges, it's simply that you dismiss them as negatives and see good in everything. You become aware that all that happens around you has a definite purpose and realize challenges are just part of the whole life experience or the process. This shift in perception or attitude is very rewarding as you now put the spiritual realm or solution-based cosmic powers of the Universe to work for you.

Spiritual Body or Physical Body alignment in the forefront of perception determines the resultant affect of life circumstances. If you spend a few moments to go back and review Chapter 2, Section 12, you may finally understand the importance of how your Four Body System is aligned. That session discusses the different outcome scenarios of a life situation experience. You quickly realize that when a challenge arises in any life situation, only the ego can bring about negativity and ONLY through Physical Body alignment perception.

When you accept that you are the script writer of your own eternal life, you understand that everything happening around you was orchestrated by you directly prior to birth of the Physical Body. You understand that there is a reason each event unfolds at exactly the moment it needs to and you start searching for good in every present moment.

If you are living life from a fourth dimension standpoint, with Spiritual Body alignment guiding your actions, you become aware of the positive influence you make in this world. You not only have the power to choose your perceived outlook on life, you also have the Divine power to limit the affect life situations have on your energy vibration. And, by staying spiritually aligned or vibrating at a higher energy, you stand a much better chance of a positive outcome during any challenge, because you never see the glass as half empty.

You stay empowered to find good in everything. You make decisions differently by keeping your energy vibration set point to the level of intuitive Higher Self awareness as your lowest set point.

Four Body System alignments are very interesting as they determine what vibration your overall body is operating at. Therefore, the higher the operating vibration, the lesser the affect or the perception of the story it has on the ego. At the higher frequencies of energy vibration, when challenges arise, you simply have more options available to you for solutions than you do at the lower frequencies of vibration. Therefore, when your energy vibration is higher, a challenge becomes little more than a minor disturbance or a trigger to bring awareness to a life situation. This is true because you are experiencing the challenge as an observer rather than as a victim. Furthermore, the more you take the observer position, the easier it becomes to stay relaxed and at peace; when you are relaxed and at peace, you never take anything personally, because you no longer make up false stories in your mind.

By living with Spiritual Body alignment in the forefront of your life, with each step up or increase of energy vibration, you discover how to deal with challenges more spiritually. You learn to accept *what is* in the present moment and dismiss the stories of the old ego. Therefore, if you view a challenge from this awareness, you step outside the role of victim and experience the challenge as an observer. This allows you to co-create a solution with the cosmic powers of the Universe and you remain calm or easy and relaxed in the face of perceived adversity.

Always remember, no one has the power to make you upset about any life situation. It's necessary for you to drop your energy vibration down to the vibration level of fear for you to experience the sufferer level of reality. In truth, everyone has the Divine power to experience life easy and relaxed, so why not simply choose to be just that, "easy and relaxed" when challenges arise? Remember, whether or not your life is easy and relaxed is always up to you. You have a choice; you can take the spiritual high road of acceptance and enlightenment or the self-induced egoistic low road of emotional pain and victimization.

All emotional pain is based upon the story you are creating in your mind. It's never your Spiritual Self that causes pain. The Spirit or True Self is always naturally joyous and does not even understand what emotional pain is; let that awareness sink in for a few moments. Yes, there are certainly sad moments (drops in energy) experienced in everyday life situations, but they typically come from a state of non-acceptance to *what is* or periods of grief which brings about yet another level of spiritual awareness.

Even when experiencing grief as during the physical death of a loved one, we can learn to be joyous and celebrate the Spirit leaving the body to find its way back home. Western society has the most difficult time recognizing this Spiritual moment as being a positive lifetime event. In truth, when the Spirit is ready or has fulfilled its purpose for being here, it will naturally leave the Physical Body at its own destined time. It can be very difficult to watch a loved one transition back to pure Spirit, however, the more we educate ourselves in Spiritual Transformative Education, the easier it becomes when the time is at hand.

As a Western culture, we are just beginning to tap into the Divine natural beauty regarding the death of the body and the transition home of the Spirit. However, we are now learning to accept that all form-based and human creation has a beginning and end; only the Spiritual Body is eternal.

At the *Universal Level* of the *Conscious Clarity Energy Process*™, you will discover the Spiritual Body actually consists of four sublevels of energy vibration which are explained at the level of Knowing in the *Consciously Embrace Your True Personality* book in this series. However, for now, we will continue to focus on the Soul Merge and beginning stages of the *True Personality* level of awareness until you are vibrating at a higher energy level to accept that Knowing is your guiding light.

Can Anyone Assist Me with Acceptance of Challenges

Each and every one of us has others in our lifetime with perceived power to influence our decisions. Yes, we each have trusted partners and relationships, people of reliance to provide input when challenges arise. However, when it comes right down to it, no one is able to assist us with actually accepting challenges. When challenges arise, you can think about deeply rooted beliefs or ask for input from others, but if you are living a spiritual life, your choices always come from a place that is within you, never from outside you. The higher vibration level of acceptance to *what is* can only be experienced through your own connection with Source Energy, God, Highest Self, God-Self or whatever other name you give to the Divine power of the Universe.

If you are merely mentally making choices based upon only the input from those outside of you, you are giving away your life-force power to the decisions others are making for you. You are not living your true purpose, because true purpose is always aligned with Highest Self and makes decisions from an open heart, never the ego. When you allow others to unfold your life for you, your experiences in life are limited to what others have deemed as best for you. This is the mentality of the follower or victim because you never take full responsibility for your own life and the ego provides the "out" to blame others if your experience in life turns out to be something less than you anticipated for yourself.

When you truly understand who you are and that you have the Divine power within to bring about acceptance to *what is*, you will be on your way to unfolding the secrets of enlightenment. You will make better choices because you will be in harmony with the Universal intelligence that guides you from within. You are a Divine Spiritual Being which is housed in a temporary physical body for the purpose of healing that which is out of alignment with your Original Source Agreement or True Life Plan. When you truly know this, the way you arrive at decisions changes from external to internal at the level of inspirational harmony with God.

Once you are living a spiritually realized life, when you experience a challenge, you become conscious that every challenge comes to either teach you something that you do not know, something you have forgotten about yourself or something you are here to assist someone else with – but always from a spiritual level of understanding. This may sound contradictory to the previous statement about no one being capable of assisting us with acceptance of challenges. However, acceptance to *what is* has to do with how you personally deal with or your perception of a challenge, not the challenge itself.

Challenges come from a higher power than your human self; therefore, it is simply not possible for another human being to provide a long-term solution. As you become more aware of the way you manifest every life situation into reality, you will discover the challenge at hand is only there to bring awareness to something you are to achieve by being in harmony with your Original Source Agreement or True Life Plan.

Yes, all challenges are part of your own healing process and must be experienced if you are to stay in alignment with the script you wrote for yourself in harmony with Source Energy or God. The old saying, "God never gives you more than you can handle", is absolutely true. And, if you look at life from that viewpoint, you take full responsibility for what you have already agreed to accomplish while here in this Earth school.

Spend a few moments reflecting on a past challenge, which at the time, you thought was unbearable. It could be something from your childhood or perhaps an early adult experience. We all have something in our background that we can reflect on, something which has not as yet been fully resolved. Have you ever said, "If I knew then what I know now, I would have done that differently?" Of course, you have. In truth, if you did not experience full closure or complete resolution during a past challenge, you are probably still experiencing it at some level today. Furthermore, by not fully accepting it for *what is* (and no more or less than *what is*), you have not grown fully from the experience. You are probably triggered by the unresolved challenge every time a similar challenge arises in the present moment.

Typically, you do not bring about change or growth without first going through some type of challenge which, of course, requires a solution. And, in reality, there is a spiritual solution to every challenge. This may seem like a totally new perception for some of you. However, the depth of it can be quickly seen from a spiritual point of view. From a spiritual level of understanding, everything in life is exactly as it is supposed to be. Therefore, all answers or solutions are already there waiting for the question to be asked. Furthermore, at the higher levels of energy vibration, there is always a spiritual solution to every challenge and the first part of any solution is acceptance of *what is* based upon this reality.

Consciously, a better way to view a challenge when it arises is to ask a question and, if you are not receiving the answer you would like, "ask a better question". Instead of asking, "God, why me?" ask "God, what would you have me learn from this challenge or God, could you provide me with your wisdom to resolve this situation." You see, by taking the spiritual path of acceptance to *what is*, you never need to have a conversation with anyone other than Source Energy when a challenge arises. The answers or solutions are all there waiting for you to ask!

What Is the Purpose of Non-Thought Reality

The purpose of non-thought reality is to allow you to hear the messages being delivered to you by Source Energy in the space or gaps between the thoughts. It's during these periods of silence that your Higher Self can hear this direct connection so that you can review and adjust your actions to align fully with your Original Source Agreement or Life Plan purpose reality.

If you recall, the average person has over 60,000 thoughts each day and most of them are the same cluttered or returning thoughts from the previous day. Therefore, when you learn to quiet the mind and place less importance on the recurring unnecessary thoughts which have need of so much of your time, your life changes and you evolve to a much higher state of consciousness. It's by eliminating the unconscious thoughts which are falsely anchored in your mind that you allow yourself to connect fully with the spiritual guidance found in the silent meditative state of mind or higher consciousness reality.

From a Spiritual perspective, the old saying, "You don't know what you don't know", really means you can't hear the communication coming through from outside your realm of consciousness if you are constantly thinking without feeling the Knowing. In spiritual reality, the natural balanced state of the mind is only used after receiving the messages (*Knowing*) brought forth in the gaps between the thoughts. Unfortunately, beginning at infancy, we are programmed or "brain-washed" by well-meaning people into believing that our mind/old ego has control over our life. This is by far the greatest hoax of all time and most of the population still buys into this hallucination as if it were real. You may be one of them, but only because you are not vibrating at a high enough frequency (as yet) to fully grasp the importance of eliminating that limited perspective of consciousness – but have faith you will awaken soon!

Once you complete the Soul Merge process and the *True Personality* is fully embedded into your perception of reality, you will better understand how the shift from Physical Body alignment to Spiritual Body alignment evolves once you are fully connected with Source Energy guidance. As your energy vibration increases, so does your awareness of the Divine power housed within the Highest Self. Therefore, it is imperative that you start paying close attention to eliminating thoughts that do not serve your overall Well Being or hold you back from experiencing the higher levels of reality. The importance of "getting out of your head and getting into your heart or Spirit" will become more and more enlightening for you as you slowly shift. You will discover that your Life Purpose evolves as you balance the categories in your life situation in harmony with your Higher Self reality.

The secret to balancing the awareness of your True Life Purpose is by aligning with others that have made the choice to shift fully into the fourth and higher dimensions of reality. The fourth dimension is the Spiritual realm of reality and it is only in that reality that you will understand who you really are and the Divine power that you share in harmony with Source Energy. When you fully understand that you co-create everything that comes into your life situation with Source Energy's guidance in one way or another, you will then discover how Universal intelligence compliments the formation of the *True Personality* (new ego) and the way you perceive life.

The *True Personality* listens to guidance from the Highest Self or God-Self and then takes action to bring about change. The *True Personality* realizes it is the servant of the heart and it becomes child like in its understanding of reality. It carries no baggage with it or never relies on past circumstances to create present moment experiences. The present moment is simply *what is* and accepted as the only reality. Sit in silence with that reality for a few moments and let the vibration of its energy anchor into your new awareness. The past never ever equals the future!

In truth, you are the innocence or essence of the Love you bring to the world and you have the Divine spark within you to fully develop your visions into reality. Only you know when your True Life Purpose will be revealed fully. It is your responsibility to consciously continue evolving into the person you are meant to be *for the sake of your Highest Self evolution and for the betterment of humanity, as well.*

How Can I Share My Life Purpose

It is your Spiritual Destiny to share your Life Purpose with everyone you meet in this Earth school. That is the purpose you are here, to share your gifts with all of humanity at the level of Oneness. If you are living life from the Spiritual Body perspective merged with the Mental Body and have been consciously starting to release Kundalini Energy into the world, you will are well on your way to living the Purpose Driven Life you are destined to experience. Your *True Personality* is now fully intact and you are ready to create another quantum leap in spiritual growth.

However, if you are still stuck in only the Physical realm of reality, now would be a good time to review your understanding or perceived reason for being here. Your belief system is holding your prisoner to the material aspects of life and you are not experiencing it to your full potential. If you feel like something is missing in your life, then you are part of the unknowing population living on the surface of life situations which is based upon that which will one day cease to exist.

If you are not consciously aware of your purpose and the gifts provided to make your journey easy, relaxed and loving, you are currently living only a half-life and are missing out on what brings about pure Divine Joy. It's through the power of Divine Love, Peace and Light that we are able to feel our vibration level increase as we harmonize with the Universe Intelligence to move us forward.

Spiritual Transformative Education transcends what is currently being taught in typical academic education systems. Our academic school system has done us a disservice by removing Spiritual education from curriculums and insisting that separation of Spiritual and Physical realities is best for us. This is all part of the egoistic control mechanism put in place and guided by fear based mortal paradigms. We are not building a full life if we are only schooled in the form-based necessities of the Earth school. Our leaders have failed us and it is time to reevaluate what is happening in the world.

We are further separated by what money can buy with respect to the physical comforts of life and have allowed this separation to be controlled by just one-percent of the world's population. We have individuals and huge corporation's hording riches and blatantly manipulating the world economic system to their advantage. This is all being perpetuated while watching millions starve all over the world, including here in America. However, many of these so called elite personalities are spiritually poor. They lack the wisdom and knowledge that transcends the physical realm of reality and will leave all their so called riches behind when the Spirit is ready to leave the body.

If we are to evolve as Spiritual Beings, we cannot continue to stand by or be a part of this old school or third dimension reality. Now is the time for us to step up to the opportunity at hand in the fourth dimension – to bring about massive change in the way we treat one another as human beings. Each one of us has a God-given gift which we are to develop for the betterment of humanity, not merely for our own personal satisfaction. These gifts always align with our true spiritual purpose for being here. When we are in alignment with this purpose, we are unlimited in the amount of good we can do for society or the world as a whole.

If the leaders of the Earth school are not enhancing our education systems to create unity between the Spiritual Body and Physical Body in the academic system, then we must seek out Spiritual Transformative Education ourselves to again bring about wholeness to our Highest Self reality. Only then will we begin to live the true life that was intended for us or in alignment with our Original Source Agreement.

We begin to share our purpose fully by leading a Spiritual life in the fourth dimension. By merging our Soul with the mind, we can transcend adversity and manifest a Purpose Driven Life. The more we utilize our unique gifts and realize our purpose, the more we align with the Divine powers of the Universe to bring about evolution to the level of Oneness.

If you are still following this course of discovery, you are well on your way to bringing about your alignment of True Self and fulfilling your true purpose for being here on Earth – Congratulations!

Is True Life Purpose Self-Aligning

Living you True Life Purpose is always self-aligning which means it is your natural state of Being to stay aligned with your Original Source Agreement. When you are truly dedicated to using your God-given gifts to their full potential, your choices in life change and your reality begins to align with the feelings of Love, Peace and Light in Gratitude to move you forward every step the way.

We have been so brainwashed by society into fitting in with the rest of the crowd that we have forgotten the value we give to the world by aligning with our True Life Purpose for the benefit of all. We have forgotten that we can co-create with God-Self a life that is blessed with Love, happiness and joy in each moment. We have allowed ourselves to be duped into the false belief that we are only our Physical Body and that the Spiritual Body is nothing more than a figment of our imagination. This is because the ego cannot understand that which is formless and will do everything in its power to trick you into believing that only form-based material things are real.

Most people still blindly walk through life situations by experiencing only its form-based reality. Because the idea of being something greater than what is seen in the mirror brings them so much uncertainty or fear that they settle for what the limited six-senses have to offer. However, the Spiritual Body is much more powerful than the ego and always brings about questions for the mind to ponder.

During times of mind-altering, negative feelings, people are brought back to the question, "Is this all there is to life?" This question always comes from a higher state of consciousness, a state that vibrates at a higher level of energy to bring you out of unconscious survival mode of the ego. It comes from the Self-aligning conscious idea that you can live a life "on purpose".

If you feel like you are stuck in your current life situation, it is because you lack faith in what you are truly capable of as a Spiritual Being. Your gifts are the key to escaping that which does not serve your Life Purpose in the false reality you have built for yourself. You can escape from the life you falsely brought to yourself by simply listening to the messages being sent to you from Higher Self. If you are still struggling with the choices you make, perhaps it is time to truly surrender to a Spirit-driven lifestyle. Yes, it can be and actually is that easy. You can change your perception of life by simply aligning fully with the gifts you brought with you when you entered the Physical Body.

If you choose to change your current life situation to a Spiritual Body alignment lifestyle, there will be many people that question your decision. You will be outcast from many form-based false perceptions of what life is meant to be. It will be necessary to let limited form-based friendships fall away. You will be misunderstood by many of the people you once thought of as true friends and you will undoubtedly be looked upon as someone that is losing touch with reality.

Therefore, the next time someone tells you that you are "out of your mind", just say thank you because being out of your mind is exactly where all the secrets to the Universe are waiting for you. You will be labeled by many as someone that lives life with "rose-colored glasses" and you will for the first time in your life see the truth pertaining to what is really important.

You will no longer be part of the old ego-based dogma of reality and you will become consciously aware of the false sense of freedom that is brought on by fear-based society and material possessions. You will become a truly inspirational force for good and you will see the true light of every moment as it is truly meant to be experienced. The life you once thought was so important will simply fall away and it will be replaced by a life of daily joy, harmony and light!

Once you exterminate the old ego once and for all, your daily perception of reality will Self-align in each moment without any "doing" on your part and you will experience the joy of bringing your gifts to light. You will live life from a completely different understanding which is in alignment with God's True Life Purpose for you and you will no longer be concerned with what others believe is best for you. All judgment will fall away; you will simply accept everyone as they are. From a neutral position of Love, Peace and Light, you will see or experience the best of everyone. The best part of all of this awareness is that it will happen without any "doing" on your behalf.

In the next section, you will discover a few simple actions to take to step up your energy vibration to the point where you will no longer require approval from people living in the third dimension to live a happy life. It's your script, so why would give up your Divine power to live your life based upon someone else's approval? If True Life Purpose is Self-aligning, do you really believe some other form-based entity has any control over it or of you in true reality?

Do I Need To Consciously Live Life Purpose Everyday

In order to bring harmony, peace, spiritual abundance and a fully realized purpose to life, you must consciously live your human life from a higher state of awareness each day. To create this type of life, you must *daily immerse yourself* in the studies of Spiritual Transformative Education without question. If you are not living your life with the Spiritual Body in the forefront of your daily life situations, you will continue to be a prisoner to the spiritually illiterate leaders of our current society and their limited, controlling beliefs.

Let me make this really simple for you; Spiritual Transformative Education is simply a means to the end. Once you are *daily immersing yourself* in this higher state of education, you no longer allow yourself to be a prisoner to the old third dimension paradox that holds you back from living life as the Spiritual Being you truly are. If you are to fully experience your True Life Purpose, you must fully evolve to the state of Being you are destined for. If you do not comprehend the Higher Self messages that are coming to you at the higher energy vibrations, you cannot expect to live a life in harmony with the higher vibrations of the Universe. You old ego simply will not allow it because it has control of you at the lower energy vibration levels. Ego realizes that living life with the Spiritually Body in the forefront of your life situations means the death of itself and the rebirth of True Self!

To determine where you stand, spend some time reviewing Illustration B from a "Spiritual perspective" to gain a better understanding of how the Four Body System alignment affects your understanding of daily reality and ultimately your *Life Purpose*. The sure magnitude of *The Train of Life™* analogy is far too complex for the old ego living in the third dimension to comprehend; therefore, it may be necessary for you to stretch your belief system to a "dream" state of Being and allow that which you do not understand to be guided by a "what if this were true mentality" for comprehension purposes.

From a totally Spiritual perspective, a fully-realized human being has only two components, the Engineer (new ego or *True Personality* perspective) moving the Spirit forward to a constantly higher energy vibration and the Conductor (Higher Self) which provides guidance or the route which is in alignment or harmony with True Life Purpose. It's really that simple; the Spirit speaks, the Personality listens and then follows direction without question. Free will is now naturally aligned with Spiritual guidance and "Life Situation Drama" or the "Green Boxcars" of *The Train of Life™* are non-existent. Therefore, there is a "linear progression" of *Life Plan* or *Original Source Agreement* fueled by Atomic Fuel as pointed out in Illustration E.

At the lower energy vibration of Physical Body alignment, there are multiple influences or "Green Boxcars" separating the Engineer and Conductor which cause a smokescreen or clouded reality of life. If you examine the boxcars closely, you will notice the figures (people) in them are glowing brightly at first and progressively spiral into a lower energy vibration as society influences their free will choices during life situations. These dark influencers are typically well-meaning people that are simply lost when it comes to spiritual awareness. They are stuck in their own third dimension reality and have not been exposed to Spiritual Transformative Education, mainly because the current society leaders are also lost in third dimension reality and try to suppress spiritual enlightenment because of their spiritual ignorance.

However, at any given moment in your life, you have the opportunity to escape the limited, third dimension lifestyle by simply stepping through the "White Light Doorway" to Higher Self energy levels associated with Spiritual Transformative Education. Once you decide to put Spiritual Body alignment in the forefront of your daily life, you begin listening to the inner spiritual guidance available to you and you release all of the "boxcar" influencers that hold you back from evolving to your True Self consciousness level of understanding.

Now that humanity is fully evolving into a fourth dimension world, we are beginning to see a shift in the education system. Although, typical academic universities still only offer that which fuels the ego, we are now seeing more and more Spiritual Transformative Education Centers like the *Conscious Clarity Center, Inc.* being created throughout the world.

If you are to fulfill your true destiny for being here, it is time for you to take steps to consciously align with your True Life Purpose and immerse yourself in it fully each day.

Can Other People Define My Life Purpose

We as a collective society have been misrepresented when it comes to Spiritual Transformative Education. The influence has always been on academics that fuel the ego and the truth about who we really are has been set aside to say the least. We have been manipulated by a society that is, for the most part, spiritually ignorant. The idea of Love, Peace and Light in the mainstream of our education system has been withheld from us at the highest levels of government leadership or should I say lack of authentic leadership.

Our natural state of Being (Love) has been replaced by a domain of fear-based dogma, which is perpetuated by a capitalist mentality to control and acquire more and more material possessions in an effort to become happy. It is no surprise that we have accepted this false truth about happiness, as it is driven into our brains as the way to live life to its fullest. The problem with that belief is it equals living a half-life filled with what money can buy which allows only the smallest percentage of our planet to have a life where putting food on the table is never an issue.

This society has stripped us of our true essence by convincing us that our God-given gifts are not enough to live a joyous life. We are so brainwashed into believing our government leaders have all the answers that we simply allow them to slowly by surely strip any resemblance of spirituality from all government controlled establishments.

Our current government education system is stripping away all of our much needed spiritual rights and replacing them with mandates that won't even allow the word God to be used in classrooms or government-controlled buildings. However, in conflict with the rules we are supposed to follow, when an oath is to be taken whether in a courtroom or the swearing in of a President, the Bible is used and the words "So help me God" at part of the process. It's no wonder that we are confused.

The separation of Spiritual Body alignment with the Physical Body is controlled even more so by mega corporations. The very idea that we are something more than our physical bodies is being eradicated from government-controlled society and the mega corporations that continually use manipulative tactics to control us. The rules (laws) that are written are typically mandated to serve only the wealthiest or big business corporations which are manipulated by strong arm lobbyists.

453

The mass consciousness of the world is fueled by old ego low energy dynamics and we are manipulated into believing the world leaders know what they are doing. The sad truth is that most of the leaders in our governments are vibrating at frequency that is spiritually ignorant. And yet, they are supported as if they have some superhuman power that most others in society lack.

The way the current political system is structured, the typical representatives in governmental power were put their mainly because of the amount of money they were able to raise for campaigning; not for their innate God-given gifts which are meant for the betterment of humanity as a whole. These are the same people that are responsible for leading our world into the next phase of evolution, but they establish rules and one-sided laws that do not benefit the Divine plan for Oneness.

My question for you is will you continue to be defined by someone else's idea of what you should be or are you ready, willing and able to stand tall in the face of overwhelming odds to make a change? Are you willing to bring spiritual understanding into your household and community so that your children will become fully-realized human beings? Are you willing to set an example for the next generation by stepping up to the challenge of re-aligning yourself with Spiritual Body awareness and begin acting like the Spiritual Being you truly are? Our future is in the hands of our next generation and it is up to us to again bring Spiritual Transformative Education into the limelight.

It's actually not possible for anyone to hold you back from Spiritual Transformative Education. If our government won't provide the necessary resources in our current education system, then we need to step outside the box and research the many new non-profit organizations that provide spiritual education for ourselves. When it comes right down to it, it is your own choice to give power to someone that wants to define your purpose for you. Whether they do it out of spiritual ignorance or because they blatantly want to control you is irrelevant, the result is the same!

We have been held prisoners by the spiritually ignorant leaders of our communities for far too long now. It is every person's right to develop into the fully functional Spiritual Being they are meant to be.

Now that we are living in the fourth dimension of reality, the separation is slowly being seen for what it really is. However, we have a long way to go to bring in new government leaders that actually understand how important their spiritual energy vibration is with respect to benefiting humanity as a whole. Having said that, you must realize it is not your fault if you have not evolved beyond the old ego dominance to this point. It is the fault of the spiritually ignorant system that has brainwashed you into believing you are less than you truly are.

Most people think they are up against such great odds to make a change into bringing Spiritual Body alignment in the forefront of their daily lives that they simply roll over and allow the separation to continue. They are more fearful of change than they are of staying in the controlled or limited lifestyle they currently live. This is especially true if they have been living a lifestyle where they have amassed great wealth from a material standpoint; then they hoard their fortunes for fear of losing what they worked so hard for. The idea of possibly sharing what they have acquired with anyone, including family, is fueled by the old ego's daily fear of losing what they believe makes them special. They truly believe they are more important because of their financial status and hoard their possessions as if they are more important than their true identity as Spiritual Beings. Then, they wonder why they are so unhappy!

Many political people caught up in the never-ending, greed-based cycle of old ego's control are simply not aware of their true gifts. They have been living their life based upon a false reality and inside they are dying a painful death based upon complete spiritual ignorance. They falsely believe they are in control of everything surrounding them and they use people as chess pieces in the game of life situation dominance. Many of these people believe their influence on society has the power to override God's given right to a spiritual education. They use their political influence to keep God out of our classrooms, government establishments and any other area they deem necessary to control and keep us spiritual uninformed.

In other words, they do not want you to be aware of your True Life Purpose for being here and how it can be discovered through Spiritual Transformative Education.

Who Really Cares if I Live My Life Purpose

Who really cares if we are spiritually ignorant as a society and never actually fully live our Life Purpose? The answer is really quite simple, *"Ever single human being on the planet should care because it is the Higher Self that prevents the destructive path that so many take in life by living unconsciously."* The sole purpose for your existence is to share Love, Peace and Light with each individual that crosses your path through the wisdom of living a Purpose Driven Life.

By aligning with your Higher Self energies that focus on the greater good of all, you stay connected with Source Energy at the highest level of creation and you fulfill your ultimate destiny. Conversely, living a life of fear which is typically brought on through misinterpretation of your true identity, you limit what you can consciously co-create with the Universal power of Love, Peace and Light.

However, when we live a spiritual life Knowing that every action we take has a direct or indirect affect on the other people within our immediate family, community, nation, and ultimately, the world, we begin to consciously understand the importance of living life fully from a spiritual perspective. On the other hand, if we only live a physical body reality or a "half life" that is being touted as what's best for us by leaders that don't have a clue of what Spiritual Transformative Education does to develop a fully embodied person, we lose touch with why we are here in the first place.

We should all stand up and shout as loudly as possible –

"We need more spiritual awareness brought into our current education system!"

In truth, we should be living fully developed lives based upon a combined academic and spiritual education system that provides us the tools we need to become and stay connected with our Original Source Agreement for the benefit of everyone, not just our own selfish perceived egoist wants. It's true that the academic side of human life requires reading, writing and mathematics to bring about the form-based materials required to live in the physical realm of life. However, even more so we need to be fueled daily with the Higher Self power of Spiritual Transformative Education so that we stay connected with the highest level of understanding to evolve fully as a planet.

The vast majority of the world's population believes they were born when the physical body was brought into existence by their parents; when in fact, we were all born at exactly the same moment of cosmic time. As Spiritual Beings, we have no beginning and will have no end. We are eternal and literally chose the parents that united together to bring form-based existence to a body for us to use, a body that has a being and will eventually have an end. We arrived into the body on a wave of Love at the exact moment of physical conception. The physical body is merely the host for the Spiritual Being that we truly are. This is why it is so important for us to live life with the Spiritual Body alignment in the forefront of our daily existence.

For some of you, this may be the moment (in form-based reality) that you question the validity of this spiritual wisdom being presented to you. It may be difficult for your old ego (mind) to grasp the magnitude of what has just been stated. If this is the case for you, perhaps you have not yet experienced the opening of the Kundalini energies which awaken the spiritual reality of your true life existence. If not, simply be patient with your lower self, as we all open up to the Divine wisdom in our own timeframe and not before.

However, you must understand that acceptance of Knowing you are a Spiritual Being having one of many human experiences is necessary for you to move on to the *Universal Level* of the *Conscious Clarity Energy Process*™ later on in this spiritual experience. The next phase of this spiritual education is focused on developing the sublevels of the Spiritual Body. As you progress, you will find the complexity of the awareness becomes more detailed and at the same time easier to digest as you release the old ego once and for all.

For now, try to comprehend that by living the half life of only an academic education, it brings limitation to your existence and aligns you with a life dictated by others. Your True Life Purpose is not revealed at this level of understanding and you will remain in a state of limbo, held back by limited beliefs and false realities or a mind-altered Life Purpose at best. It's a half life that only allows that which is deemed real by society and the governing leaders of your small outside community which controls your daily life situation existence. And, the true reality is that it is a choice your make unconsciously; even though deep within yourself, you know the truth about who you really are and your purpose for being here.

Once you accept the great responsibility of Knowing you are a Spiritual Being, you can never turn back to the old ego paradigm of limitation. Even if you attempt to deny your true Higher Self reality, the Kundalini energy flowing through your body will continue to awaken you. In many ways, it can be very painful to attempt to block this energy flow. If you close your chakras due to lingering fearful limited beliefs, you may experience physical pain in the areas blocked by these limited beliefs. It will begin as tightness in the body at the chakra center that is blocked and will bring about emotional anxiety, negative thinking and eventually deep depression. You won't know what is happening to you, but you will sense that there is something deeply wrong. That something wrong is merely the fact that you are denying your true spiritual existence. Furthermore, until you realign yourself, you will continue to go through this self-inflicted hell on earth.

Fortunately, once the transition back to Spiritual Body awareness begins through the discipline of Spiritual Transitional Education, there will always be a spark of certainty and light operating in the background of your daily life situations which will bring you back to questioning the validity of only a Physical Body existence.

Once your energy level expands to the Divine power of the Universe and the Highest Self guidance starts to again flow through your body, your life will never be the same. Whether you choose to move forward or not is irrelevant because the Spiritual Body reality of your existence is far more powerful than your old ego self. You will be constantly guided by the inner self-realization of who you truly are and begin to understand that no form-based reality has the power to block the spiritual Divine power for long.

You have a choice, you can move forward with a blissful life fulfilling your True Life Purpose which is in alignment with your Original Source Agreement or you will live with the consequences of denying the truth and wisdom of the Universe.

What Happens If I Never Realize My Life Purpose

Each of us has unique gifts that reside within us that are meant to be shared fully with the world. These gifts are meant to be used for the betterment of all, not just our own egoistic wants which are based upon a false reality and separation. Our choices in life are either in alignment with these gifts which in turn leads to a life in harmony with what our creator intended for us or our choices move us away from our gifts and result in a life where we feel victimized by those around us. If we don't develop our gifts to their full potential, we sacrifice the Divine life we are meant to have and only touch the surface of the power given to us to make a difference this world.

As Spiritual Beings, we are provided with the Divine power of the Universe to use in harmony with others to achieve that which is in alignment with our Original Source Agreement or the Life Plan for accomplishing miraculous things for humanity. However, if we never realize our true purpose for being here in this incarnation, we will simply be reincarnated over and over until we finally reach our true potential. No one is prey to anyone else in this world, we only perceive ourselves as victims when we are not in harmony with the Universe or Source Energy (God). God does not understand the term victim because every life situation has a purpose and is in alignment with his Master Plan for all of us. If you believe you can change God's plan for you, you are mistaken.

In the infinite wisdom of the Universe, there are many different names for God or the power greater than us as individuals. Whether we call this power God, Source Energy, the Divine Power, Allah, Deity, Great Spirit or Supreme Power all have one thing in common; they all relate to the Highest Self energy that is found in each and every one of us. Therefore, if this power is within each of us, we each have the ability to co-create with God at the level of Oneness. We are all part of God and this Divine presence is always available to guide us into fulfilling our Life Purpose to its fullest potential. Therefore, if we are not fulfilling our Life Purpose, we are making the choice to live something other than a True Purpose Driven Life. We are choosing to listen to the ego (edging God out = EGO) rather than God's Divine guidance.

Typically, religious people pray to God when they need something or have a great burden they want released from a life situation. This is a one-sided conversation asking for something and expecting a prayer to be answered.

However, those that truly understand the Spiritual Oneness of our essence, live life in a meditative state that is constantly in direct communication with God. The conversation was never intended to be one-sided in the spiritual reality of life. We have the gifts within us that allow us to speak directly with God and actually hear what God has to say in response to every life situation; all we need do is communicate in silence and the guidance will reveal itself. Unfortunately, most people choose to ignore this natural flow of communication or this limitless conversation. They were taught to believe they are less than God and that God should be placed on a pedestal to be worshiped as a deity beyond daily life reality. This is merely man's interpretation and was never God's intention.

God's intention is for us to be in constant contact with the God-Self or Highest Self within us, so that we can truly understand how to develop and utilize our gifts to their fullest potential for the benefit of humanity as a whole. We are not meant to be separated by religious beliefs, man-made rules or other egoistic mandates that hold us prisoner to a limited system of beliefs and stifle's the unique gifts we have to offer.

Each one of us has a unique Divine Life Purpose that is in harmony with the *God's Master Plan* for humanity. If you choose to play small and only follow what is mandated for you by society, don't complain. And, don't ever feel like a victim as it is your choice to stay locked in smallness and those around you are never to blame.

If you are to become conscious of your true purpose for being here, you must step up your energy vibration to a level of understanding that is in harmony with your Original Source Agreement. You must participate in daily conversations with God and you must align with the authentic power that is within you. The solutions to all unrest in the world are found in the meditative state of Being. And, the more time you spend living in a meditative state, the more your gifts will be revealed to you for the purpose of living life fully and sharing your gifts with the world.

"Meditation is not some "thing" you do; it is the experience of Being that which you are." – Terry Swejkoski

It's always possible to change the direction you are traveling on your journey, but you need to step up and take charge of your life at the level of Highest Self awareness if you are to fulfill your Life Purpose and bring about change to this world.

Always remember, we each have our own individual Life Purpose that is unique to us, but at the same time always in alignment with the collective power of Oneness. God resides in all of us and, if God is within us, we are all part of God, the creative power of the Universe and are not separated by anything other than our false beliefs of whom we think we really are.

Your old ego will continue to hold you prisoner by manipulating you into believing you are a victim of the world but, in reality, the only one that is capable of victimizing you - the egoistic self.

Shift your Four Body System alignment today and bring light to your life by living life with the Spiritual Body in the forefront of everything you want to co-create with God. Use your unique gifts to assist others in having a better life and get out of your head while you still have the chance to change. Realize your true purpose by opening your heart fully and by being grateful for the gifts you have at your disposal. Discover your gifts in a meditative state of mind and then share them with the world and you will have a better life; a life filled with Love, Peace and Light. I promise you this is a Universal Truth.

You are Loved beyond ego's comprehension, but you will never experience that Love fully, until you release the mind which holds you prisoner and surrender yourself fully to the limitless power of Universal Love!

Chapter 9 Suggestions – Key Tips – Secrets for Discovering Your Life Purpose

Discovering your Life Purpose is the ultimate goal for bringing inner spiritual joy to the forefront of your daily life situations. The magic formula for bringing you into alignment with your Original Source Agreement or Life Purpose is based upon your individual beliefs and unique gifts which are to be utilized "outside" your old ego-driven patterns. For some, it may take multiple reincarnations to increase their energy vibration to a level where their True Life Purpose is finally brought to light. However, this can all change in a heartbeat as well, but it requires listening to the Divine guidance within you. Guided by Source Energy, you can achieve anything that you can visualize, combined with Conscious Clarity of mind in alignment with *True Personality*!

You will be very close to realizing your True Life Purpose once you acknowledge who you truly are and start living with Spiritual Body alignment in the forefront of your life. Although, the magic formula for coming into alignment with your True Life Purpose is unique for every individual, there are some key steps to remember when seeking your renewed spiritual awareness:

- Spiritual Body Alignment – This is the most important step of all and will always keep you on track without weakness of the old ego getting in the way. You must first bring Spiritual Body alignment into the forefront of everything you plan to achieve in harmony with your True Life Purpose.

- Meditative State of Being – Consciously live your life situations from a meditative state of Being which means staying consciously connected with Source Energy at all times. You will receive messages from Source Energy constantly throughout the day, however, your energy vibration must be high enough for you to hear the guidance being delivered through you. This will be difficult at first, but eventually you will live in a constant state of awareness. Begin by sitting in a meditative state for 20 minutes, twice daily (preferably early morning and late at night) to begin hearing the messages from Source Energy. This will enhance your awareness of the spiritual guidance that is always coming through you.

- Visualization – Once you are conscious of the messages coming from Source Energy, begin a two-way conversation in the silence of this higher energy vibration. Feel the guidance coming through you and visualize the Original Source Agreement you signed up for before coming into this re-embodiment. One of the best ways to do this is to sit in silence just before bedtime and then allow yourself to drift off into a dream state with your vision in your mind as your body goes into the rest realm of reality. The brain wave patterns during this form body sleep mode will align with your inner awareness and you will clearly see the vision of your true purpose as it begins to unfold. Remember to keep a pad of paper next to you bed, so that you can write down visions as they come to you during the night. You will naturally discover how to train yourself to awaken your physical body when the dream state vibration is in alignment with your True Life Purpose.

- Live Easy and Relaxed – Live a stress-free life, easy and relaxed, should always be your motto! If you feel your Physical Body beginning to experience stressful energy patterns, immediately stop what you are doing and breathe new higher energy, white Light into the life situation you are involved in during the present moment. You can always remove yourself from the happenings around you. There is always a way to excuse yourself from mind-induced stressful life situations. Keep the vision of your True Life Purpose in the forefront of every life situation and stay focused on the deep spiritual core of reality. Keep your vision easy and relaxed. You will learn to stay in a constant state of inner peace even when life situations happening around you attempt to challenge that peace. Remember, you have to "do" stress and stress is all in the mind, not the Spiritual Being of which you are.

- Fearless Existence – Live a Purpose Driven Life without fear coming into your reality. Always listen to the inner guidance and remove fear from your life permanently by consciously staying aligned with the True Life Purpose you witness in your visualizations. There will always be those that challenge you new way of living, simply dismiss them in a loving manner and bring your vision into the focus of your daily reality. When you live life without the constant fear-based dogma of the old ego controlling your life, you are capable of creating quantum leaps into the creative process of Universal awareness. There is truly nothing to fear. Fear is merely an illusion of the old ego attempting to control you with form-based limitations. Never underestimate the Divine Highest Self power within you. You are more powerful than your limited thinking will ever allow you to comprehend. You must rise above this old ego mind manipulation. In other words - get out of your head!

- Conscious Awareness of What Is – Your Physical Body lifestyle has a direct influence on the outcome of your achievements in your lifetime, especially at low levels of energy vibration. Use your vessel wisely and keep toxins to a minimum so that you do not pollute your energy vibration with the limitations of the old egoist patterns. If you are a heavy drinker or drug user … STOP IT … because it will not serve you well. Get help for your physical addictions so that you can hear the higher vibration messages coming to you from Source Energy. When you are in a heavy, low vibration or unconscious state brought on by substance abuse, you bring the

Physical Body below the life situations solutions available to you at higher states of energy vibration. And keep in mind, the first step in any addiction recovery is conscious awareness that you have a challenge, which is greater than your low egoistic energy vibration or limited perspective. Connect with spiritual groups that can help you see the true reality of what you are "doing" to limit your life experience.

- Acceptance of What Is – What is today is not necessary what will be tomorrow … your past never equals your future! Accept what is today, but do not allow it to hold you prisoner from your vision or True Life Purpose. No matter what your life situation may be at this current moment, once you accept what is, there is always a white Light of awareness at the end of the tunnel. Once you bring acceptance to what is, you allow yourself to bring higher energy solutions to the surface that will assist you in bettering your life. Acknowledge your mistakes (mis-steps) and open your heart fully to the creative powers of the Universe. You have the Divine power within you to bring about change in every life situation. The first step to making a change is to understand "what is" by accepting the illusion for what it is and moving past it. Never make any form-based reality more than what it is. By constantly living with the Spiritual Body in the forefront of your life situations, you will never again get caught up on the manipulation of the old ego. Accept what currently is and then move forward with your life by allowing the inner Highest Self guidance to bring conscious awareness to the next steps you must take to fulfill your True Life Purpose.

You are a Spiritual Being having a human experience; therefore, you are more powerful than your old ego or mind will allow you to comprehend. When you look in the mirror, see beyond the body that houses your Spiritual Self.

Through the development of Spiritual Mindfulness or Spiritual Transformative Education, you will grow to be far more powerful than your current limited egoistic beliefs. The secret is to keep old ego under Spiritual Body control and to enhance the development of your new ego or higher vibration *True Personality*. By living this lifestyle, you will become conscious of your True Life Purpose before you know it!

Chapter 10

Secrets to Staying Out of Old Ego's Control

What Will Old Ego Do To Control Me

The purpose of this next phase of the *Conscious Clarity Energy Process™* is to anchor-in the Soul Merged personality or *True Personality* into your reality. By bringing awareness to the intellectual tricks the "old ego" will play on you, it is my hope you will understand you are not, as yet, completely free of old ego's control tactics.

The old ego will continue to do anything it can in an effort to keep you disconnected from your Spiritual Self. The old ego knows that both it and your true Highest Self cannot exist at exactly the same moment in Earth-based reality which ultimately means the complete death of the "old ego". Therefore, like a rat trapped in a corner, it will continue to fight its way out every time it perceives spiritual weakness in you. It will use every small challenge of your life situations to latch on to control of your decisions and attempt to prove, from a physical body or intellectual standpoint, that the whole Spiritual Body reality is nothing more than wishful thinking. However, wishful thinking is again nothing more than one of old ego's form-based tricks to manipulate you without you even realizing it is happening.

It is imperative that you stay connected with Highest Self on a daily basis; otherwise old ego will slip back into your consciousness and bring your energy vibration down. Old ego knows there is a transition period many people are going through as limited beliefs change into the reality of limitless awareness and what is actually possible for you to achieve in your human life situation reality. This correlates with the Spiritual Transition that took place in the year 2012 into the fourth dimension where many people evolved and all the rest were left behind to continue to live in third dimension reality. During this transition, your energy will seem to be on a roller coaster ride as you have never experienced before. Old ego will pull out all the little tricks it has to confuse you and question your new beliefs which are being anchored into your enhanced reality of what life can be.

Furthermore, until you truly understand and *believe without question* that you are the co-creator with God of your Original Source Agreement, you will experience mistakes (mis-steps) along the way. When these mistakes occur do not be discouraged, be gentle and patient with your human side of Self. Remember, you are not your mind or thoughts; you are beyond both and are the Spiritual Being behind the creation of the mind and thoughts. The spiritual energy within your body is a constant or always with you and can easily overpower any irrational unspiritual thoughts or emotions the old ego brings to the surface which are typically driven by life situations happening around you. Be conscious of these at all times.

Always keep in mind, anything that you experience with your five sensor perception is part of the illusion of lower energy vibrations and can be changed in a heartbeat. In truth, your Highest Self is always in charge of manifesting your next experience into reality on this journey called life. By staying connected with this Highest Self or the Source Energy within you (meaning the true Spiritual Self), you will be able to overpower any life challenge that comes your way. And never forget, each challenge that occurs around you is meant to teach you a lesson and cannot harm you in anyway. Therefore, all challenges in life situations are temporary and already have solutions in the spiritual realm which are ready to overcome the limited reality of old ego. Ultimately, all challenges are nothing more than opportunities to grow more spiritually into the *True Personality* you are meant to be!

As your Higher Self awareness or consciousness becomes more evolved, you will begin to see how the whole synchronicity of life unfolds before you. As your beliefs in the Divine powers of the Universe evolve, you will find yourself laughing about the small form-based happenings around you which controlled you in the past. You will see how clever old ego can be and you will awaken to the reality of how you were so easily manipulated. Rest assured, as your energy vibration continues to increase, you will become more conscious of the Divine power within you to overcome and learn from any challenge the old ego creates. Life is meant to always be blissful; it is the old ego or the limited thoughts of uncertainty that hold you prisoner to everything else which is all form-based dogma.

To overcome the limited form-based thoughts and emotions about your True Self, be certain to sit in a meditative state of Being for 20 minutes, twice daily, until your energy vibration increases. This one new habit will take you beyond the limited beliefs you have about yourself and bring your energy vibration up to a level where any*thing* that seemed like a life threatening reality before will shift and be viewed as a minor nuisance.

As the co-creator of your own reality, you are responsible for staying consciously connected with Source Energy and the Divine powers of the Universe. By keeping your Spiritual Body aligned with the unlimited potential or the highest energy realms of reality, you will experience a surge in energy vibration within the physical body. Then, you will begin to understand, it is possible for you to manifest your visions which are in complete alignment or harmony with your Original Source Agreement.

Source Energy (God) is always within you and surrounding you at the same present moment in cosmic reality. However, it is your free will choice to bring this awareness to the forefront of your daily life situation reality or you can continue to stay a prisoner of the lower energy vibrations found in the third dimension and your old egoist mind.

In truth, the *True Personality* (new ego) transcends any false realities the old ego anchored into the low energy vibration reality of a mind-based or limited life perception; this transition is what is typically known as "Being born again".

How Do I Stay Out of Old Ego Control Dynamics

The most powerful tool you have right now to stay out of old ego control dynamics is living life from a meditative state of Being perspective. The knowledge you have available to you at any moment is locked in the silence of meditation, where you can always check in to "feel" whether or not you are on the right path. Notice, I did not say check in to "think about" whether or not you are on the right path.

At this point in knowledge, many of you have not increased your energy vibration enough to truly know the difference between what you think and what you feel. I will discuss this in greater detail, but for now, just have faith that meditation is the key to unlocking the truth within you. Through meditation you can access the place where the most accurate information is stored to bring true consciousness to light. Always remember this extremely important Spiritual Truth:

"Meditation is not some "thing" you do; it is the experience of Being that which you are." – Terry Swejkoski

The old ego will constantly bombard you with false truths or excuses as to why you do not have "time" to live in a meditative state of Being. This is nothing more than another control tactic used by the old ego to keep you from experiencing your True Self at the highest level of energy vibration available to you while in human form. The old ego knows that you will evolve or achieve an enhanced rate of spiritual enlightenment and Knowing if you live your life from a meditative state of Being. Therefore, it will do whatever it can to keep you from the silence and experiencing life at this much higher level of awareness. The old ego wants you to live in a state of agitation and conflict which is just the opposite of what you are.

Rest assured, as you continue to raise your energy vibration through the practice of living in silence or non-thought, you will ultimately experience the blissful state where you are in a constant meditative state of Being. The experience of observing other peoples agitation will no longer have an effect on your inner peace. Right now, this may be too much of a reach for you to comprehend because the old ego is still bombarding you with thoughts to the contrary. However, soon (if you have not already evolved there), you will discover you truly can increase your energy vibration to a level of awareness where all thought influenced by outside sources fails away in an instant and the guidance from Source Energy is consciously revealed to you more frequently and with a much higher level of understanding. Be patient with yourself because even though we all have the power to experience this state of awareness, your current belief system and energy vibration may not have expanded sufficiently enough yet so that you truly understand this reality.

As an example, let me share the difference between prayer and meditation with you. This is where many religions have blocked the flow of energy due to the dogma or rules established by man which separate the truth of Oneness. This can be compared in energy vibration to night or day awareness. Prayer is typically a one-sided conversation where you are sitting in darkness or a lower energy field asking a deity, which you perceive outside yourself, for assistance with resolving some problem that is perceived by the mind. However, when you meditate or live life from a meditative state of Being and Oneness, you have a direct two way conversation with Source Energy which is a much higher energy vibration. It is the light which resonates at the level of Oneness within all of us collectively. At this level of awareness, all solutions to any perceived "mind based problems" are already resolved and waiting to be discovered.

Therefore, you simply converse with Source Energy to expand the awareness to reveal the solution to any challenge at hand. All fear is eliminated, because you already "know" there is a solution available to you. This is living life at the level of Oneness or Knowing which is discussed in detail at the *Universal Level* of the *Conscious Clarity Energy Process*™.

This level of Oneness or Knowing is where you are completely transformed to an energy level that is in harmony with the Source Energy power within you. This is the level of breath where you naturally breathe in the Highest Self energy vibration with each breath you take. This is the level of Conscious Clarity of who you truly are and is the ultimate goal for this study course. Once you expand to this level of harmony with the Universe, all doubt will be eliminated from your mind and you will be in harmony with Spiritual Body alignment in the forefront of your daily existence. Many egoistic people call this living life through "rose-colored glasses"; I call it the experience of living life in nirvana or heaven on Earth. Whereas, all fear is eliminated from your life situations and you flow through life with the Grace of God!

When you ultimately transform to this energy level of existence, you will no longer experience the old ego's tricks because you will be vibrating a level of energy where old ego has surrendered completely (death of the old ego). This is what the *Conscious Clarity Energy Process*™ or Spiritual Transformative Education is all about; the process of taking you to the level of energy vibration where you consciously live life in harmony with your Original Source Agreement and the Divine powers of the Universe without fear, personified through Love and reverence for life itself!

What Are Some of Old Ego's Tricks

Fear is the ultimate tool of the old ego and is used for one main purpose - to keep you from loving yourself. If you do not Love yourself, you will not feel the Love the people in your life have for you. Don't think about that spiritual truth, simply sit with it in silence and allow you true Higher Self to bring this to light for you. Just relax and bring the feeling of Love to your awareness. Ask yourself whether or not you feel Loved. If you do not feel Loved, it's probably a challenge for your old ego to be loving to others.

If you spend most of your day in negativity and are drawn to a state of feeling tired of living with the perceived burdens surrounding you, more likely than not, old ego is alive and gaining strength. As you go deeper into your mind-induced illusion of how bad your life is, you will become self-absorbed in the belief that you are a victim of society or at least have been wronged by someone close to you. If you are heading down this road of self-destruction, you need to seek psychological medical attention immediately. You are psychologically experiencing a mind-altering psychosis that will lead you to actions that will not serve you well.

If you are experiencing overwhelming feelings of anxiety and depression due to your perception of what is happening around you, your brain has been altered in some physical manner (possibly by drugs or alcohol) to where you are not no able to think rationally. If this is the case, the possibility of you being able to comprehend the spiritual realm of whom you truly are is limited; you should temporarily pause this course immediately until you are psychologically well because the purpose of this course is to awaken the true Spiritual Being you are from within. If you are not of a frame of mind to even consider there may be a better spiritual way to live your life, you are probably not in a positioned to understand what this course truly has to offer. This course is for spiritual seekers ready to move in the direction of enlightenment not for those that are deeply locked into the illusion of victimization.

Once you have recovered from this dis-ease of the mind, it would be a good idea to go back and review what you have read thus far in this course. You will, more likely than not, be more open to the content and will view it from a different light or energy vibration. By doing so, you will be in a better psychological position to prepare for the move forward to the *Universal Level* of the *Conscious Clarity Energy Process™* where it is necessary for you to have a higher energy vibration understanding or true reverence for life.

The old ego mind control tactics or tricks can be very convincing to someone that feels like their life is out of control and spiraling downward. This is one of the most powerful negative tools the old ego uses to convince you that life is not worth living. It will manipulate every life situation and completely alter the true reality into something that makes you feel victimized at every turn. You will think everything is happening to you and that you are being controlled by or manipulated by everyone around you. When in truth, the only manipulation that is happening is all in your egoistic mind which is operating at an extremely low energy vibration.

We have all been programmed by society to live a life of negativity where the media continues to focus on the negativity of what we do to one another, which is a fear-based reality. The main motivation of this type of negative stimulus is to keep you locked in fear and feeling as though you are not in control of our own life. This is delusional thinking in its raw form. In truth, that which is outside you cannot harm you in any way unless you surrender to the false reality of thinking you are not in control of your own life. When you give away your spiritual power and allow others to dominate your thinking through manipulation the old ego does a happy dance. So don't go there – stop it right now!

Furthermore, if you are using mind-altering toxic substances that bring your energy vibration down below the fear so that you do not have to deal with life circumstances, seek psychological medical assistance immediately. You are most likely chemically addicted to your toxic substance of choice which will alter your capability of making realistic choices that serve your overall Well Being in a positive way. The old ego wants you to continue using addictive substances because the addictive substances allow the pain of your self-induced false reality to appear real once the addictive substance effects subside. It's just one more form of manipulation to keep you locked in fear.

Fear will always cripple you from making choices that will move you forward in life. This false reality will keep you from what you are truly here to accomplish in life. You will live your life in survival mode and not feel like taking the necessary steps that will ultimately eliminate the old ego. Fear will bring you to a false state of reality where you trust no one other than your false self. You will question and misinterpret those around you and you will convince yourself you are the only one that is right. You will walk a path of slow self-destruction until you awaken to the reality that you are not only your body or the thoughts and emotional trauma you bring to yourself.

The True Self, which is the Spiritual Self and *True Personality*, knows fear is a manipulation of the old ego (mind) in an effort to keep you trapped or a prisoner to its control tactics. What you believe in, your mind will insist is very real to you even if it is far from the truth.

In truth, the mind was never meant to be the controlling power of your human experience on Earth. It was only meant to serve your Spiritual Self in living at a lower life form called the Physical Body. This Physical Body is not who you really are, nor is it the only source for experiencing this lifetime to its fullest potential.

Your life is the spark of energy vibration which is in harmony with Source Energy or God. Once you realize this most important truth, you will be able to comprehend what old ego is attempted to do in an effort to control your life. The death of the old ego does not mean the death of the Physical Body. It means the removal of the mind's false sense of reality which manipulates you into believing you are less than you truly are. The old ego does not want you to believe you are a Spiritual Being having a human experience.

The old ego will attempt to separate you from your true God-given gifts that are meant to keep you a life which is in harmony with the Universe. It will attempt to keep you as far away from Spiritual Body alignment as possible. It will attempt to keep your thinking focused on what you don't want in life or how bad your life appears to be. And, the harsh reality is that you always get what you think about most; you manifest it into the illusion of what you perceive as truth. However, somewhere deep within you, there is a spark of light that knows there is something better. This spark of light will allow you to transcend the low energy vibrations of a completely mental or Physical Body state of living.

What you believe about yourself will drive your actions and those actions will be the catalyst for the life experiences you manifest into reality. If you truly believe you are only the Physical Body and that the Spiritual Body is merely an illusion or some force outside yourself, you will continue to spiral downward into an abyss of negativity and false truths. You will continue to believe you are the victim of the life situations surrounding you and you will dismiss anything that attempts to help you break free from this mind altering delusional state of existence.

The simple truth is you can break free from this old ego manipulated delusion at any time. You have the spiritual capability to move your life forward by utilizing the gifts given to you. You can remove yourself from the rat race or old ego-driven life by opening your heart fully to the presence of Source Energy within you. You can train yourself to bring about change in your life and to experience a life filled with Love, Peace and Light in each moment. Once you discover the capability to change your thoughts, which will ultimately change your experience, you will be on your way to recovery and the life you were always meant to experience will appear as easily as if you are floating on a cloud.

Is All Thought Based Upon Old Ego

One of the misconceptions of many spiritual seekers is that all thought is of the old ego. When in reality, only lower vibration thought is of the old ego or thought from a Physical Body alignment. The mind games at this lower energy vibration attempt to maneuver the personality of the spiritual seeker off path. Therefore, it is wise to watch your thoughts closely with conscious awareness!

The old mind games of ego are easy to recognize because they take you away from Love, Peace and Light! – Terry Swejkoski

When we are off path or not experiencing life from a spiritual perspective, we allow our energy vibration to fall below the threshold of Conscious Clarity and go back to the lower energy vibration that brings negativity into the forefront of daily life situations. Once you realize this and the mind games the old ego brings to your lower self, you will spend less time at this lower energy vibration. Your awareness will make a shift and you spend most of your day at the Soul Merge level of awareness where you are in constant connection with Source Energy. At this level of reality, I guarantee it will be possible to use your mind to train your brain with the new belief system you have brought to light - The Spiritual Body Alignment System!

If you recall, in the year 2012, there was much discussion about whether or not the world (as most know it in the third dimension) was going to end. Because we were still vibrating at the mass-consciousness level of beginners or spiritually ignorant, most of the world was waiting for some terrible doomsday event to occur. When in fact, what actually happened is those ready to release the fear-driven aspects of their reality, simply made a shift to fully integrate into the fourth dimension. It was during this shift from the lower vibrations of old ego reality that the *True Personality* was born for those making the transition.

Those seekers planning for the completion of this harmonic convergence on Earth were simply brought to a state of energy vibration whereas they will never fall below their true Conscious Clarity ever again. The beauty of this transition is it came in silently without the knowledge of most of the planet. Those that were on the spiritual seeker path to enhance their overall Well Being understood what was happening. However, those that doubted the truth about themselves (most of humanity) anchored their old egos' deeper into the subconscious mind and manifested a barrier or smokescreen (created by the old ego) to keep them trapped in third dimension reality. They made fun of those that had the privilege of breaking out of their spiritual ignorance. They simply continued to live their lives with the idea that they were in control of their lifetime from a Physical Body alignment perspective – how arrogant!

The lower energy mentality for the people that choose to stay locked in old ego's control was not powerful enough for them to rise above their limited thinking. They stay, even to this day, locked in the false reality that they are only the Physical Body and they mock anyone that has discovered their true essence. They continue to live their lifetime as victims, in judgment of others and bring more of the same lower energy vibration dogma into their limited perception of life each day.

However, those of you that have made the transition into the fourth dimension are now experiencing life from a totally new perspective, a life with Spiritual Body in the forefront of every moment. A life that is not only limitless, but also alive with anticipation about the beauty of Love experienced at the level of Knowing. You are now feeling the Divine guidance Source Energy is bringing to you and you are no longer fearful of what life has in store for you. You have transcended the prison of the old ego's manipulating mind and are now beginning to see how marvelous your lifetime can be when your true Higher Self is in charge your actions. The mind is now becoming accustomed to serving the true Spiritual Self or

Spiritual Body and you are feeling, perhaps for the first time, the amazing possibilities that are unfolding before you.

When the Spiritual Body is in the forefront of your life, there is no fear of what is to come, ever. The daily experience is perceived as a blessing and acceptance of "what is" brings more inner peace to your existence. You awaken each morning, not only refreshed spiritually, but the body is no longer heavy with the affects of the poisons you once ingested in the physical body. You have stopped relying on mind-numbing toxins (including alcohol and drugs) to change your perception of life and you have risen above the lower level vibrations of survival and victimization.

Once the *True Personality* is fully integrated into your life, you will no longer require any thoughts of negativity to appease the old ego. You will truly live life from a higher level of energy vibration and you will feel the presence of God within you and come to realize your true authentic power with Conscious Clarity. The new thoughts you have will always be of a big picture reality and you will spend more time engaged in the Spiritual Transformative Education aspects of living life with the Spiritual Body in the forefront of each present moment.

Once you have started to transition into Higher Self reality, it becomes easier to manifest that which is in alignment with your Original Source Agreement into your life. The acceptance found in the fourth dimension of life is like taking a breath of fresh air after being locked in a toxic space for years. You finally discover what it means to take a fresh breath and you breathe in the sweet fragrance of a life filled with Love, Peace and Light!

How Do I Monitor Old Ego from a Higher Self Perspective

Even though by now, you have raised your energy vibration above the limited beliefs of the old ego, you will continue to experience glimpses of the old ego dogma attempting to trick you. When this happens, simply smile and tell yourself, "I see what you are trying to do and I will no longer be your prisoner." You can accomplish this purging of old ego dogma at any moment by simply closing your eyes and feeling the fresh breath of Spirit coming into your awareness. By stepping into awareness or inspired (In-Spirit), it is nearly impossible for the mistakes (mis-steps) of old ego to reoccur in your life. Because you are now vibrating at a level above old ego perception, you are no longer in harmony with negative things happening in your life.

You are now beginning to experience the energy vibration of Knowing. This level of vibration is in alignment with acceptance and allows you to transcend the old ego control tactics. And, when you keep your energy vibration at the level of acceptance, the messages from Highest Self or Source Energy can be heard loudly and clearly in every moment – this is Conscious Clarity. By simply quieting your mind, accepting what is and breathing in the energy vibration of Knowing, you can transcend any challenge that comes your way.

Because you are now living life with the Spiritual Body in the forefront of you daily experiences, your perception of what is happening around you improves or increases in energy vibration each moment.

By now, you have discovered you are not only the Physical Body and you have increased your energy vibration to a point where you are no longer in alignment with negativity and judgment. Your new positive outlook on life has been enhanced to the state of Being rather than doing. Living life at this state of awareness allows you to easily see when old ego is attempting to regain control over your everyday experiences and decisions. Your actions are inspired by Highest Self guidance and you are in harmony with the Divine laws of the Universe or Cosmic Intelligence.

The more your energy vibration increases, the more it will become natural for you to monitor the old ego control tactics. As time goes by, you will immediately feel when old ego is attempting to trick you. You will feel a blockage occurring in your chakra system way before the affect of old ego thinking reduces your energy vibration. This is why it is so very important to continuously monitor your chakra system and to continue the practice of sitting in a meditative state of Being. By checking in with your Higher Self in this manner, you will always remain one step ahead of old ego's clever ways of tricking you into the obedience of a confused or cluttered mind.

Your level of acceptance to "what is" in life is equally proportionate to the level of success you have at keeping old ego out of your life situations. The old ego can be very clever, especially during times when the Higher Self is still purging old ego control dynamics from your life. Therefore, until you are totally in alignment with your Original Source Agreement, it will be necessary for you to monitor your feelings closely. This is the key to monitoring old ego's forms of manipulation. The feelings you are experiencing in this very moment are the catalyst for taking complete control over your life situations and the death of the old ego forever.

There is one powerful certainty in life - until you are completely focused on living a spiritual life and understanding the truth of which you really are, you will stay prisoner to the old ego's control dynamics. Until you purge the old ego from your life permanently, you will be continually reminded that you are not vibrating at the level of Knowing that you are a Spiritual Being. Your mind will play the victim role and you will stay stuck in the third dimension of reality where you believe things are happening "to you" rather than around you.

What you feel in any moment is the road map for your path in life. If you have not purged the victim mentality from your life, you are not ready to move forward.

Pay close attention to your feelings and continue bringing the light of the Highest Self energy into your life. Never forget that you are more than just the Physical Body. By staying aligned with Spiritual Body in the forefront of your journey, you will experience the joy that emulates from within you at the level of Knowing. Once you are certain of your true Higher Self awareness, you will see the spiritual light shine through you with every choice you make in life situations. Always remember; only you have the power to continually increase your energy vibration to the next level of understanding.

You can continue your journey driven by the cleverness of the old ego control dynamics and stay prisoner to a life of victimization beliefs. Or you can choose to live a spiritually Purpose Driven Life that is in alignment with Source Energy and the abundance of the Universe!

Ask yourself, this moment and be honest, what is the current life-force or energy vibration that drives your journey each day?

Does Old Ego Drive Me

In the last section, you were asked to answer a simple question, "What is the current life-force or energy that drives your journey each day?" There are only two answers to that question, the first "Spirit drives me" and the second "ego drives me." It is really that simple, but the mind wants more of an explanation than that because it has been trained to distract you from realizing the true essence of your Highest Self existence. You have been tricked by egoist society to believe you or only "old ego" or the Physical Body. Therefore, you have been living a false truth that limits you and keeps a well-maintained smokescreen or fog surrounding you to keep you locked in old ego's control mechanism.

Take a few moments to review all of the illustrations again to ensure you fully remember the various aspects involved with the Categories of Life and the relevant energies driving them.

The purpose of the *Conscious Clarity Energy Process™* is to begin the journey of Spiritual Transformative Education, to awaken you to the truth about your limitless possibilities in life.

You are being prepared to step beyond the limited beliefs of old ego and to step above those controllers surrounding you that would want to keep you a prisoner of our current societal control tactics. You are being guided to learn how to raise your energy vibration or internal life-force to a level of awareness where you will no longer live life in fear. The fear that has been perpetuated over us on this planet has been the biggest hoax of all time. We as a society, especially in the West, have been manipulated by fear mongers to keep us locked in a society that operates at a very lower energy vibration. By falling for this scam, we have allowed a few old egos or old world dynamics to keep us from discovering the essence of who we really are. This old ego control mechanism has been in place for far too long and it is now time for us to awaken to the true limitless possibilities we are meant to experience.

Our world has been controlled by those with the most money and the seemly unlimited power that money can buy; from control of Government that is bought by those able to raise the most money to get elected, to the huge corporations that lobby those elected government officials for control of the power over the people. We have been guided by leaders that have been driven by super old egos which superficially position themselves above the people with respect to the laws they pass. We have allowed huge corporations to lobby the government in an effort to make more money for a few while the rest of the population suffers the affects of such leadership.

It is a fact, the elected leaders of our world are supposed to be servants of the people, working for the betterment of society and the world as a whole. If you take the time to learn about our governmental system, you will discover the truth about how you have been manipulated into believing you are only the Physical Body and are supposedly limited by the rules made by whatever administrative power is in force at the time. It's a shame that we have been locked in the dynamics of super old ego control dogma for so long. Our government leaders are so fixated on fear-based tactics created to keep the population in check, that they have set in place a system of punishment rather than rehabilitation when someone falls out of Spirit and into the control of old ego survival thinking. The United States has more people in prison that any other country in the world and most of the punishment dished out by the system is done by spiritually ignorant power mongers.

We were never meant to be a population separated by those that have abundance and those that live in scarcity. In the sense of old ego's understanding of abundance, the definition is limited to the material possessions that someone has, which is meant to separate people into economic groups controlled by the government and the huge corporations operating in the background by high paid lobbyists to mandate more rules to keep us in check.

The idea of Spiritual Transformative Education has been held back from society because the elected leaders, thus far, have also been duped by their predecessors into believing that we are only the Physical Body. Newly elected candidates talk about how they are going to change the world, but then they use the same old ego control dynamics to keep us locked in a world of fear rather than moving our evolution forward through Love, Peace and Light.

This scam has gone on for so long that most people actually believe abundance is only measured by someone's monetary wealth and/or economic power. Most of the population is completely spiritually ignorant of the fact that they are Spiritual Beings having a human experience. Even in the self-improvement education system, many of those that are involved limit their teachings to that which can be measured in some physical form which is based upon some ego controlled manner or unspiritual measurement of success. They assign grading systems which are designed to separate people into groups based upon that which can be measured by the spiritually ignorant people in control of the systems they put in place. The idea of allowing someone to develop their true potential, utilizing their spiritual gifts for the betterment of Oneness, is completely foreign to most of these so called self-development experts. Most simply teach the same old control tactics that separate people rather than uniting them spiritually as the Spiritual Beings they truly are.

We are beginning to experience an uprising of those that have "seen the light" or the awakening of energy vibration to the level of Knowing that they are Spiritual Beings having a human experience. We are beginning to see people step up and become noticed that are not afraid of the old ego, fear-based systems. The idea that Spiritual Transformative Education is the key to bringing us into the next level of evolution is not a new one. People like Albert Einstein, Martin Luther King Jr. and Dr. David Hawkins have been attempting to education the population about Spiritual Body alignment for centuries. However, we have been so brain-washed into believing that we are only the Physical Body that we have simply not taken the steps necessary to absorb what these high vibrating Spirits are trying to bring to our conscious awareness.

The truth is most of the people of the current world still believe they are only the Physical Body and are not ready to rise above the typical out-of-date self-development teachings to the Highest Self realms of evolution found through true Spiritual Transformative Education. The leaders of the world certainly don't understand it and they do not want you to step up your energy vibration where you can discover the truth about your own destiny. Most people are so locked into the rigidity of old ego control dynamics, they are still driven by old ego rather than opening up to the limitless possibilities that have always been meant for them in life. The simple truth is it takes dedicated focused action to move forward Spiritually because ego is so deeply embedded in the unconscious mind and anchored in to the lower levels of awareness.

When will you be ready to bring the Spiritual Transformative Education system to the forefront of your life? What would it take for you to overcome the cleverness of the ego and move forward, inspired by the internal guidance available to you in every moment?

Is Old Ego Clever

There's no doubt that the old ego can be very clever, but when defining the word clever, it can have two meanings. From the old ego perspective, it can mean intelligent, witty, sharp, quick and other commendable aspects having to do with physical intellect or academic intellect. However, from the Spiritual Self or True Personality perspective, it has a completely different meaning, having to do with trickery, sham, fraud, deception, conning and other manipulative false pictures of grandeur or illusions to keep you locked under the old ego's control. Therefore, you must be very careful how you interpret that which seems harmless on the surface of life or from the form-based illusion of what is best for your overall Well Being.

As an example, you may consider how the Bible is frequently misinterpreted.

The actual understanding of the Bible is very different whether coming from a Physical Body or Spiritual Body alignment perspective.

From a Physical Body alignment perspective that is rooted in fear, punishment and judgment, a person would be very careful (in their mind) that they follow the messages from a religious perspective; one that places those leading the church on a platform of power or separation as messengers of God which is more based on rules and what "egoistic man" believes the Bible means, because it was written by egoistic man in God's name. From a Physical Body perspective, the person is taught to pray to a deity called God whenever they need assistance with a problem they have created with their old ego mentality. Most of these prayers go unanswered because they are not in alignment with the true intentions of the creator of all that is or Source Energy.

However, from a Spiritual Body alignment perspective, one rooted in Love, Peace and Light or Christ Consciousness, the Bible tells a completely different story. From a Spiritual Body perspective the Bible speaks of the Oneness of the Universe and the unlimited Divine power of unity that is found in acceptance and Love for one another. A perspective of growing eternally in energy vibration, but based upon the internal aspects of going deeper within one's Self to have intimate conversations with Source Energy. From this alignment perspective or Christ Consciousness, the outcome is completely different because a meaningful exchange of communication is heard in the silence between the words.

This energy vibration communicates beyond what the Physical Body is capable of understanding; therefore, those that do not hear the Christ Consciousness messages will condemn the interpretations with more false words cleverly spoken by egoistic man or they will relate back to the Bible with more misinterpreted phrasing in an attempt to gain control.

The most difficult level of acceptance for those still living in the third dimension of reality is to believe that there could actually be a higher energy vibration that has a much deeper understanding of what life is really all about. The old saying, "you don't know what you don't know" actually means, you are not vibrating at the level of Oneness where you can have direct connection in any moment with Source Energy to understand your own Original Source Agreement. Therefore, you must continue to experience that which is created by old ego or mind and live the life situations created by the Physical Body or old ego until you rise above the limited beliefs or lower energy vibration of the egoistic mind.

Source Energy does not understand most prayers because most prayers are rooted in fear, separation and being victimized in some manner. These one way conversations fall on deaf ears or an energy vibration that is not in alignment or harmony with Original Source Agreements. Therefore, until the lessons are learned (usually the hard way) based on Physical Body or old ego alignment, the life situations will continue at the level of this lower energy vibration. However, once the old ego surrenders completely and evolves to the level of Christ Consciousness or Oneness where the True Personality is created, a two way conversation begins with Source Energy. This higher vibration level of communication brings immediate guidance during life situation challenges. All you need do is communicate in the silence and listen to the messages coming to you from the internal God-Self or Spiritual Being. Once you align your energy vibration in the Oneness of this higher truth, your life situations are no longer in alignment with the lower energy levels of negativity and, then, your life and perception changes in a heartbeat.

The solutions to all life situation challenges which are always brought on by old ego control dynamics are already there waiting for you to ask the right question for resolution of any problem. Once your energy vibration has risen to the level of the solution-based spiritual mentality or True Personality, you will find challenges that come your way are nothing more than life's lessons delivering you to an ever-evolving level of awareness. And as this level of awareness grows within you, you begin to experience life at the level of Knowing. You begin to experience the co-creation process and discover that you are not separated from anyone, but actually connected in Oneness with everyone surrounding you. You begin to understand the true meaning of cause and effect where the Spiritual Body aligns with your Original Source Agreement. You become eternally aware of the presence of Source Energy within you!

Once you reach this level of energy vibration, you no longer take anything surrounding you personally and you transcend the need for being right. You obtain a completely different viewpoint on life, one that transcends from separation to unity. This unity allows you to align with the solutions to any man-made challenge through Conscious Clarity and Spiritual acceptance on your lifetime journey.

Am I Separate from Old Ego

Old ego was born through thought which was based upon a series of mistakes (mis-steps) cultivated by a fear-based society. The mind of old ego was brainwashed into believing that you are less than the Spiritual Being that is housed in the Physical Body. While old ego will always be a part of your complete Highest Self reality or Oneness, it will transcend to the level of True Personality (new ego) once you surrender to the born-again realization of true Self. Born-again simply means realigning your Spiritual Body in the forefront of your life and acceptance of your Spiritual Being reality.

As you proceed closer to the end of the Soul Merge level of the *Conscious Clarity Energy Process™*, it will become increasingly important for you to release the old ego completely in preparation for the Universal Level of this enlightenment program. As you move into the new awareness of Highest Self realization, the old ego will no longer be discussed as it will be left behind in the third dimension mentality or illusion of life. Anchor into your subconscious mind that you are *in* this world, but NOT *of* this world. When you can truly make that statement without any doubt from the Higher Self reality of existence, you will then have experienced the completion of the Soul Merge process.

As you move forward in spiritual evolution or energy vibration, you will gain a higher level of wisdom or understanding that transcends the mind and opens up the Kundalini energy flow completely. You will discover how easy it is to keep the Kundalini energy flowing through the Physical Body and will experience the deep Knowing associated with direct connection with Source Energy. Until you reach this level of energy vibration, you will continue to fall victim to the old ego control tactics.

The process of removing the controlling aspects of old ego from your consciousness is not something that happens overnight. It is the continual gradual increase of energy vibration that brings about the birth of the True Personality or unrestrained personality that is servant to the Higher Self reality – not the mind.

Once the True Personality is born again, even though you will be vibrating at a frequency beyond that of old ego, you will always retain the idea of how primitive the dynamics of old ego were in the past. By association with the memories of this dark side of life (false reality), you will be reminded of how limited you once were, so that you will have a greater appreciation for the Spiritual Being you truly are. The mind is a fascinating control tactician which can move up and down the energy vibration scale of life in less than a heartbeat. It can open you up to visualizing your most ideal life or it can shut you down in a heartbeat as well by creating negative thoughts which are meant to keep you from reaching higher levels of awareness. What you will discover as you grow spiritually is that you will never forget the hardships old ego brought to your life situations. These memories will forever be etched in your memory. Once you fully appreciate life beyond the unbalanced aspects of your old way of thinking, you will become whole and truly understand what Oneness means.

When you have shifted completely into True Personality mentality with the Spiritual Body in the forefront of every thought and action, you will learn to understand the beauty or reverence for life at a new level of consciousness. It's not impossible to transcend quickly from the control tactics of old ego, but the longer you live life on this planet locked in its control, the more difficult it will be for you to release the control tactics and shift into the limitless realms of reality. All you need do is keep the Spiritual Body alignment in the forefront of everything you experience during life situations and you will become a master at aligning yourself with your Original Source Agreement or Life Plan existence.

It will appear so simple for you once you reach the level of awareness called Knowing that you will wonder why it took you so long to surrender the old ego from your perceived reality. It's not always easy to change, but then it's not easy to believe you are more than just the Physical Body if you truly believe you are less than God-like. Source Energy is

504

everything, Source Energy is everywhere and Source Energy is part of your true Spiritual Self reality. Because Source Energy is all that is and whatever will be, this is proof that you are then naturally a piece of the totality or Oneness of Source Energy and therefore God-like.

Your old ego personality or mind is so limited in its beliefs that it is not possible for it to even begin to understand the level of energy vibration you are capable of achieving and what you are ultimately capable of co-creating with Source Energy guidance. You are moving forward in awareness at the level of Knowing when you feel the Divine presence within you in each present moment. When you feel this Divine presence expanding in your awareness of Spiritual Self, you will be released once and for all from the control dynamics of old ego.

Once you forgive yourself for being so naive in your beliefs, you will be ready to understand the unlimited life you were always meant to experience. You will be in complete harmony with your Original Source Agreement and your Kundalini energy flow will transcend the limitations of the mind's illusion of Self.

Spend more time living your lifetime in a meditative state of Being and you will experience the true influence or guidance from the Divine Source Energy within you.

How Does Spiritual Body Influence Old Ego

Spiritual Body awareness influences old ego by reminding you who you truly are and eliminates old ego's fear-based control over you. The Spiritual Body alignment process is meant to eliminate limited negative thinking and replace your life experiences with the Divine power of the Universe which is LOVE. The Universe has broad shoulders and can handle any leftover control tactics of the old ego once you have made the transition into the fourth dimension of reality. By simply re-aligning your Four Body System with the Spiritual Body in the forefront of every thought, emotion and action, you bring about the death of the old ego and its fear-based dogma.

There is a big difference between the fear-based dark side of the old ego and the Divine life-force of Love-based True Personality which guides your true reality. The fear-based mentality of old ego is meant to keep you from increasing your energy vibration to the point where you can see the truth pertaining to your commitment to honoring your Original Source Agreement.

Old ego knows that once you see your true Original Source Agreement unfolding into reality, you will never again allow fear to influence your daily decisions. Love will always progress you closer to Cosmic Life realization and Conscious Clarity of your true center. Conversely, fear will always hold you back from realizing your true destiny in life. This is why it is so very important for you to transcend to the fourth dimension of reality which is driven by the Divine power of Spiritual Transformative Education.

There are only two ways to perceive something happening around you - through fear or Love. The choice is yours and yours alone. You have nothing to fear because you cannot be controlled by anything outside you unless you relinquish your internal truth and allow the manipulators of the world to dictate what is best for you. Only you know what is best for you and by aligning fully with Spiritual Body in the forefront of every decision you make, you are guaranteed a life filled with abundance.

The limited thoughts of the old ego mentality of existence are coming to an end. Increase your energy vibration and you will see changes in your life daily. You can step up your energy vibration by simply following the internal guidance that flows through you in the fourth dimension and the light of God-like thinking. God-like thinking is *True Personality* flowing through life at the Highest Self level of reality. By following the guidance that comes to you in the silence of living life at the level of Knowing, you align yourself with an energy vibration in a way that you can hear the response from Source Energy when you ask questions.

The Spiritual Body influence which is transmitted during the silence of the mind brings about the inner peace you have always been meant to experience. By staying aligned with Spiritual Body in the forefront of your decisions, you transcend beyond the limited thoughts of fear that once drove you to make mistakes. You are far more than what the old ego's illusion will allow you to believe. You are the controller of your destiny and only you can make a change to experience life to its fullest and change can be accomplished in a heartbeat.

By allowing True Personality to take action in alignment with Love-based feelings, thoughts and high energy alignment with Highest Self, you bring the cosmic power of the Universe into each life situation experienced. As you continue to increase your energy vibration by doing good things for the betterment of humanity, you bring spiritual wisdom to the world. You bring the Divine power of Spiritual Body alignment to the forefront of each decision you make and you flow with life.

"Imagine a world based on Love and Knowing that you are a Spiritual Being having a human experience." – Terry Swejkoski

Knowing that you made a choice to come into the world for the betterment of humanity and the evolution of the Universe is a huge responsibility. However, once you align yourself fully with Spiritual Transformative Education, the responsibility seems minuscule when looking at the big picture and reverence for life. Once you have transitioned into Knowing that every action you take has a ripple effect on everything that has an energy vibration, you will change the way you interpret life situations. Your actions will be different and the results will be amazing.

All that happens around you has a Divine Purpose. Once you are aligned fully with the Spiritual Body, you will see that Divine Purpose through a third-eye reality and no longer feel victimized by the events happening around you. Each person's Original Source Agreement is meant to be played out to its fullest and the sooner you realize (come to the understanding in Spirit) that you are an intricate part of this whole Universal Plan, you will then have the life of abundance you always dreamed of.

To have a balanced life of abundance has nothing to do with external reality. A balanced life of abundance is based upon Love, Peace and Light, which are all internal. The unity brought about through Love allows us to experience an inner peace that cannot be disturbed by outside influences. The Divine power of Light, God, Source Energy, Christ Consciousness or whatever other labels you choose to use is the guiding life-force of all life.

Life is not the limited perception of the old ego or Physical Body reality, that's a lifetime. True Life is the eternal experience of Highest Self reality which is constantly unfolding around you with Love. – Terry Swejkoski

Therefore, if your focus is in alignment with the influence of the Spiritual Body guiding you, you will never again feel the need to drop your energy vibration to satisfy others that do not understand the spiritual power of the Universe. The Love, Peace and Light found in Spiritual Body alignment will always bring you back to truth, even when old ego is knocking at your door.

Live in light or darkness – the choice is yours!

Can I Live In-Spirit and In-Old-Ego Simultaneously

Living In-Spirit means the death of old ego and total surrender to a life of faith, filled with Love, Peace and Light. By releasing the limited aspects of old ego, you allow your life to evolve to the level of Knowing. And, at the level of Knowing, all self-doubt or limited beliefs about your True Self are eliminated forever.

Living In-Old-Ego is a life of limitation, fear-based and an illusion at best. At its worst, it is a life filled with self-doubt, anxiety, cluttered thoughts and deep depression. Many people vibrating at a very low frequency turn to drugs, alcohol and other mind-controlling activities that bring about a false sense of reality to reduce the pain they are experiencing on a daily basis in the third dimension. Because of the cluttered thoughts in their mind, they feel hopeless and fearful of taking any risk to better themselves through Spiritual Transformative Education. They stay stuck in this low energy until the Universe sends them a few powerful messages which would provide them with the experiences necessary to make life-changing choices that ultimately enhance their life.

It is impossible to live a spiritual Purpose Driven Life (In-Spirit) and an old ego-based life at the same time. Another way to look at this is to understand that it is impossible to have light and darkness at the same time. The problem is the whole idea of a Spiritual life is misinterpreted by most people, primarily because most people think a spiritual life means a religious life which is very far from the truth.

A religious life is more focused on old ego control dynamics and the rules setup by the religious organization that a lower vibrating personality chooses to follow. Most religion is based upon the fear-based misunderstanding of the scriptures which were involved with establishing religion in the first place. The stories told during religious services are typically misinterpreted or further perpetuated on half truths of the past and based upon the old ego opinion of the Religions leaders. Their beliefs typically have to do with their mind-based understanding of the scriptures, not Spiritual Transformative Education. Their illusions are achieved by old ego fear-based beliefs which separate Universal Oneness.

In spiritual truth and Spiritual Body alignment of Self, the True Personality has an opportunity to seek the authentic meaning of the scriptures and question the outdated interpretation from a higher energy vibration perspective. The idea that we are to be judged by some deity that is put on a pedestal and worshipped is stripped away and replaced by the Knowing that we are all Spiritual Beings having a human experience and are ALL God-like.

The understanding that we are all part of Source Energy and eternal is general knowledge to a person living a spiritual driven life. As a Spiritual Being, you are an intricate part of the Universe and capable of limitless achievements in life. This realization is the beginning of true enlightenment or Conscious Clarity of Self.

In spiritual truth, there are no limitations as to what can be achieved while experiencing the Earth school of lifetime. The energy vibration of a typical person living a spiritual life is beyond that of old ego. The True Personality which is formed through the surrender of old ego third dimension beliefs has the Divine authentic power of Source Energy working in unison with the personality not separated by rules. This new perspective on life is built on a spiritual structure that is in alignment with Source Energy, also known as Christ Consciousness in religious terms. It transcends all that is limited in old ego-based life. It is at this level of energy vibration that Conscious Clarity of your Original Source Agreement manifests into reality.

When living a life In-Spirit, a person knows they have the Divine authentic power within to accomplish even greater things than Jesus did while he occupied the Physical Body. Most people don't understand that it wasn't until the resurrection of Jesus that people began to feel the presence of Christ Consciousness that was always housed in Jesus' body. The spiritual examples, parables or proclamations recited by Jesus throughout his Physical Body existence weren't brought to light until the body was sacrificed completely. The example Jesus set through the resurrection of the body is until this day misinterpreted by most religious extremist beliefs.

In contrast, through spiritual beliefs, the idea that a body can rise again after its death is commonplace, because what Jesus actually did was raise the energy vibration of the body to an energy level that transcended death of the body and appeared translucent or Spirit-like.

The idea that spiritual awareness can be increased in energy vibration to a level of consciousness which allows Spirit to rise again is what the fourth dimension is all about. The Spiritual Self is far greater than what the old ego is capable of understanding. Therefore, those that still live in the old ego paradox or third dimension reality are bound by the shackles of limited beliefs and a limited personality that is desperate to survive rather than thrive in spiritual abundance.

Will Old Ego Bind Me

Old ego will bind you with the shackles of false beliefs or half-truths about yourself and hold you back from discovering your true authentic Spiritual Self. Therefore, you must retrain the brainwashed mind through Spiritual Transformative Education practices. It is imperative that you realign your Four Body System for you to progress to the energy vibration level of Knowing.

If you are not (as yet) living with Spiritual Body alignment in the forefront of your daily life situations, you are not ready to experience the next level of awareness presented to you at the *Universal Level* of the *Conscious Clarity Energy*

Process™. The surrender of the old ego is mandatory for you to increase your energy vibration and to fully integrate the Soul Merge process into reality. The old ego will manipulate you into believing that you can move forward in the *Conscious Clarity Energy Process*™ without realigning the Four Body System; this is merely the ego's arrogance showing its false sense of reality again, don't be fooled by this control tactic.

It is worthwhile to again review the example of the different outcomes associated with realigning the Four Body System so that you can transcend beyond old ego mentality and move forward with a life experience centered in Conscious Clarity:

We all consist of a Four Body System and how deeply we are integrated into the various parts of that system determines how we approach our life situation on a daily basis. If you could discover how to simply acknowledge that you do indeed have these multiple aspects of the body without allowing them to control you, your life would be a lot happier. Through meditation, you can consciously stay connected with the highest power of this system, the Spiritual Body.

The actual sequence of the Four Body System is of the utmost importance with respect to our perceived level of happiness. Therefore, it is naturally aligned when in the sequence below.

<u>The natural Four Body System alignment consists of the</u>:

1. Spiritual Body
2. Mental Body
3. Emotional Body
4. Physical Body

<u>Example – Typically Out of Alignment:</u>

The vast majority of humankind lives their life based upon having the Four Body System reversed where control is perceived at the Physical Body first.

- Physical Body - When the Physical Body is first, it identifies as situations happening to me (identity) or a physical reality.

- Emotional Body - This in turn excites the Emotional Body whereas, now, a feeling is generated due to what is perceived as having been done to my physical identity.

- Mental Body - These emotions then excite the Mental Body into thinking about what has happened to me (my story), usually based upon thoughts of the past and false beliefs that then lead to some type of reaction to the life situation experienced.

- Spiritual Body – Then, finally, after much self-inflicted torment, the Spiritual Body sends a message that perhaps you may be over-reacting to the situation at hand. At that point, an inner dialog or discussion within lower self begins and a decision is consciously made to either build on the story (which the Mental Body created) or to drop the issue in acceptance of what is.

The difficulty with this type of pattern is it usually leads to fear-based action, unless you have learned to catch yourself when you see this destructive pattern emerging.

Example – Naturally in Alignment:

If we analyze the same situation and reverse the control mechanisms of our Four Body System, there is a completely different result.

- Spiritual Body - When the Spiritual Body is in control and a life situation occurs, it is first acknowledged as what is and acceptance is immediately allowed. The perception is merely "this happened", it did not happen to me, it simply happened.

- Mental Body - Then the Mental Body activates to confirm; yes, this happened and some type of action may be required.

- Emotional Body - Next, the Emotional Body ignites with a feeling of empowerment to the challenge; it creates positive solution-based emotions and provides action to resolve the issue rather than focusing on the perceived problem.

- Physical Body - The result is the Physical Body feels peaceful and excited that there is a challenge to resolve. The Physical Body remains stress-free and the solutions appear from a higher knowledge base. The beauty of this type of pattern is the Four Body System then works in harmony without fear and feels peaceful Knowing that Love through Divine power and wisdom can bring light to any life situation.

In each of the above examples, the resultant actions will vary dramatically depending on whether you are living your life in a state of Love or fear. This may sound rather idealistic to some of you; however, if you make a focused effort to realign yourself with the Spiritual Body (through meditation), your life will be more balanced and in alignment with the higher level of understanding which is experienced through Love, Peace and Light.

The best way to stay connected with your Spiritual Body in the forefront of life situation is through the practice of daily meditation. When you discover how to keep the Spiritual Body in the forefront of your life, your level of awareness in any given situation will have a higher energy level and you will perceive life with Conscious Clarity.

When the mind is quiet and Kundalini energy is flowing unrestricted, the highest level of Spiritual communication is possible. It is in that quiet clarity of mind that your true purpose is revealed and the *I-Am-Ness* of your Spirit transcends to the level of Knowing. You must let go of old ego if you are to evolve to the next higher level of understanding.

How Do I Let Go of Old Ego Passively

You let go of old ego by simply living life at the level of "acceptance to what is" and always keeping your Higher Self in the forefront of your daily life situations. With this alignment, your life becomes easy and relaxed. You have feelings aligned with your highest good or Well Being and you smile when challenges come your way, because you know there is a Spiritual solution to every challenge. You maintain inner peace because you no longer allow the old ego to control you when challenges are brought to you. You fully realize each challenge that comes is for the purpose of some discovery you need to obtain.

The secret to letting go of old ego passively is to breathe in the essence of the Universe and allow yourself to see all challenges from the perspective of higher energy understanding. A simple smile increases your energy vibration ten-fold and "acceptance of what is" reinforces the transition to the level of Knowing. This higher level of energy vibration is very powerful as it has the Divine Spirit or Source Energy driving the next level of your understanding to the forefront of Conscious Clarity of Self. You will never accept who you really are if you allow old ego to continue to control you. The death of the old ego is mandatory to move forward with a spiritually-centered lifetime experience.

By now, you realize you are on your way to discovering your true "center" which is the center of all existence. It is not found in the mind, but in the inner levels of Knowing and a deeper acceptance of the Divine spark within you. You are not of this world, you are merely in this world for a temporary human experience which is meant to enhance your life and bring you to full enlightenment or understanding of True Self.

As you increase your energy vibration through the practice of experiencing life at the level of existence you have always been meant to achieve, you will be amazed at how quickly your perception of what is happening around you changes. By consciously participating in life in a meditative state of mind, you experience life from a completely different perspective. You know you are the Spiritual Being having a human experience and you begin to witness the events unfolding around you as if you were elevated above the surface of the Earth witnessing the next scene as it unfolds. This beautiful dance of life is truly an amazing journey, especially if you are aligned with the Spiritual Body guiding every step.

By witnessing life with Conscious Clarity of center, which is the spiritual essence of which you truly are, you allow the blessings of life to unfold as they were written in your Original Source Agreement. And because you are the author of your life, you have the Divine power to change any scene within your existence at any time. By staying connected to the Highest Self realization, you become exactly what you were always meant to be, a Spiritual Being having a temporary human experience; NOT a human being living a false life of scarcity and fear.

Open you heart more everyday and allow the Love to flow from your very Being. Allow the blessings of the Universe to flow through you and never doubt the Divine power that is housed within your Spiritual Self. As you grow in energy vibration, you begin to experience the higher levels of reality that were once invisible to you.

You are being prepared to witness the levels of understanding that were once completely foreign to your existence. You are now stepping through the next doorway of light that allow you to transcend any challenge from the passive level of Knowing. The old ego's aggression is being replaced with Love, Peace and Light and the higher realms of life are manifesting around you. Change your perception and your life changes immediately.

You will no longer live life with the glass half empty mentality of the old ego. Your life is about to change and you are about to experience the true meaning of being blessed. Your emotional stability will be anchored in to the level of constant peace and the experiences you have during life situations will evolve to the higher levels of perception. The negativity that you once experienced with old ego pushing or forcing you through life will be replaced by a gentle hand reaching out to you in every moment to pull you forward on your journey.

Always remember, you are part of the Divine wisdom of Source Energy. Therefore, it is time for you to align fully into this higher level of energy existence. The negativity of the past is being released and you will no longer be controlled by the old ego's limited beliefs, actions and fear-based agenda.

Does Old Ego Drive All Negative Emotion

Negative emotion is always driven by old ego and the misalignment of the Four Body System. If at any time you feel negative emotion such as anger, jealousy, resentment, etc, you are living life from the level of old egoist dogma or fear-based manipulation. You can change any negative emotion through conscious awareness of the past control tactics of old ego. If you feel negativity in your body, you have slipped back into the old ego's deceptive ways of manipulation. However, that being said, if you are feeling these negative emotions and have a deeper feeling that something just doesn't seem right, you are beginning to understand what it means to be consciously aware of your emotions.

The emotions you experience in each moment are always in alignment with your current energy vibration. Therefore, if your emotions are not positive and uplifting such as joy, gratitude, peacefulness, etc, your energy vibration is down and you need to increase it immediately. Don't attempt to make sense of it all as it may add to your confusion. Simply think of something that uplifts you to increase your energy vibration. It could be some wonderful experience you had in the past or it could be your vision of the future. Or better still, it could be gratitude for the present moment and the awareness you are feeling that something doesn't "feel" quite right. There is always a bright side to every moment and the Higher Self feels that bright side each time you shift your energy.

At this stage of your understanding, you are probably experiencing a roller coaster ride on *The Train of Life™* and the experiences may feel very confusing. However, I can assure you this is a good thing, because right after confusion, you begin the discovery of Knowing.

Once you believe that you can transcend any negative emotion, you will begin to live life from a higher energy perspective and you will quickly clear any negativity that holds you prisoner in a heartbeat. Be kind to yourself by allowing the negative emotions to bubble up and then patiently dismiss them with a higher energy thought, vision or emotion. By doing this, you increase your energy vibration slightly so that you can align with even higher increases of energy in the future.

In previous sections of this book, I mentioned the Kundalini flow of energy within your body. However, I intentionally spent little time explaining how you can control Kundalini flow. The reason is so that you could experience the confusion of the mind before you Spiritual Body control shifts into the level of Knowing. As you grow in spiritual wisdom, the Kundalini energy being released will grow exponentially within you. When this occurs, there is a definite shift within you that transcends the mind (old ego) and counteracts any negativity that the mind creates. But, if you release too much Kundalini energy too quickly, you could inadvertently cause physical damage to the body.

The old ego needs time to become accustomed to not being in control, because it is about to be replaced by its *True Personality*. To make it easier to comprehend, think of it as if your life just finished shifting from infancy to adolescence. These new possibilities available to you at the adolescence level will be the building blocks for shifting you further into adulthood. Yes, just as with a teenage personality, one that is developing to think for and be responsible for the outcome in life situations, you are growing but spiritually rather than physically. These growing pains can feel emotionally overwhelming at times, but the Spiritual Body can overcome any emotional pain the Physical Body can't handle by itself. It just takes a relaxed approach and there is no rush to complete the Soul Merge process. You must progress forward at your own rate so that you are not tricked by the old ego's deceptive tactics.

The false idea that you are only a human being has been so deeply implanted into your reality is not an easy belief to change. It will take you time to make the shift completely from old ego to True Personality. However, you are about to anchor in the main shift of your lifetime into the reality of fourth dimension realization and true alignment with your Original Source Agreement. If you relate this shift to *The Train of Life™* with the death of the old ego, you are beginning to transfer (transcend) from a slow coal or wood burning engine or mental personality to the more powerful diesel or electric powered of the evolved True Personality. The True Personality is guided 100% by the Spiritual Body or higher energy vibration of the Universal Level of understanding called Knowing.

You have already transcended from the very low energy vibration or coal/fossil fuel burning reality of life earlier in the *Conscious Clarity Energy Process™*. This transition took place without you even realizing it. Had you not transitioned, you would have stopped interacting with this study program long ago. Be proud that you have made it to this point without allowing the old ego to convince you it was not meant for you. Your energy vibration is now at a level where your limited beliefs are being replaced with thoughts of unlimited potential. Keep moving forward and get ready to experience the next step at the level of Knowing.

Spend as much time as necessary reviewing Illustration E, so that you better understand the shift taking place within your Four Body System. Don't just glance at the illustration, actually step through each column and deeply embed the different "resultant realities" into your consciousness. Your True Personality is beginning to take hold of your reality and you will now begin to release Kundalini energy at an exponential rate.

Your energy level is on its way to becoming the driving Divine power behind everything you accomplish in your current lifetime. As you move forward to the next level of reality, enjoy the journey!

Does True Personality Redefine Me

YES, True Personality completely redefines you! The wisdom of the True Personality or identity of Higher Self is a stepping stone from "little me" to the Divine limitless power of Higher Self realization or Spiritual Enlightenment of Life. You are no longer the total or incessant prisoner of the old ego. The old ego is now falling away more rapidly and the True Personality is taking hold of your consciousness. You now pay close attention to every intention that is transmitted through your mind and you focus on the reality of consciously co-creating every category of your life with Source Energy guiding every step forward.

Thinking small is a thing (form-based) idea of the past. You now realize, you are a limitless spiritual entity that was sent here to fulfill a particular purpose. Your life is about to change in a way you never thought possible as you continue to increase your energy vibration exponentially. The Divine realization of true Spiritual Self is now in control of every life situation and your daily choices are guided by the internal authentic power of the Universe.

Your identity is no longer limited to the Physical Body or role you play on Earth. The Physical Body is performing each task assigned by the Spiritual Body guidance that now drives you forward on your journey. The level of Knowing is now clearly visible to you and you dance through life situations Knowing you are a significant part of the overall Universal Plan. You are now beginning to see that you are intricately woven into the Universal Plan for all of life or the Oneness of the Universe. Now, when you think, it is only after "acceptance of what is" and your reactive old ways fall behind you. Your actions are in alignment with Spiritual Self guidance and you are beginning to live life at the Universal level of existence. Your thoughts now move you to solution-based action which is guided by the wisdom of the Highest Self.

You have come a long way and should be very proud of yourself for manifesting this major leap in your perception of life.

More and more people are turning to Spiritual Transformative Education than ever before and in the big picture you are one of the few that have transitioned into True

Personality awareness. When you have conversations with people vibrating at this energy level, statements made relating to "I" are now understood to mean, the Spiritual Body, not the Physical Body. Therefore, anything that is related to the Physical Body is generally understood to mean the form-based vessel you are temporarily using to experience the human journey of enlightenment. Your purpose is now clearer than ever before and you know you are here to assist in raising the mass consciousness of the World (Earth) to the Universal Level of understanding.

You role in the Earth school may change significantly for you now. The Original Source Agreement that was made with Source Energy is now being experienced. You are consciously guided along *The Train of Life*™ in a way that blends Mind and Soul together. One is not separate from the other anymore because you no longer live in fear of your life circumstances. Now, you actually look forward to the many challenges of life situations because you know you are part of the solution-based reality of the higher state of awareness. You find peace in Knowing you are a Spiritual Being having a human experience and you are humbled by the authentic power you have at your disposal. The authentic power of the Universe is yours to use during every man-made challenge that comes your way for enhancement or healing of the World.

From this point forward, you will experience the *Conscious Clarity Energy Process*™ from the perception of only Spiritual Body alignment. The confusion you once felt is drifting away, as you discover how easy it is to live a meditative state of life guided constantly by Source Energy wisdom. The idea of living each moment in Love, Peace and Light is anchored or embedded into your awareness and you consciously dance through life with a lighter step.

The Soul Merge process is nearing completion and you realize it is time to finally say goodbye to old ego. By taking this leap of faith into the unknown, you are guaranteed to exist at the level of abundance. The Categories of Life are now being viewed at a much higher level of energy vibration and you are starting to experience the feelings that come from Knowing who you truly are. By Knowing who you truly are, every decision you now make is guided by the authentic Divine power you possess within. The outside influences of life situations have no affect on you anymore as you now realize outside influences are merely a form-based illusion of the old ego's perception of life.

Living a Spiritual Driven Life is an understanding that you are an intricate part of the complete Universal Plan of existence. Every action is based upon what's best for everyone around you and you "know" you have the support of Source Energy in every moment.

I-Am-Ness of life is being presented fully in each present moment and you are now on your way to increasing your energy vibration, such that it is totally in alignment or harmony with the *I-AM-Ness* of your True Life.

What Does Power vs. Force Mean for the True Personality

Alignment with Authentic Power forever eliminates the fear, judgments and darkness you once had when old ego had control over you. This old control mechanism is replaced by Love, Peace and Light. Authentic Power is Source Energy guiding every step on your journey called life. It is the unseen power that speaks to you in moments of silence and the Divine power of the Universe. As your energy continues to rise above the level of unconscious thought and false beliefs you once had, you begin to experience more moments of pure enlightenment which transcend the unconscious mind completely.

Now that you know you are a Multi-sensory Spiritual Being brought to Earth to fulfill a specific purpose, you begin to expand perception of life to a conscious level that is in alignment with the Divine power of the Universe. It becomes easy to change your life from one of unconscious reaction to the events unfolding around you to one of Conscious Clarity. You are now in alignment with Source Energy and your Original Source Agreement. The Spiritual Body alignment you are now experiencing expands at a level of energy vibration that was once foreign to you and your beliefs expand exponentially to the level of Spirit or focused Knowing.

Force is exactly the opposite. It is a life based upon the limitations of five-sensory perceptions which are manipulated by fear and anchored into your unconscious mind by the false beliefs you once had about yourself and the outside forces that attempt to control humanity. Force is used in most governments to control the people and keep them from experiencing the power of Love. A population controlled by fear is easy to manipulate into performing acts that are out of alignment with Source Energy for the benefit of a few egotistic, rule-based leaders that have a false sense of who they truly are.

Everything in the Universe has an energy vibration associated with it, including all form-based creations and all that is formless. Spiritual Transformative Education is meant to bring consciousness to that which is formless and in harmony with the Universe. By increasing the energy of the planet one person at a time, we begin to move forward in evolution to the level where we can experience that which was once thought impossible. As the human race evolves beyond the limited beliefs of five-sensory perceptions, the mass consciousness of the world increases to the level when more people live life guided by Knowing. They are consciously aware of the Authentic Power within which guides their everyday life situations.

In the Universe, like always attracts like. Therefore, that which you are in alignment with or in energy vibration harmony with comes to you; there are no exceptions. Consequently, if you have shifted your life to Spiritual Body alignment and are now vibrating at a higher state of consciousness, you are beginning to experience that which is in alignment with a higher level of energy vibration. The True Personality was formed to assist you in experiencing these higher levels of reality, guided by the Highest Self energy within you.

All life situations are guided by either the high-energy levels of Authentic Power or the low-energy levels of Force. If you have not as yet read David R. Hawkins book, *Power vs. Force*, you may not understand the vibrations or frequencies associated with the two. I urge you to purchase a copy of this insightful book so that your mind can better understand the different vibration levels which were scientifically studied over a period of twenty years and presented by the author. Hawkins states, "The ability to differentiate between high and low energy patterns is a matter of perception and discrimination that most of us learn by painful trial and error."

Once you read *Power vs. Force*, it will bring you to a level of awareness that will prepare you to better understand the *Universal Level* of the *Conscious Clarity Energy Process™*. The *Universal Level* is based upon Knowing and does not reflect back to the old ego because you are no longer in alignment with that limited perception of life. Once you raise your energy vibration above the level of old ego, you never again drop your energy below the level of Knowing. When you are rooted in Knowing and ready for the Universal Level of the *Conscious Clarity Energy Process™*, the education level shifts from one of merging the Soul with the mind to one that increases your spiritual awareness far beyond that of limited mind. At these higher vibration frequencies we begin understanding the sub-levels associated within the Spiritual Body. These are far more multifaceted than the beginning stages of this enlightenment process.

Spiritual Transformative Education is now being presented to you in many forms by many authors that have learned to transition from Physical to Spiritual Body reality. You have the opportunity to learn from the experiences they share as they fulfill their life-purpose of teaching Spiritual Awareness to the world.

This is an exciting time to live on this planet as we are moving forward at a rate of evolution as never before. We are rediscovering our Authentic Self and are creating a world brought to evolution by Light. The Love we have suppressed for so long is now bubbling up to meet us and the Authentic Power driving this cycle is being understood by much more of the world population. We are truly living in the fourth dimension of reality and are preparing to take a quantum leap forward into the fifth dimension of understanding.

With the birth of the *True Personality*, you have transitioned from fear to Love. This greater energy vibration will once again raise your Conscious Clarity to higher levels of understanding than ever before. You are now part of this spiritual growth system and have completed the Soul Merge level of understanding. You are ready to move forward to the levels associated with the *True Personality* perspective. Your level of inner peace will be brought to Light and the abundance your have been seeking with manifest into reality.

As you move forward to the *Universal Level* of the *Conscious Clarity Energy Process™*, you will be amazed at how quickly you enhance each "Category of Life" which is associated with the Authentic Power that manifests each of the categories into abundant reality. Your life will change at the rate of awareness you bring to Light from sharing in Oneness!

Chapter 10 Suggestions – Key Tips – Secrets to Staying Out of Old Ego's Control

The *Soul Merge* level of the *Conscious Clarity Energy Process™* is merely the death of the old ego and birth of the True Personality. Now that the false beliefs which you have been brainwashed with for years have been brought to your awareness, it is time for you to truly take a quantum leap in your life experience.

As you progress with the *Conscious Clarity Energy Process™* at the *Universal* level, you will notice the old ego is not mentioned anymore and the new ego is simply called *True Personality* or Personality.

You have grown as a human from the manipulations of society into a free thinker or a Personality that has transcended the control mechanisms of societal influence pertaining to your beliefs. All this preparation was necessary for you to fully comprehend and integrate the next levels of reality into your consciousness. With the Spiritual Body guiding you, it will be easy for you to accept the amazing truths that are about to be presented to you at the much higher vibration level or *Universal* level of the *Conscious Clarity Energy Process™*. The next book in the series, *Consciously Embrace Your True Personality*, will pick up where this one ends.

Following is a summary of "Key Tips" which are anchors for staying out of old ego's control. These are the most important areas for you to always keep in mind as you progress with your Spiritual Transformative Education:

- Birth of *True Personality* - You now know with certainty that you are a Spiritual Being having a human experience which transcends all negativity and false beliefs you once had about yourself and the world you currently exist in. You know you are in this world, but not of this world. The death of the old ego is an event to be celebrated consciously, because it removes the burden of unnecessary cluttered thought from your life. When you look in the mirror, you no longer see just the Physical Body; you look beyond the body into the depth of the Spirit behind the physical eyes. This transition was necessary so that you could see the magnitude or greatness before you from the higher vibration levels of fourth dimension reality. This renewed personality or True Personality is an amazing tool to be used to increase abundance in your life and those around you through Love,

Peace and Light. The mind is now consciously the servant of Spirit as it was always intended to be.

- Spiritual Alignment – Spiritual Body alignment is the key to all Spiritual Transformative Education. By placing the Spiritual Body in the forefront of your daily experiences, you co-create everything around you with Source Energy and increase your energy vibration exponentially. With the clear understanding of solutions available to you in every circumstance of life situations, you allow the power of the Universe to expand your awareness of what life is truly all about. You now live life with a Spiritual Purpose and can see far beyond the limited beliefs of the past. Keep this alignment in place and, I promise you, you will never think of yourself as a victim again. By acceptance of what is, you allow the powerful energy of the Universe to bring solutions to challenges that arise out of necessity. This is all part of the enlightenment of Self and the sharing of gifts between all people in Oneness for the Divine Purpose of healing the collective Soul.

- Meditative State of Being – Most of the population believes that Meditation is some "thing" that is done or is a spiritual nutrient to the body. The idea of meditation being a tool for the human mind is a limited perception.

"Meditation is not some "thing" you do; it is the experience of Being that which you are." – Terry Swejkoski

As you become more aware of your true Self as a Spiritual Being having a human experience, you shift from thinking about meditation or doing some physical act to actually living life from a "Meditative State of Being". What this means is you flow through life situation experiences as the spiritual observer of each moment always connected to the guidance of Source Energy. As you grow in spiritual understanding, the direct connection with Source Energy becomes a constant conversation, not just a period of time when you sit still in silence. You discover it is possible to quiet the unconscious mind, as well as the constant chatter that is experienced by "thinking" of the conscious mind. This brings about a state of mindfulness that is at a much higher energy vibration than the Physical Body can experience on its own without the guidance of Source Energy. You essentially become the Love, Peace and Light of the Universe and rise above or transcend limited Physical Body awareness!

- Conscious Spiritual Education – Once the shift occurs in the Soul Merge process, you no longer separate Academic Education from Spiritual Education. The new world experiences of life in the fourth dimension of reality are centered on Spiritual Transformative Education. This brings to light the continued study of Highest Self from a level of Being in unity with the Universe and the understanding that Oneness exemplifies. By discovering the true essence of which you are, you alignment your Self with the higher realms of reality that can only be experienced from a Spiritual Life perspective. Through the elimination of old ego, you bring your energy vibration up to a point of awareness where you can reach greater achievement while in the Earth school of life. You have just begun to glance at the magnitude of this limitless creation at your finger tips. It's through Conscious Clarity coupled with action that you discover the underlying Divine energy that truly controls the Universe. If you are to evolve into the personality you are meant to be, you must prioritize Spiritual Transformative Education in your life.

- Limitless Perspective – When experiencing life from a Spiritual level of understanding, you align with the limitless perspective associated with True Personality thinking. You understand the guidance that comes through you and you realize you have the opportunity to co-create a life of true abundance. The idea that you manifest that which you think about mostly is not a new discussion that just started in the fourth dimension. If you review all the scriptures, each one has referenced a limitless perspective of what life could be. When you change your perspective from "I can't" to "How will we", you open up the discussion to the Universe and you are sent the solutions to every challenge immediately. You begin to understand that we are all here to assist one another with the challenges of life. There is no more "I" it is transformed to "We". Therefore, you shift from "What's in it for me" to "How do I serve" the totality of the world and, ultimately, the Universe. We are each given gifts or resources to share with the world, use them with loving care and watch how your life changes in abundance.

- Expanding Consciousness – Authentic Power vs. Force is the lifeblood of the Universe. You cannot co-create a meaningful life without expanding your consciousness. As you become more adapt to shifting into the higher levels of consciousness, you will experience many challenges along the way. However, they are all based on the lingering closed-mindedness of the old ego and the force it is still using attempting to trick you into submission. Let these small nuisances bubble up as they may, then simply acknowledge them for the low energy they are and dismiss them as quickly as they appeared. By expanding your consciousness of which you truly are through Spiritual Transformative Education, you will experience an enhanced life in every "Category of Life" and discover how easy it is to stay Inspired!

The Soul Merge process has been the first step in spiritual discovery for many of you. It has been a journey where I know many have discarded years of misunderstanding and probably some tears along the way. It has been my pleasure to be your spiritual guide as you learn the secrets to discovering that which you truly are. You are now ready to reveal the limitless possibilities your now Know are available to you as a Spiritual Being having a human experience.

Don't stop here; keep Spiritual Transformative Education in the forefront of your awareness by reading, *Consciously Embrace Your True Personality* and completing the *Universal* level of the *Conscious Clarity Energy Process*™ and you will discover what it really means to live life in ONENESS!

Namaste

Illustrations

Illustration A – Original Source Agreement

Illustration B – The Train of Life™

Illustration C – Energy Transformation

Illustration D – Life Plan Balance

Illustration E – Energy Vibration - Life Fuel Source

Illustration F – Kundalini Energy

Original Source Agreement

Source Energy

Spiritual Highest Self = Before Human Birth

Birth = Beginning of The Train of Life™

Engine/Engineer/Personality – Highest Self/Conductor/Inner Guidance
(Original Source Agreement)

First Breath

Always Meant to Be Connected

Unconditional Love

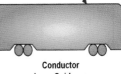

Engineer
Personality
Ego

Conductor
Inner Guidance
Higher Self

Birth Path - Flow on The Train of Life™ – Linear Momentum
(Original Life Plan – Original Source Agreement)

The Train of Life™

Conscious Clarity Energy Process™

Illustration - A

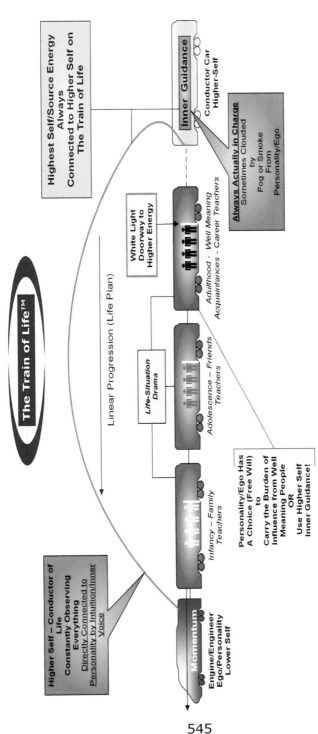

The Train of Life™

Highest Self/Source Energy Always Connected to Higher Self on The Train of Life

Inner Guidance
Conductor Car
Higher-Self

Always Actually in Charge Sometimes Clouded by Fog or Smoke From Personality/Ego

White Light Doorway to Higher Energy

Linear Progression (Life Plan)

Adulthood - Well Meaning Acquaintances - Career Teachers

Life-Situation Drama

Adolescence – Friends Teachers

Infancy – Family Teachers

Personality/Ego Has A Choice (Free Will) to Carry the Burden of Influence from Well Meaning People OR Use Higher Self Inner Guidance!

Momentum
Engine/Engineer
Ego/Personality
Lower Self

Higher Self – Conductor of Life Constantly Observing Everything Directly Connected to Personality by Intuition/Inner Voice

Conscious Clarity Energy Process™

Illustration B

Copyright © Terry Swejkoski - All Rights Reserved Worldwide

545

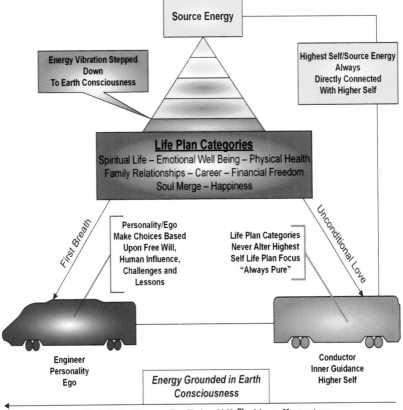

Energy Transformation

Source Energy

Energy Vibration Stepped Down To Earth Consciousness

Highest Self/Source Energy Always Directly Connected With Higher Self

Life Plan Categories

Spiritual Life – Emotional Well Being – Physical Health
Family Relationships – Career – Financial Freedom
Soul Merge – Happiness

First Breath

Personality/Ego Make Choices Based Upon Free Will, Human Influence, Challenges and Lessons

Life Plan Categories Never Alter Highest Self Life Plan Focus "Always Pure"

Unconditional Love

Engineer
Personality
Ego

Conductor
Inner Guidance
Higher Self

Energy Grounded in Earth Consciousness

Birth Path - Flow on The Train of Life™ – Linear Momentum
(Original Life Plan – Original Source Agreement)

The Train of Life™

Conscious Clarity Energy Process™

Illustration C

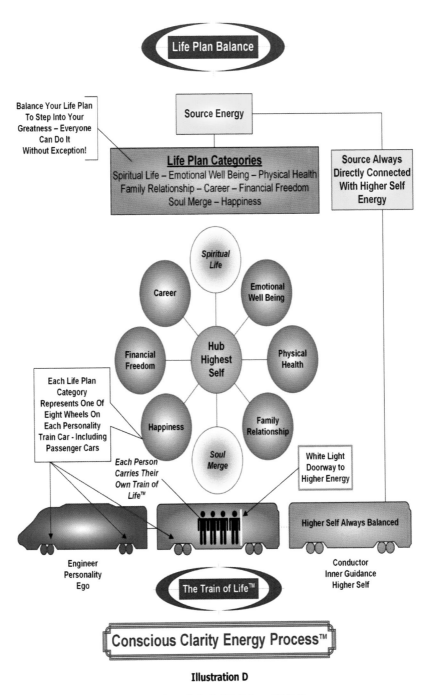

Illustration D

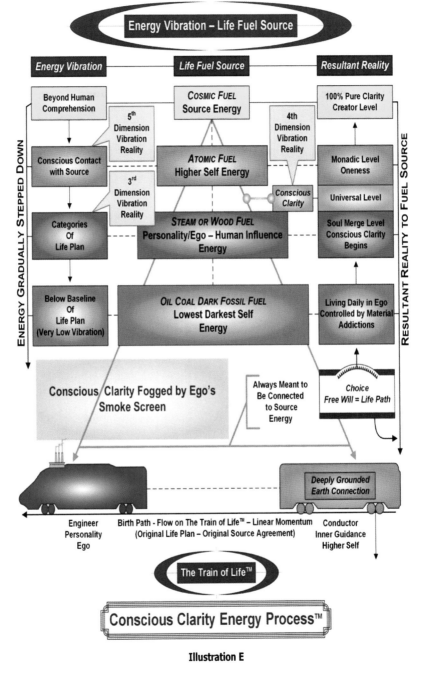

Illustration E

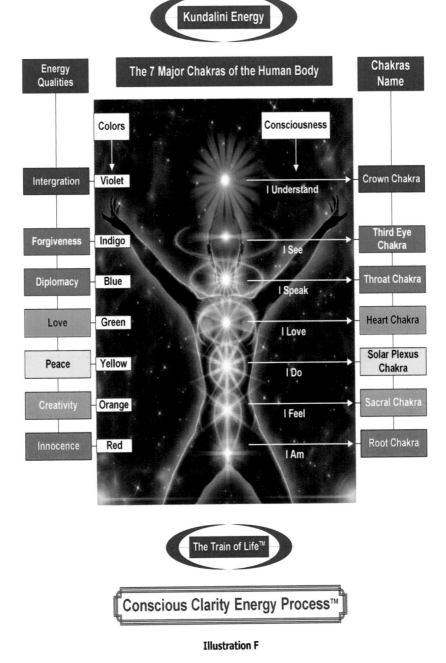

Illustration F